MODELING FINANCIAL MARKETS

Using Visual Basic.NET and Databases
to Create Pricing, Trading, and
Risk Management Models

BENJAMIN VAN VLIET
ROBERT HENDRY

McGraw-Hill

New York   Chicago   San Francisco   Lisbon
London   Madrid   Mexico City   Milan
New Delhi   San Juan   Seoul
Singapore   Sydney   Toronto

Ben Van Vliet: To my parents

Bob Hendry: To Caroline and Cassandra

2 3 4 5 6 7 8 9 0   DOC/DOC   0 9 8 7 6 5 4

P/N 143818-1
PART OF
ISBN 0-07-141772-9

This publication is designed to provide accurate and authoritative information in regard to the subject matter covered. It is sold with the understanding that neither the author nor the publisher is engaged in rendering legal, accounting, or other professional service. If legal advice or other expert assistance is required, the services of a competent professional person should be sought.

—*From a declaration of principles jointly adopted by a committee of the American Bar Association and a committee of publishers.*

 This book is printed on recycled, acid-free paper containing a minimum of 50% recycled de-inked fiber.

McGraw-Hill books are available at special quantity discounts to use as premiums and sales promotions, or for use in corporate training programs. For more information, please write to the Director of Special Sales, Professional Publishing, McGraw-Hill, Two Penn Plaza, New York, NY 10121-2298. Or contact your local bookstore.

Library of Congress Cataloging-in-Publication Data

Van Vliet, Benjamin.
    Modeling financial markets : using Visual Basic and databases to
create pricing, trading, and risk management models / by Benjamin Van
Vliet and Robert Hendry.
        p. cm.
    ISBN 0-07-141772-9 (cloth : alk. paper)
    1. Investment–Mathematical models.   2. Financial engineering.   3.
Microsoft Visual BASIC.   I.   Hendry, Robert.   II. Title.

    HG4515.2.V36 2004

CONTENTS

SECTION FOUR

SECTION FIVE

ACKNOWLEDGMENTS

Andrew Kumiega, Nithiphong Vikitset, Anton Karadakov, David Norman, Keith Black, Pamela Reardon, Alex Deitz, Melanie Winter, Siriporn Treetanasawat, Mulianto The, Debbie Cernauskas, Michael Modica. Jerold Lavin, Duana Wooters, Thomas E. "Burma" Shea, Sagy Mintz, Kenneth M. Horjus, Mark McCracken, Julia Spaulding, Dave Kuipers, Rich Pombonyo, Paresh Akbari, Cliff Ensing, Brain Huyser, Mark Groenenboom, Bruce Rawlings, Gary Lahey, Hank Perrit, Jack Wing, Varsha Pitre, Michael Ubis, Jason Malkin, and Irma Baines.

Trading System Development

I project that, [in the next ten years], the majority of money managers wil completely automate their trade entry decisions. . . . So, in the very near future, if you have a mouse in your hand, you will be too late.

Blair Hull

CHAPTER 1

Introduction

Although this book follows the layout of a programming book, the underlying theme is financial modeling and quantitative trading system development. In a sense, this book really marries four disciplines—computer science, quantitative finance, trading strategy, and quality development—into one, financial engineering. The following chapter, Chapter 2, outlines the Kumiega–Van Vliet Trading System Development Methodology, which as you will see provides the underlying structure for the rest of the book. As the chapters progress, we present gradually more complex programming ideas along with mathematics and trading applications to illustrate the steps along the Kumiega–Van Vliet paradigm. So this book is not just about Visual Basic.NET (VB.NET) and databases. It is about modeling financial instruments in code and putting the pieces, or models, together to create an automated trading or risk management system using a programming language, which in this case is VB.NET. Let's get started.

Financial markets are in a constant state of evolution, from buttonwood trees to trading floors to computer screens. Over the last 40 years, owing to the invention of computers and the development of quantitative tools for market analysis, the pace of this change has increased dramatically. The revolution in derivatives market analysis really got into full swing in the early 1970s when, soon after the Chicago Board Options Exchange (CBOE) began listing options on equities, Texas Instruments developed a calculator to price options using the Black-Scholes formula (Berstein, 1996, pp. 310–316). Over the coming years, one major outcome of this revolution may very well be a complete automation of the trading process (Norman, 2001, p. 236). In the future, computerized investment models and trading algorithms and instantaneous trade execution could render human traders completely obsolete (Van Vliet and Kumiega, 2000).

Human traders, using strategies based on technical indicators, fundamental factors, or even plain old market savvy, are becoming increasingly scarce. More and more each day financial engineers are quantifying trading systems that can watch hundreds of securities and derivatives in real time and execute hundreds of strategies instantaneously and simultaneously. The trend that started decades ago with Moore's law (a doubling of speed in computer processing power about every 18 months), coupled with the decreased cost of technology and market data, means that in the future all profitable trading strategies may be, through mathematics and statistics, quantifiable and programmable.

The equities trading industry caught on several years ago with program trading and index arbitrage, using computers to generate hundreds of orders simultaneously. The options exchanges, however, have in the past prohibited automated order entry in an effort to protect market makers. But it appears now that such rules may very well be abolished in the near future, if they have not already been by the time this book is published. The Boston Options Exchange (BOX), which will be opening for business in mid-2003, currently has no bylaw prohibiting automated order entry, which will likely have the effect of forcing the other options exchanges to amend their rules.

Whatever the future holds, however, make no mistake—the trading game will be as it always has been: The first person, or computer, to recognize a profitable opportunity and execute a trade wins. It's just that being first is no longer measured in the split seconds it takes to click your mouse button, but rather the milliseconds it takes a computer to react. The financial engineer who can program a computer to recognize profitable trading opportunities and execute trades is really the trader of the future (Van Vliet and Kumiega, 2000).

In the trading industry, a key job performed by financial engineers, among other things, is to formalize trading strategies based upon quantitative research, back-test algorithms against historical data, construct or supervise construction of necessary software for automation of order execution, and, after implementation, manage the risk of the trading system. Of course, not all these duties are always performed by just one person, but rather, usually, by a team of financial engineers and programmers.

If you intend to have a career in trading in the financial markets, you will likely work on such a team, which will require that at some point you will be required to either write computer code yourself, manage programmers, or work and interact with programmers on projects. This will necessitate an understanding of, at the least, Microsoft Excel spreadsheet and the Visual Basic for Applications (VBA) environment, but likely also Visual Basic.NET or a higher-level language such as C/C++ or Java. In addition you will need to understand how databases are constructed and accessed using computer code to do financial research and develop trading and risk management algorithms and systems.

All financial research requires data, and the efficient management and storage of data is crucial to the profitable operation of a trading system. "Data is the lifeblood of electronic markets," as David Norman states in his book *Professional Electronic Trading* (2002). Industrial-strength relational database management systems, such as Oracle or MS SQL Server, can store gigabytes of such things as historical market data and firmwide trade and position information (Norman, 2001). Often, historical market data is simply the opening, high, low, and closing prices or other time-incremented data such as implied volatilities, but it could also be more qualitative, economic, or fundamental data such as earnings report data, stock splits, or Fed actions. Whatever the case, analysis of data requires not only the knowledge of quantitative methods, but also the programming tools to implement that analysis in a real-life environment. This book addresses topics that are critical to these aspects of trading system development.

Top financial engineers estimate that only a fraction of financial engineering actually deals with mathematics. The lion's share of time applies to the actual construction and analysis of models and forecasts and technology development.

This majority of a financial engineer's time engaged in construction, though, is not simply spent coding. Rather, the entire development process requires this amount of effort; actual time spent coding should be just a part of it. As you grow in your understanding of programming and trading and/or risk management system development, you will become increasingly aware that comprehensive blueprints, or plans, or development methodologies, of a project must be laid out before any nails are hammered or computer keys pressed. The value of a development paradigm cannot be underestimated.

A good methodology, though, does not mean that an engineered trading system is infallible. Not every trade and not every system makes money. There are certainly dozens, if not thousands, of examples or anecdotes trotted out by "nonquant" market participants that attempt to disprove the ability of automated systems to outperform human traders over the long run. To be sure, the markets are "replete with examples of 'fat tails'—unusual and extreme price swings that, based on a reading of previous prices, would have seemed implausible" according to Roger Lowenstein in his book *When Genius Failed* (2000, p. 229). In the past, quantitative systems, like that of Long Term Capital Management, which were built on historical data have blown up quite spectacularly during financial meltdowns, or tenth standard deviation events, when all correlations go to 1, as they say. But we don't stop engineering bridges just because one in London fell down. No matter what anybody says, using a bridge to cross a river is still an improvement on taking a boat across. Over time, with more experience and better engineering, financial models and forecasting will improve and become more able to weather those once-a-millennium floods that seem to come around every couple of years. A computer can't beat Kasparov at chess yet. But give it a few more years. Our money is with Deep Blue, or Deep Junior as the case may be, over the long haul.

The real strategy for quantitative trading systems is to know ahead of time, through research, the probability of the success of a particular trade or series of trades, and assuming the odds are in your favor, to play as often as possible, all the while keeping a close eye on risk and the changing trade winds (Lowenstein, 2000, p. 134).

Developing a profitable trading system is no small task, however. One options trader we talked to estimates that it takes a

$10 million investment just to get in the game. That $10 million pays for building a network infrastructure, hiring high-level quantitative analysts and programmers, and conducting at least a year of research and development before you even make your first trade. Much of this expense, though, may be dedicated to creating and installing proprietary software and hardware that connects to exchanges through their application programming interfaces (APIs). APIs can be thought of as "pipelines" to the market over which third parties, such as exchange member trading firms, can access exchange data and place orders electronically. Installing and maintaining a communications network for data and order execution, however, involves a terrible tangle of inter-connecting hubs, routers, switches, and fiber optics, not to mention constant software redevelopment as exchanges upgrade their APIs (Norman, 2001).

Rather than incurring the time and expense it takes to build from scratch, it is also possible and much less capital-intensive to license third-party trading software and take advantage of the exchange connections and built-in functionality for data feeds, order entry, and risk management. Then proprietary analytics and trading algorithms can be added on top of this software via their own APIs. Many of these third-party vendors have over 10 years' experience building front-end systems for futures and options traders and are, in terms of development, well ahead of even some major U.S. trading houses (Norman, 2001).

In this book, we will show you how to use Visual Basic.NET and several quantitative tools to begin development of some trading strategies and to analyze data, and we will share some ideas about how to connect to industry software via APIs to monitor financial markets and execute trades. Figure 1.1 shows graphically how to implement a trading system in this way. In this figure the arrows represent APIs.

One limitation to this architecture, however, is that no single front-end trading system connects to all markets around the world. So it may necessary to create proprietary software that connects to a multiplicity of front-end trading system APIs to provide access to all the different markets and products (Norman, 2001, p. 175).

F I G U R E   1.1

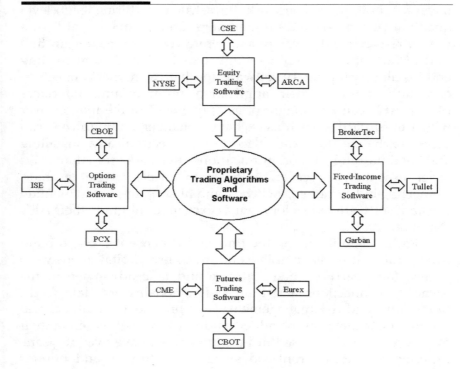

The term *front-end trading system* refers to the "client workstation [and software], or order entry point, on the exchange member local area network (LAN) that a trading firm uses to access electronic exchange services" (Norman, 2001, p. 242). An exchange "back end" is the point where an electronic order reaches the exchange and passes through to the exchange's matching engine (Norman, 2001, p. 242). Electronically routed orders pass from a firm's front end to the exchange back end and then, once the trade has been executed, again to the front end as a trade-fill confirmation (Norman, 2001, p. 243).

In derivatives markets, related products are often traded on different markets. For example, Dow futures trade on the Chicago Board of Trade, S&P 500 futures trade on the Chicago Mercantile Exchange, and S&P 500 cash options trade on the Chicago Board Options Exchange. Shares of IBM stock trade on the NYSE and other stock exchanges, while IBM stock futures trade on One Chicago and NQ_X and options on IBM trade on the various options exchanges. Given the disparate technological infrastructures and trading rules for the different exchanges, connecting to all of them for automated trading of related products can be somewhat of a nightmare.

So as you may be able to see from Figure 1.1, it is possible, for example, to build an automatic hedging device through the type of framework we described. MicroHedge is a popular institutional software package with connections to the options markets. And Trading Technologies' X_Trader software is a popular front-end software system for futures trading on electronic markets. Thus, we could create a system to trade the CBOE's S&P 500 cash options, via a market connection through MicroHedge's API, that could also provide real-time delta hedging with the E-Mini S&P contract on the Chicago Mercantile Exchange via connection to Trading Technologies' API (Norman, 2001).

As we mentioned earlier, there are four disciplines that go into automated trading strategy development: computer science, quantitative finance, trading strategy, and quality development. This is a lot to learn. We do not attempt teach you all of it. Rather we bring together some important ideas from math, technology, project management, and the financial markets that are required to build a real-world automated trading system.

CHAPTER 2

Development Methodology

So what is an automated trading or risk management system, and what process do we go through to create one?

A trading or risk management system, as we define it, consists of the rules for automated entry into and exit from a position or positions and the technology used to make them happen. These rules are a set of logical or mathematical operations that can be based upon qualitative, technical, or quantitative research. Many books and papers currently available outline stock and futures trading system development from a purely technical analysis standpoint, often using a retail software package to optimize a set of trading rules based upon moving averages and oscillators. In this book, however, we will focus on quantitative analysis of equities, equity indexes, and options on equities and the programming of professional, proprietary software using Visual Basic.NET.

Several steps are involved in creating a quantitatively based trading system, and while clearly not exhaustive since there are literally an infinite number of potential quantifiable trading strategies, this book presents some of the necessary steps to create an automated system, with lots of code examples along the way. Before we begin, however, we should define the steps to go through or the process of creating an automated system.

In their paper "An Automated Trading System Development Methodology" (2003), Andrew Kumiega and Ben Van Vliet propose a process for trading system development that consists of four phases: research and documentation of calculations, back testing, implementation, and portfolio and risk management.

KUMIEGA–VAN VLIET TRADING SYSTEM DEVELOPMENT METHODOLOGY

By their nature, all implemented and functioning automated trading or risk management systems must manage two concurrent processes: (1) trade selection and (2) portfolio and risk management. However, prior to implementation the process of development should follow a well-defined, well-documented flow of steps along a development methodology. In 2001, Kumiega and Van Vliet first proposed a software development methodology for financial markets that laid out the steps to codify trading and risk management algorithms. This earlier model is encompassed within this broader methodology, which outlines an entire trading system development paradigm.

Kumiega and Van Vliet propose a standardized model for the development of automated trading systems that will ensure rapidity, desired by senior management, and consistent quality standards, desired by financial engineers. While the idiosyncrasies of the securities and derivatives trading industries require a unique system development paradigm, this methodology owes a large portion of its structure to a combination of the traditional waterfall model (Royce, 1970) and the evolutionary spiral models (Boehm, 1988). The combination of these two models seeks to gain from their respective strengths as well as to overcome their respective weaknesses.

Waterfall Methodology

The traditional waterfall model is a very powerful software development methodology and consists of four phases that, in general, map to the four phases of the Kumiega–Van Vliet model— analysis, design, implementation, and ongoing system testing. At the completion of each phase, the waterfall model requires a decision by management prior to advancing to the next phase. This decision is whether or not to continue development of the system based upon the potential for profitable implementation.

In a nutshell, the waterfall model forces financial engineers to think about the system to be built and to come up with a plan for building it, before they begin construction. By following this model, we can force ourselves to use a disciplined approach to the process of development and to avoid the pitfalls of creating a system and writing computer code before the blueprints of the project are well defined and precisely laid out.

The waterfall methodology does have a major drawback though: It puts too much emphasis on planning. The waterfall model necessitates that all details and all plans be defined up front before design and implementation begin. That is to say, there is no room for error and no process for handling feedback or problems that occur down the road. In the fast-moving financial markets, where trading opportunities come and go quickly, the waterfall model may not be able to react quickly enough.

As an example, suppose we find in an implementation phase that a coherent trading idea will be impossibly complex in terms of the technology needed to make it happen. As a result the project fails. Had the financial engineers been aware of this fact in the analysis phase, they may have been able to modify the system design so as to enable successful construction. The waterfall model has no way of handling these types of situations. Furthermore, technology these days is changing just about as fast as the market itself. The danger with the waterfall methodology is that by the time a trading system is ready for implementation, the technology it was built on may be obsolete and there may be a better, faster, easier technology already on the market.

To overcome the shortcomings of the waterfall model, the spiral model was developed.

Spiral Methodology

In the spiral methodology a small amount of time is initially devoted to each of four phases: research, planning, implementation, and testing, followed by several repetitive iterations or cycles over each of them.

As the cycles progress and the spiral gets larger, more detail and refinement are gained in each phase. At some final point, it is hoped, each phase will be complete.

In this way, the spiral method allows for feedback as problems in the system are detected. A problem can be dealt with either by correcting it or, if the problem is fatal, by scrapping the entire trading idea. Of course, the truly fatal problem is the prospect of losses. If the system cannot or will not be profitable, for whatever reason, it will be discarded. So intermittent or prototype implementations can provide feedback about the viability and profitability of the trading system. Also, as new discoveries in quantitative methods and system design are made, the system's blueprints can incorporate them as they arise.

As with the waterfall method, the spiral method is not without its drawbacks. The primary problem with the spiral methodology is that the number of cycles can grow without end, using up resources. There are no inherent constraints or deadlines. This can lead to loss of project focus, messy logic, and extraneous or unnecessary digressions. This is often called *scope creep*, when the scope of the projects gets continuously larger.

As a result, the blueprints may never present a clear and concise architecture of the trading system. So in the spiral model, the cycling process must have a clear condition for termination. This lack of termination is common in Excel-based trading systems.

To overcome the problems with each of these methodologies, Kumiega and Van Vliet have combined them into a single paradigm for trading system development. As Figure 2.1 illustrates, the four phases progress in a traditional waterfall, but within each phase, four elements are connected into a spiral structure. At the completion of each phase, management must make a decision before proceeding to the next phase. After completing the fourth and final phase, the methology calls for financial engineers to repeat the entire waterfall process for continuous improvement. The phases are as follows:

Phase I.   Research and Document Calculations
  1. Describe trading idea.
  2. Research quantitative methods.
  3. Prototype in Excel.
  4. Check profitability.
Phase II.   Back-Test
  1. Gather data.
  2. Clean data.
  3. Perform in-sample/out-of-sample test.

4. Check profitability.

Phase III.   Implement

   1. Build vision and scope document.

   2. Build objects and program document.

   3. Program and document the system.

   4. Paper-trade and check profitability.

Phase IV.   Manage Portfolio and Risk

   1. Monitor portfolio statistics.

   2. Perform value-at-risk calculations.

   3. Document profit and loss attribution.

   4. Determine causes of variation in profitability.

Repeat the entire waterfall process for continuous improvement.

Here is some brief discussion on the 16 elements listed in the Kumiega–Van Vliet methodology.

F I G U R E   2.1

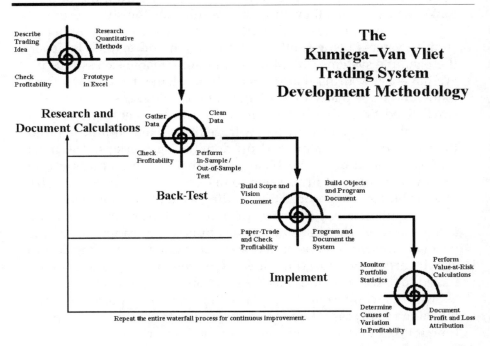

The Kumiega–Van Vliet Trading System Development Methodology

PHASE I. RESEARCH AND DOCUMENT CALCULATIONS

The first of the four phases consists of researching quantitative algorithms for a trading system.

Describe Trading Idea

There is an old saying in the trading business, "Got a hunch, bet a bunch." As with most old sayings, this one is based more on fact than fiction. In most human endeavors it is more fun to do than to plan. This trait is very human and is only driven out of people by years of schooling and life. There are two problems with planning in finance. One problem is that most traders want to trade, not plan. And the second problem is that most planners never get to trade since management in financial firms mainly rise from the trading ranks, which means they strive to optimize for the short term.

Therefore, in financial markets we have a large number of simple systems being built again and again and again. However, these simple systems do not result in maintainable excess returns. We have a few firms that do actually implement their long-term plans, and these plans do result in maintainable excess returns. The small-sized firms that become mid-sized firms eventually end up being sold to large firms. The few large firms that continue to build their proprietary systems end up dominating markets. The most interesting feature of the business is that the best trading and money management firms seem to understand this, given the size of their budgets for proprietary trading system development.

Complex trading systems are built one step at a time, evolving along the way. The first step toward building a trading system is normally the hardest one. It may seem elementary, but being able to clearly articulate a trading idea is extremely important. Being forced to describe an idea has the effect of clarifying your thoughts, as well as communicating plans and defining goals and the meaning of success. The more complex the trading idea, the more time it takes to define and communicate it clearly.

The description of the trading idea should contain the answers to several basic questions:

1. What market or markets will be traded?
2. What capital will be traded?
   a. Short term
   b. Long term
   c. Midterm
3. Whose capital is it? Proprietary or investor capital?
4. How will success be defined? Is there a benchmark against which to compare the results? Are there competitors against which to compare results?
   a. Best/worst/average returns for a group
   b. Sharpe ratio
5. What is the strategic advantage over the competition?
   a. Data
   b. Calculations
   c. Speed
   d. Capital cost
6. What is the expected time horizon for launch of the initial paper trading?
7. What is the expected time horizon for full-scale trading?

The goal of this stage of the project is to focus attention on the long-term features of the trading system. As with most business ideas, a focused, well-defined plan is essential, especially in a start-up phase. Due to the low barriers to entry, one common situation in the trading industry is the existence of multiple trading firms with little or no focus and, to make matters worse, meager start-up capital.

Research Quantitative Methods

Research into quantitative methods may be in the form of the derivation of proprietary algorithms or the application of publicly available research or white papers. Furthermore, this research may also include gaining an understanding of the methodologies of other successful systems.

To be successful at quantitative research, you should take full advantage of the available resources such as the Internet and libraries of academic publications. Building a proprietary library of quantitative methods is key to long-term system and firm success.

Books and papers in this library should be cataloged by the author, the firm, and the nature of the quantitative method discussed.

Prototype in Excel

Excel is the most rapid development environment for testing trading ideas. However, large spreadsheets, especially those that contain historical data, can become increasingly difficult to document and manage.

Check Profitability

At any point in this or any other of the four stages, profitability testing may show system failure. That is, the trading system may not be profitable. This will necessitate a looping back to previous stages. The goal is to quickly stop development on trading systems that have a low probability of success.

PHASE II. BACK-TEST

A back test is a simulation of an automated trading system against historical data. A back test determines what buys and sells would have been made according to a prescribed set of algorithms. Successful system analysis and design necessitates research into past market movement as a way to analyze and validate the system. But not only should back testing confirm the validity and accuracy of a system's algorithms; it must also confirm risks and rewards of competing alternative algorithms.

Gather Data

It may seem obvious, but being able to gather the necessary market data is very important. Oftentimes data required may not exist at all or may be too expensive.

Clean Data

One of the major obstacles to building a profitable trading system is the unavailability of clean and timely data. Many systems that are dependent upon the analyses of historical data are never fully implemented because data is either too expensive or not obtainable altogether. Therefore, prior to starting a project, the data feeds and their prices should be determined.

Perform In-Sample/Out-of-Sample Test

Financial engineers are keenly aware of the extent to which in-sample results of model fitting differ from results obtained on out-of-sample data. Trading algorithms and quantitative models must be examined against out-of-sample data prior to moving to the implementation stage. A well-developed system will perform similarly out-of-sample as it does in-sample. It is of course important to save some of your historical data for out-of-sample testing.

Check Profitability

Again, checking the profitability of the system will prevent additional time and resources from being spent on unprofitable projects. We may need to loop back to the initial research phase and reassess the quantitative methods and algorithms.

PHASE III. IMPLEMENT

Implementation of an automated trading system will require connectivity between and interoperability with disparate software systems for trade execution and other processes such as optimization. This will require the creation of plans and blueprints before programming in a language like VB.NET begins.

Build Vision and Scope Documents

The purpose of the vision and scope documents is to ensure that management fully understands the end goal along with the expected costs of the project before construction starts. The vision document provides both the financial engineers assigned to the project and management a brief overview of the current project. The information listed on the vision document should be at a very high level so that the entire form can be completed in a couple of hours.

The scope document should clearly define the steps for the project along with the documentation of all the detailed information about a calculation. After management has approved the initial project concept and the vision document, then the scope document can be completed. A full-blown scope document can range from 2 or 3 pages to over 20 pages depending on the level of detail provided. Its design should allow for multiple revisions along the way. This is important in finance since many of the key items of a project get revised regularly as the details get flushed out with prototypes.

The following samples of vision and scope documents provide some basic information about the project in a consistent manner from project to project.

Project 1
Vision Document

Project Leader: **Andrew Kumiega** Date: 03/01/03
Project Originator: Ben Van Vliet
Sponsor: Bob Hendry

Project Definition:
This section should include a one-paragraph definition of the project.

Major Objectives:
This section should list the major objectives of the project.

Impact:
This section should define and forecast the success of the project.

Priority/Deadline Issues:
This section should list all deadlines, known priorities, and other issues relevant to the project.

Constraints:
This section should list any known constraints for this project.

Analysis of Product:
This section defines how we intend to test the implementation of the completed product, including white- and black-box testing.

Resources:
This section should list the financial engineers involved in the project as well as other support personnel, including additional programmers and hardware support.

Project Type: _____Formal _____Ad Hoc

Initial Priority: A B C D E

Approved By: _____
Approved Date: _____

Project 1
Scope Document

Project Leader: **Andrew Kumiega** Date: 03/01/03
Project Originator: Ben Van Vliet
Sponsor: Bob Hendry

Project Definition:
This section should include a one-paragraph definition of the project. Also, the project definition should be updated as additional specifications arise or changes to the specifications are made.

Functionalities:
The entire list of functionalities of the application should be fully documented in this section. Beyond whatever may be the obvious functionalities, here a few important things to remember:

- Management will likely still want printed reports.
- Bulletproof error handling must be incorporated to prevent trading errors due to bad data or erroneous human interaction.
- The algorithms should be clearly explained.
- The graphical user interface, as simple as it may turn out to be, should be fully laid out.
- A complete data dictionary should to be built along with a data flow map.
- Speed of execution is critical for many applications, and so competing methods of implementation may need to be analyzed.

Steps and Milestones:
The purpose of the Steps and Milestones section is to keep the project on track. The goal is to document at a high level all the major steps and milestones that are required to complete the trading system. A simple, but key, element of the documentation of the steps is color-coding of work

items. These steps should be updated at least weekly as progress is made on the project.

- Standard black text is used to list steps and milestones that are progressing as planned.
- Blue text is used to show steps and milestones that have been completed.
- Red text is used to show steps and milestones that have stopped and are currently placing the project at risk.
- Green is used to show scope creep.

As we have discussed, scope creep can be the most dangerous portion of a project as stakeholders request additions to the project. Unnecessary digressions can doom a project, and so it is important to focus on specific and relevant functionalities. However, as is typically the case, rejected additions will be used as an excuse if the trading system loses money.

Future Features:
This section should describe any additional features that should be started after the initial project is completed. The goal of this section is to contain scope creep.

Schedule:
A schedule should be presented in this section done in project management software such as Microsoft Project.

Detailed Documentation of Key Functionalities:
Key functionalities of the trading systems should be fully documented—for example, data, I/O, GUIs, calculations, error handling, and reports.

Build Objects and Program Document

Building a trading system in code is a bit like building a building. The bigger and more complex the building, the more important blueprints are to the success of the project. Likewise, the more complex a trading system becomes, the more important it is to create detailed architectural plans before construction in code begins. But how do we create these blueprints? The answer is the Uniform Modeling Language (UML). UML is the software industry's graphical language that enables project designers and programmers to communicate the details of software design.

Through the use of UML, programming problems can be solved in an object-oriented way before programming begins. As you can imagine then, financial engineers who want to use UML must be familiar with object-oriented programming and the process of abstraction and application modeling. (Don't worry. If you are not familiar with these concepts, we will show you them over the course of this book.) Models written using UML will help us visualize and document the structure of a software application.

Program and Document the System

Having proved the trading system to be successful through in-sample and out-of-sample testing, we proceed with the crossover stage of the system development process. In this stage we cross over from Excel's cell-based environment to VB.NET by converting the system's functionalities into programming code.

Paper-Trade and Check Profitability

This time when we check profitability, we will have some real-time, live data to go on. The last step prior to opening an account and turning on a trading system is paper trading. Placing simulated trades against real-time market data will give us a true and final test of the potential of a trading system.

PHASE IV. MANAGE PORTFOLIO AND RISK

Apart from the simplest trading systems, no individual trade exists in a vacuum. Rather, all the trades and subsequent positions will be viewed as a portfolio of positions.

Monitor Portfolio Statistics

Portfolios of securities and derivatives require constant monitoring. No system, no matter how well planned or well built, should be left unattended. A system for monitoring trade limits, risk factors such as portfolio delta and gammas, and drawdowns should be implemented and followed strictly.

Perform Value-at-Risk Calculations

Value-at-risk calculations will give management a snapshot of the potential losses given a portfolio. However, while methods for dealing with extraordinary occurrences may be built into a trading system, overnight volatility in the form of opening gaps may render them useless.

Document Profit and Loss Attribution

A good way to monitor the success of a system is to keep track of individual trades and their respective payoffs. These will be valuable when reevaluating the underlying premise for the system.

Determine Causes of Variation in Profitability

Profitable trading systems will not be so forever. Eventually, the market will close the door on our trade. So systems will need to be continuously tweaked, and in the end scrapped.The goal here is to quickly stop trading systems that lose their edge before they cause losses. A successfully implemented trading system always requires ongoing profitability assessment.

Repeat the Entire Waterfall Process for Continuous Improvement

Continuous improvement consists of an ongoing effort toward bettering our trading systems. When applied to a trading environment, a continuous-improvement strategy involves both management and financial engineers working together in trading teams to make small improvements continuously. It is top-level management's responsibility to cultivate a professional environment that engenders constant improvement. A culture of sustained ongoing improvement will focus efforts on eliminating waste in all trading systems and processes of a trading organization. Intelligent company leadership should guide and encourage trading teams to continuously improve profitability, increase efficiency, and reduce costs.

Through small innovations from research and entrepreneurial activity, trading firms can discover breakthrough ideas. These ideas include, among other things, the creation of new trade selection algorithms, the application of existing systems to new markets, and the implementation of new technologies for more efficient trade execution.

SUMMARY

The advantage of the Kumiega–Van Vliet approach is that it allows financial engineers to quickly deliver a prototype for evaluation and specifications prototyped in Excel that are scalable into VB.NET or some other implementation language. If the trading system is deemed to have a high probability of long-term profitability, financial engineers can proceed down the waterfall.

There are four distinct advantages to using this methodology for trading system development:

1. The research and documentation stage along with its Excel prototyping approach provides a mechanism for documenting the system requirements and for gaining buy-in from senior management. Financial engineers

should be able to explicitly state and demonstrate the algorithms and profitability of a trading system prior to implementation.

2. The iterative framework of documentation, prototyping, and testing of intermediate-level working versions of the system allows for feedback and reduces risks before they become problematic.

3. This methodology allows for step-by-step testing of coded algorithms against Excel's built-in functions.

4. Time to market is greatly reduced since the Excel prototype demonstrates the profitability of a system in a short amount of time.

The process of doing quantitative research in financial markets requires the completion of these four phases of development resulting in four models: the algorithms model, data model, implementation model, and risk management model. Over the remainder of this book, each of these phases, and their subphases, will be addressed. Along the way, we will learn a great deal about quantitative finance, Visual Basic.NET, ADO.NET, databases and SQL, object-oriented programming, XML, and UML.

PROBLEMS

1. When developing financial models in Visual Basic.NET, how do we test whether or not our algorithms are correct?
2. What is a trading system?
3. What is meant by continuous improvement?
4. What are vision and scope documents?
5. What is UML used for?

Introduction to VB.NET
Algorithm Development

The ability to learn faster than your competitors may be the only sustainable competitive advantage.

Peter Senge

CHAPTER 3

Getting Started with VB.NET

In this chapter you will learn how to maneuver around the Visual Basic.NET integrated development environment (IDE) and how to customize it to your liking for efficient development. While we will only be writing a smidgen of code, we will be creating a professional-looking program and learning a few simple techniques that are big time-savers.

DIFFERENT VERSIONS OF VISUAL BASIC

There are different versions of Visual Basic. This book presents the latest version, Visual Basic.NET. If you are using Visual Basic 6.0, we suggest you upgrade your software to take full advantage of the .NET environment. Since many readers are probably already familiar with VBA (Visual Basic for Applications), which is very similar to VB 6.0, this book will be particularly valuable in converting spreadsheets and VBA macros into professional stand-alone software. While VB.NET does support some backward compatibility, we have in all cases used .NET constructs and have left COM to the scrap bin.

THE VB.NET INTEGRATED DEVELOPMENT ENVIRONMENT

Visual Studio.NET enables you to program visually, dragging and dropping controls, like buttons and text boxes, into place rather than creating them in code. In this way, visual programming greatly increases programmer productivity. Visual Studio.NET also includes several advanced tools for writing and debugging your program code. Let's jump right in.

Step 1   Before you open Visual Basic.NET, you will need to create a separate folder on your hard drive to hold all the files for all the projects in this book, so create a folder called "C:\ModelingFM."

Step 2   Now go ahead and open Visual Studio.NET.

Step 3   When the Start Page opens, click New Project.

Step 4   Give the project the name "Test" and the location of the ModelingFM folder. Also, we will be using Visual Basic.NET for the projects in this book, and so leave Visual Basic Projects highlighted (see Figure 3.1), as well as Windows Application as the template. Later in the book we will look at some of the other templates.

F I G U R E 3.1

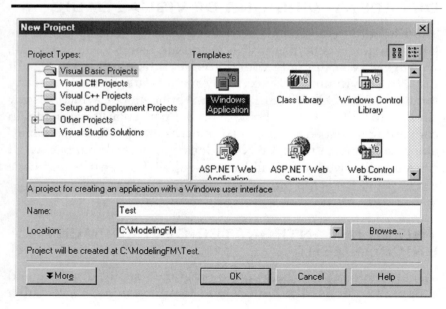

When a new project is created, VB.NET automatically places all the files associated with your new project within a folder of the same name. So the path to your new project should be C:\ModelingFM\Test\. If you take a look at the contents of this folder via Window Explorer, you will notice that several files and subfolders have been created to contain all the elements of our project. Visual Basic.NET applications that we build consist of several files. We will learn more about some of these files in later chapters. For right now, just be aware that programs consist of several files in a folder. To later reopen the project for further development, click on the file with the .sln extension.

Let's take a look at the VB.NET IDE that should now be visible on your screen (see Figure 3.2). Notice that the development environment consists of several windows, which are all either dockable or free-floating, allowing you to customize the environment to your liking. The form in the center, labeled Form1, is where we will actually build the graphical user interface (GUI) for our program.

Menu Bar

Across the top of the screen is the menu bar. Take some time to peruse the menu bar and become familiar with the types of commands that perform various actions. Many of these commands also have corresponding shortcuts, through either keystrokes or menu bar icons or both. As you will no doubt discover as you gain experience in programming in the .NET IDE, there are often several ways to accomplish the same task.

Toolbox

Written vertically down the left side of the screen should be the Toolbox button. If you do not see it, click on the Toolbox icon in the upper right-hand corner. It's the one with a hammer and wrench in an X-shaped design. When you open the Toolbox, you will see the lists of tools, called controls, that you see in Figure 3.2. We will often

F I G U R E 3.2

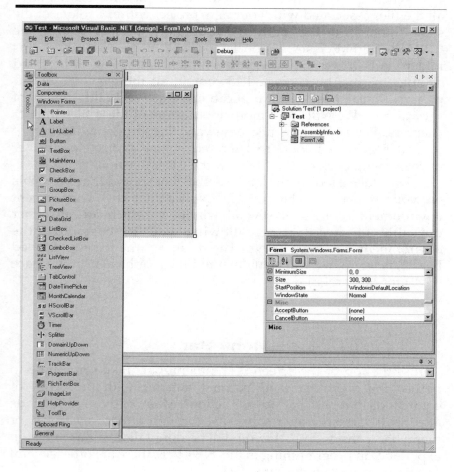

be adding controls, by dragging and dropping them into our forms, to rapidly build programs and GUIs. You may want to spend a little time investigating each of the tools before you proceed.

Solution Explorer Window

The Solution Explorer window, shown in the upper right corner, enables you to access the different parts of your project. If the

Solution Explorer window is not visible, click on the Solution Explorer icon; or on the menu bar, click View and Solution Explorer. In our applications, we almost always have several forms and classes and program modules. The Solution Explorer gives us instant access to any part of our project at any time. To close the Solution Explorer, click the X button in the upper right-hand corner.

Properties Window

In the lower right corner is the Properties window. Again, if it is not visible, click on the Properties window icon on the toolbar, or select View and Properties Window from the menu bar.

Properties are attributes, like size and color, of the objects we use in programs. Since each control, or tool, from our toolbox is an object and has its own set of properties, we can see all the properties associated with each of them in this window. You should familiarize yourself with the different properties associated with the different controls as we use them throughout this book. The left-hand side of the Properties window column lists the individual properties, and the right-hand column lists the value of each property. You will need the Properties window to set the initial values of these properties at design time, and as you will later see, we can change properties at run time using VB.NET code. As with Solution Explorer, we can close the Properties window and reopen it from either the View menu or the menu bar icon.

As we will see in Chapter 7, other, nonvisible objects we create in our programs will also have properties associated with them. When we cannot see the objects, it gets slightly more difficult to understand properties. For example, in finance, a call option could be an object. An option object in our program would certainly have properties, like an option symbol, strike price, expiration date, and implied volatility.

Events

Besides properties, controls also have events associated with them. An event is triggered when something happens to a control. The button "click" event is probably the most easily understandable example of an event. Later we will learn how to program things to happen when events are fired.

Methods

Objects, like controls, also have to perform functions of their own. It isn't usually enough that an object simply exists. After all, the whole point of creating a control is that the object does something useful. These additional functions are known as methods in Visual Basic.NET terms. Whereas properties are thought of as nouns, methods are often thought of as verbs. Later, we will learn how to create our own objects and add methods to them.

Visual Studio.NET Help

There is no way that any book can hope to cover all the features of Visual Basic.NET or all the potential instances you may uncover for using them. Finding and solving new problems quickly is one of the joys of programming. Fortunately, Visual Studio.NET provides a vast array of help features. Knowing how to find what you need in the Help files is one of the most valuable skills you can gain to improve your expertise. Again, you should investigate the Help files on your own and become comfortable accessing the Help index and Dynamic Help. Most often, programming questions that arise are covered extensively in the Help files, almost always with code examples.

CREATING AN EXECUTABLE PROGRAM

You will write many different applications as you go through this book. Creating an executable program allows you to run your application as a single .exe file from the Windows environment without having to be in the VB.NET IDE. In order to create an executable file, VB.NET programs must be compiled into machine language.

Compiling a VB.NET application is a two-stage process. First, the program is compiled into Microsoft Intermediate Language

(MSIL). Then second, another compiler translates this MSIL code into a single, executable file in machine language. In this way, Microsoft's .NET framework provides language interoperability. Programs that are written in different languages, such as C#, Perl, or Python, can all be first compiled into MSIL. So different parts of a program, written in different languages, can be combined to create a single program. In fact, any .NET-compliant language can be compiled into MSIL in this way, and thus .NET is said to be language-independent.

Step 5   Make sure your form, known by the default name "Form1" in your project, is active by clicking on it. You can change the size of the form by pulling on the highlighted corners or sides. This will automatically cause the Size property of the form to change. Now, in the Properties window, change the value of the "Text" property to read "My First VB.NET Program" without the quotation marks. When you press Enter, you will see the title on the form change to the new text.

Step 6   In the Toolbox, click on Label and "paint" a label on your form by holding down the left mouse button and dragging over the form.

Step 7   This new label is now known by the default name Label1, as you can see in the Properties window. Make sure the label is selected, and in the Properties window, change the Font property to Garamond, Bold, size 36. Also, change the Text property to Buy Low, Sell High. Change the TextAlign property to MiddleCenter.

Your form should now look like the one shown in Figure 3.3.

Step 8   Now to run your program, click the Start button on the menu bar, or under the Debug tab, click Start. The Start button is the one that looks like a blue arrow, next to the word Debug. Your program should take a few seconds to compile, and then it will run. You can close the program by clicking on the X.

F I G U R E 3.3

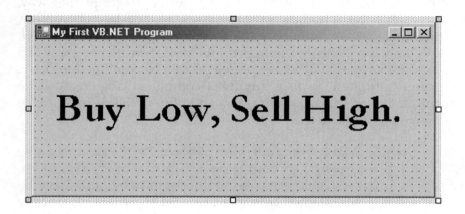

Step 9   In Windows Explorer you can find the executable program Test.exe in the Test folder, subfolder bin. The path to the file in its entirety should be C:\ModelingFM\Test\bin\Test.exe. If you close down the Visual Basic.NET IDE, you can run this executable program by double-clicking it. Furthermore, you can drag the Test.exe icon onto your Windows desktop. You can even email it to your friends so that they never forget how to make money in the markets.

Now let's take a little deeper look at the VB.NET IDE.

Step 10   If you have not already done so, close the program, so that you are back in the VB.NET IDE. In the Solution Explorer window, click on the View Code icon as shown in Figure 3.4.

Step 11   The Form1 code window will appear (see Figure 3.5). This is where we write VB.NET code that is associated with the controls we place on Form1, including code that runs when events happen, as previously discussed.

F I G U R E 3.4

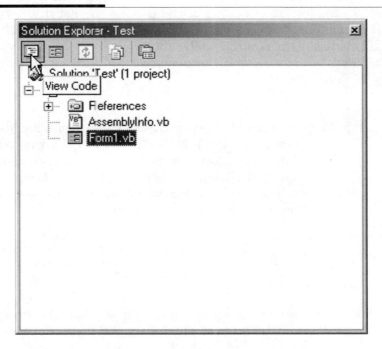

F I G U R E 3.5

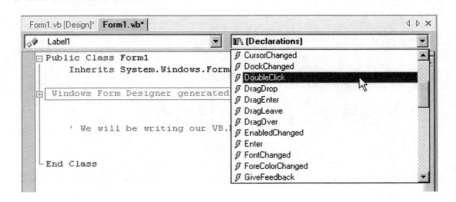

In the combo boxes across the top of the code window, click on Label1 in the left-hand combo box and open the list in the right-hand combo box. This is a list of all the events associated with our label, Label1. All the controls in the Toolbox have events associated with them. When an event happens, we can add code to make something happen.

Step 12 For example, select DoubleClick from the list of events for Label1. Notice that VB.NET writes a stub of the event code for us. In the event code routine, type Label1.Text = "Sell High, Buy Low." The underscores you see below allow us to wrap long lines of code onto the next line.

```
Private Sub Label1_DoubleClick(ByVal sender As Object, _
                              ByVal e As System.EventArgs) _
                              Handles Label1.DoubleClick
      Label1.Text = "Sell High, Buy Low."
End Sub
```

Step 13 Run the program again. Notice that the program runs the same as previously. But if you double-click on the label in the form, an entirely new way to profit in the markets appears (see Figure 3.6).

F I G U R E 3.6

SUMMARY

Visual Basic.NET makes every effort to provide us with the tools that simplify and speed the process of creating our own applications, or solutions as they are known in VB.NET. If you already program in a previous version of Visual Basic, you will notice several similarities in the new .NET IDE. If you are new to programming, you will be able to turn out professional-looking applications even while you are learning VB.NET.

Make sure you practice using the Help files. Practically everything you need to know is included in there somewhere. You might have to dig for it, but it is in there.

In the example program in this chapter, we looked at the label control and the properties and events associated with it. We even wrote a brief statement to change the text property when the double-click event is fired.

PROBLEMS

1. Where does VB.NET store the various files associated with your program?
2. Where will you find the controls used to create a graphical user interface?
3. If the Properties window is closed, how can you reopen it?
4. How do you create an executable program?
5. What are properties, events, and methods?

PROJECT 3.1

Create a graphical user interface like the one pictured in Figure 3.7. Use a tab control with three tab pages named Stocks, Options, and Futures. On the Options tab page, place 4 combo boxes with sorted items, including 10 stock tickers, Put/Call, 12 expirations, and 10 strikes. Also, place labels on your tab forms with Fixed3D border style and custom background colors. Name the colored labels lblBidQty, lb1BidPrice, lb1AskPrice, lblAskQty, and lblLast. Try adding some controls and changing the fonts to enhance the appearance and user-friendliness of your GUI. Also, on the Stocks and Futures tab pages, add similar content for financial instruments of these types. For right now, to keep things simple do not add any code to handle any of the events associated with the controls on your form.

PROJECT 3.2

Use buttons, group boxes, and radio buttons to create the GUI pictured in Figure 3.8. The default checked property for each of

F I G U R E 3.7

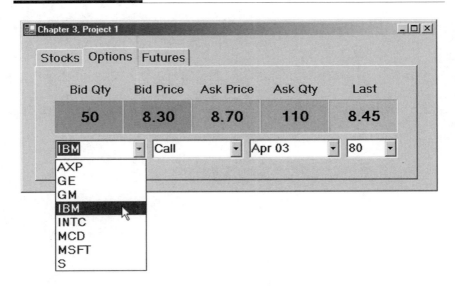

F I G U R E 3.8

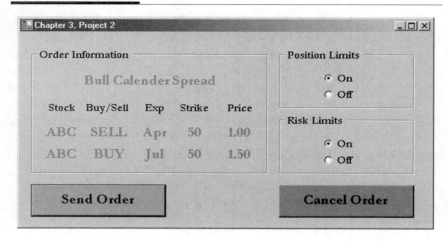

your On buttons should be set to True. When you run the program and check the False radio buttons, the True buttons should turn off automatically because they are grouped together. For right now, to keep things simple do not add any code to handle any of the events associated with the controls on your form.

CHAPTER 4

Value Types and Operators

Most financial programming involves making mathematical calculations. As in algebra, we often use variables in computer programs to hold different values we need for calculation. In this chapter, you will learn how to declare variables and perform calculations in VB.NET.

DECLARING VARIABLES

To a computer, primitive or simple value types, called variables, are actual, physical spaces in memory that store data for use by our program. Before we can use a variable, we need to declare it using the Dim statement. That is, we have to tell the computer to set up a space in memory with a specific name. In programming, the variable names we use are usually descriptive of the contents they hold. For example, a program to analyze stock returns might contain variables like this:

```
Dim sglMondayClose, sglStockPrice As Single
Dim dblCallDelta As Double
Dim strTicker As String
```

These lines of code set up variables, physical places in memory, that will be known by the names sglMondayClose, sglStockPrice, dblCallDelta, and strTicker. Furthermore, the types of data that will go into each of these containers will be things called a single, a double, and a string. Single, double, and string are value types, which tell us what kind of data the variable can hold. Here is a list of the different value types supported by VB.NET, with descriptions:

Value Type with Identifier	Range	Note	Example Using Naming Convention and Value Type Identifier
Boolean	True or false	16 bits. Stored internally as either 0 or 1	Dim blnBuySell As Boolean
Char	Any Unicode character	Character codes 0 to 65,535	Dim chrExpMonth As Char
Date	1/1/0001 to 12/31/9999 and 0:00:00 to 23:59:59	64 bits. Holds dates and times	Dim dtExpDate As Date
Decimal@	$1.0E - 28$ to $7.9E + 28$	128 bits. Large numbers	Dim decCovar As Decimal or Dim decCovar@
Double #	$+/- 5.0E - 324$ to $+/- 1.7E + 308$	64 bits. Double-precision floating-point variable	Dim dblCallDelta As Double or Dim dblCallDelta#
Integer %	$-2,147,483,648$ to $2,147,483,647$	32 bits. Integers only. No decimal numbers	Dim intNumShares As Integer or Dim intNumShares%
Long &	$-9,223,372,036,854,775,808$ to $9,223,372,036,854,775,807$	64 bits. Big integers, but still no decimal numbers	Dim lngNumTrades As Long or Dim lngNumTrades&
Short	$-32,768$ to $32,767$	16 bits. Small integers only. No decimal numbers	Dim shtNumContracts As Short
Single !	$+/- 1.5E - 45$ to $+/- 3.4E + 38$	32 bits. Single-precision floating-point variable	Dim sglStockPrice As Single or Dim sglStockPrice!
String $	Varies based upon the number of characters	Character data	Dim strTicker As String or Dim strTicker$

When a variable of any type is created, its default value is 0. We can define or change the values of our variables this way:

```
sglMondayClose = 10.12
strTicker = "MMZR"
```

Alternatively, we could declare and define a variable in the same line:

```
Dim sglStockPrice As Single = 4.92
```

In Visual Basic.NET all variables must be declared before they can be used. Later in the book, we will show you that this helps avoid common programming errors.

CONSTANTS

If the value of a variable is not going to change over the life of our program, we should declare it as a constant, rather than a variable, like this:

```
Const DIVISOR = 1.8
```

Declaring a value as a constant protects it against accidentally being changed down the road.

VARIABLE SCOPE

Variables and constants can also be declared using an access modifier. Access modifiers serve to specify the scope and accessibility of the variable. The access modifiers are Friend, Private, Protected, Protected Friend, and Public. Here is an example:

```
Public strExchange As String
```

In later chapters, we will discuss access and scope in more detail. For now, be aware that the scope of a variable refers to the parts of a program that can access a variable. Not all variables are accessible everywhere. Variables in Visual Basic.NET can have the following scope:

Scope	Accessibility or "Visibility"
Class	Accessible in what is known as the declaration space of the class
Module	Accessible to all functions and procedures defined in the module
Global or Namespace	Accessible anywhere in a project
Block	Accessible only within the block of code in which they are declared

Variables should always be defined with the smallest possible scope. Variables with global scope can make the logic of an application extremely difficult to understand and make the reuse and maintenance of your code more difficult. In a Visual Basic.NET application, global variables should be used only when there is no other convenient way to share data between parts of your program. When global variables must be used, it is good practice to declare them all in a single module, grouped by function. For now, just be aware that not all variables are accessible from everywhere in our applications. The access modifiers will limit the visibility of variables.

REPRESENTING DATES AND TIMES

When making financial calculations, we also often need to represent dates and times in our programs for things like interest accrual and trade time stamps.

```
Dim dtMyDate As Date
dtMyDate = #01/02/03#
```

Visual Basic.NET is sensitive to the cultural differences in date representation. For example, if you are working in the United Kingdom and rerun the above example, the first four numbers are interpreted as, the first of February rather than the American second of January.

OPTION STRICT

An Option Strict On statement should always appear in the declarations section of a module. Option Strict On prevents Visual Basic.NET from making implicit type conversions that may involve loss of data. For purposes of demonstration in this book, however, we will leave the default Option Strict Off. Just remember, in the real world you should always have the Option Strict On statement at the top in your programs.

STRUCTURES

Generally, when a group of data fit together, but consist of different value types, we may prefer to create our own variable type, called a structure. Visual Basic.NET allows us to create our own user-defined value types using the Structure statement. Our structures will generally contain more than one element, and each element must be declared with an access modifier. Here is an example of a user-defined data type called QuoteData:

```
Structure QuoteData
        Public dtDate As Date
        Public dblOpen As Double
        Public dblHigh As Double
        Public dblLow As Double
        Public dblClose As Double
        Public lngVolume As Long
End Structure
```

We can then declare a variable of the type QuoteData in the following way:

```
Dim qdStockPrice As QuoteData
```

Much in the same way we reference properties of objects, such as controls, we can reference the individual elements of a structure value type like this:

```
Text1.Text = qdStockPrice.dtDate
Text2.Text = qdStockPrice.dblOpen
```

ENUMERATIONS

Enumerations are integer value types that have a limited set of acceptable values. VB.NET allows us to create enumerations using the Enum statement, the integer value type—byte, short, integer, long—and the acceptable values.

```
Enum TradeStatus As Short
        Filled
        Open
        Partial
        Canceled
        Rejected
End Enum
```

We can use this enumeration by calling on one of its member names in code as follows:

```
Dim myTrade As TradeStatus = myTrade.Partial
```

Enumerations make it easier to understand the purpose of variables with a limited number of allowable values as opposed to the integer values.

OPERATORS

Visual Basic.NET has a wealth of operators to handle mathematical calculations and other logical operations. As we go through the book, we will be making extensive use of operators as we write programs. Most of them are self-explanatory, but some may not be. You can use this section as a reference as they come up over the course of the book.

Arithmetic Operators

Math Operator	Name	Example	Description
^	Exponentiation	x^y	Raises x to the power of y
-	Negation	-y	Negates y
*	Multiplication	x*y	Multiplies x and y
/	Division	x/y	Divides x by y and returns a floating-point result
\	Integer division	x\y	Divides x by y and returns an integer result
Mod	Modulos	x Mod y	Divides x by y and returns the remainder
+	Addition	x + y	Adds x and y
−	Subtraction	x − y	Subtracts y from x

Comparison Operators

Comparison Operator	Description	Example
=	Equal	sglStockPrice = 5.67
<>	Not equal	intNumShares <> 500
>	Greater than	dblCallDelta > .5
<	Less than	intVolume < 10000
>=	Greater than or equal	sglClosePrice >= 52.50
<=	Less than or equal	sglHighPrice <= sglPreviousClose

Assignment Operators

Assignment Operator	Example	Explanation	New Value
Assume that sglPrice = 10.00 and strTicker = "PKR"			
+=	sglPrice += 3	sglPrice = sglPrice + 3	sglPrice = 13.00
-=	sglPrice -= 2.00	sglPrice = sglPrice - 2.00	sglPrice = 8.00
*=	sglPrice *= 1.15	sglPrice = sglPrice * 1.15	sglPrice = 11.5
/=	sglPrice /= 2	sglPrice = sglPrice / 2	sglPrice = 5
\=	sglPrice \= 3	sglPrice = sglPrice \ 3	sglPrice = 3
^=	sglPrice ^= .2	sglPrice = sglPrice ^ .2	sglPrice = 1.5849
&=	strTicker &= "Q"	strTicker = strTicker & "Q"	strTicker = "PKRQ"

Logical Operators

Logical Operator	Description	Example
And	Evaluates to True only if both conditions are true	dblPrice > 55 And dblPrice < 56
AndAlso	Evaluates to True only if both conditions are true	dblPrice > 55 AndAlso dblPrice < 56
Not	Reverses or negates the meaning of an operand	
Or	Evaluates to True if one or both conditions are true	dblPrice > 55 Or dblPrice < 40
OrElse	Evaluates to True if one or both conditions are true	dblPrice > 55 OrElse dblPrice < 40
Xor	If both are true or false, evaluates to False	dblPrice > 55 Xor dblPrice < 60

Concatenation Operators

Concatenation Operator	Description	Example
&	Concatenates or binds a number of strings together. (Preferred)	strTick = strSymbol & "Q"
+	Concatenates or binds a number of strings together	strTick = strSymbol + "Q"

STOCK INDEX FUTURES

The most widely traded equity index futures contract in the United States is the S&P 500. The futures contracts on the S&P 500 index are traded at the Chicago Mercantile Exchange (CME). The value of the contract is $250 times the futures price. The CME's "e-Mini" contract is a smaller, electronically traded version of the original pit-traded contract and has a value of $50 times the futures price. So if the futures contract were valued at 1000, it would have a notional value of $250,000 and the e-Mini a notional value of $50,000. The CME also trades options on these futures contracts. The Chicago Board Options Exchange trades options on the cash S&P 500 index. The S&P 500 index consists of 500 stocks, each selected for its market size, liquidity, and industry group. Also, the S&P 500 is a market value–weighted index where the market value of an individual stock is the stock price times the number of shares outstanding. Each stock's weight in the index then is proportionate to its market value. The weights for the individual stocks change as their respective prices rise and fall relative to other stocks in the index (Kolb, 1997, p. 334). Alternatively, an index could be price-weighted, where the index weights are proportional to the stock prices. The Dow Jones Industrial Average is an example of a price-weighted index.

Here is an example of a formula for the calculation of the *cash* value of a market value–weighted index:

$$\text{S\&P } 500 = \left(\frac{\sum_{i=1}^{500} N_i P_i}{\text{O.V.}} \right) \times 10$$

where:

> O.V. = original valuation
> N_i = number of shares outstanding for the ith firm
> P_i = price per share of the ith firm

Let's build a simple program that will calculate the price of a market value–weighted stock index. In this example, we will demonstrate the simplest type of computer program, one that uses procedural programming techniques. Procedural programs are those written as lists of instructions divided into sections or units of code called the main block, plus subroutines and functions, which we will look at in Chapter 6. Procedural programming works well for small projects because it is very intuitive. Moreover, machine code is procedural, and so compiling procedural code is very efficient.

> **Step 1** Open the Visual Basic.Net IDE. For this exercise we are going to create a new console application, so click on the icon named Console Application and name the project "IndexFutures." A console application is the simplest type of VB.NET program and contains only text input and output, as you will see. The interface will be a command, or console, window.
>
> **Step 2** When the project IDE opens up, you will be presented only with a window in which to write code. Within the Sub main() procedure, we need to create the necessary variables and algorithms to make our calculations.

For simplicity, we will assume that there are two stocks in this index, known as stock A and stock B, and that it is a market value–weighted index like the S&P 500. Also, to keep things simple, we will not add Option Strict to our code.

> **Step 3** Now, let's add some code to calculate the index value. To do this, we will need to declare and define some variables and use some mathematical operators according to the formula.

```
Module Module1
    Sub Main()
        Const ORIGINALVALUE = 2000        ' Index original value
        Dim dblIndexValue As Double
        Dim intSharesA% = 1000            ' 1000 shares of A outstanding
        Dim intSharesB% = 2000            ' 2000 shares of B outstanding
        Console.WriteLine("Please enter the price of stock A:")
        Dim dblPriceA# = Console.ReadLine
        Console.WriteLine("Please enter the price of stock B:")
        Dim dblPriceB# = Console.ReadLine
' Calculate the value of the index and print it to the screen.
        dblIndexValue = (((dblPriceA * intSharesA) + (dblPriceB * _
                        intSharesB)) / ORIGINALVALUE) * 10
        Console.WriteLine('The value of the index is' & dblIndexValue)
    End Sub
End Module
```

You will notice in the code above, we have included some sample values for the Original Value and the number of shares outstanding. We will allow the user to enter the prices of stocks A and B when the Console.ReadLine statements are executed. Notice that we have used the double value type for our variables using both the type name and the identifier for illustration purposes. Also, we have declared the original value of the index as a constant.

Step 4   Once your code is finished, run the program by selecting from the menu bar Debug > Start Without Debugging. This will cause the program to pause before it closes the console window so we can examine the results of our program (see Figure 4.1).

Let's augment this program to calculate the fair value of a futures contract on this index. We can calculate the fair value using the cost-of-carry model (Kolb, 1997, p. 340):

$$F_{0,t} = S_0 \left(1 + R\frac{T}{360}\right) - \sum_{i=1}^{n} D_i\left(1 + R\frac{\tau_i}{360}\right)$$

where:

$F_{0,t}$ = index futures price at time 0 and expires t days in the future

S_0 = value of the market value–weighted cash index at time 0

R = interest rate

T = number of days till futures expiration

F I G U R E 4.1

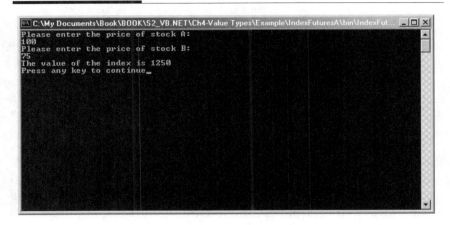

D_i = amount of the ith dividend

τ_i = number of days the ith dividend will be invested from receipt until futures expiration

Step 5 Change the code so as to calculate the fair value of a futures contract.

```
Module Module1
    Sub Main()
        Const ORIGINALVALUE = 2000              ' Index original value
        Dim dblFairValue, dblIndexValue As Double
        Dim dblDaysTillExp As Double = 90       ' 90 days till expiration
        Dim dblRate As Double = 0.10            ' 10% interest rate
        Dim intSharesA% = 1000                  ' 1000 shares of A outstanding
        Dim intSharesB% = 2000                  ' 2000 shares of B outstanding
        Dim dblDivA# = 2.00     ' 2.00 dividend 40 days from now on A
        Dim dblDivB# = 1.00     ' 1.00 dividend 50 days from now on B
        Dim intDaysDivAInvested% = 50
                     ' ( 90 - 40 ) = 50 days to invest dividend
        Dim intDaysDivBInvested% = 40
                     ' ( 90 - 50 ) = 40 days to invest dividend
        Console.WriteLine("Please enter the price of stock A:")
        Dim dblPriceA# = Console.ReadLine
        Console.WriteLine("Please enter the price of stock B:")
        Dim dblPriceB# = Console.ReadLine
' Calculate the fair value and print it to the screen.
        dblIndexValue = (((dblPriceA * intSharesA) + (dblPriceB * _
                        intSharesB)) / ORIGINALVALUE) * 10
        dblFairValue = (dblIndexValue) * (1 + dblRate * dblDaysTillExp _
                     / 360) - (dblDivA * (1 + dblRate * _
```

```
                intDaysDivAInvested / 360) + dblDivB * (1 + _
                dblRate * intDaysDivBInvested / 360))
        Console.WriteLine("The fair value is" & dblFairValue)
    End Sub
```

Step 6   Run the program by selecting from the menu bar Debug > Start Without Debugging (see Figure 4.2).

Although we are finished programming for the chapter, let's take a little more in-depth look at the fair value of a futures contract on a stock index.

No-arbitrage conditions prevent the value of the index futures contract from moving too far away from the fair value. Cash-and-carry strategies prevent the futures price from getting too high relative to the cash stocks, and reverse cash-and-carry arbitrage strategies prevent it from getting too low. Identifying opportunities for cash-and-carry arbitrage, however, necessitates the technological infrastructure to monitor the 500 stocks in real time and execute trades simultaneously. These types of trading strategies are often referred to as "program trading" since they are computer-generated.

In the following two examples illustrating index arbitrage, we assume that the prices of the underlying stocks A and B do not change over the 90 days, although the profit or loss does not in either case depend on the stock prices at expiration. Rather, the

F I G U R E   4.2

profit arises from a discrepancy between the futures price and its fair value on day 0 (Kolb, 1997, p. 342).

The futures price must be equal to the cash index price plus the charges to carry the cash index forward to expiration (Kolb, 1997, p. 71). The carrying charge is the interest lost by being long the underlying stocks. If the prices do not fall in line with the cost of carry, a trader may attempt a cash-and-carry or reverse cash-and-carry arbitrage.

Cash-and-Carry Arbitrage

A cash-and-carry arbitrage strategy involves buying the stock and selling the futures contract in a similar but opposite fashion (Kolb, 1997, p. 343). Here we replicate the index by weighting our portfolio with three parts stock B, $750, and two parts stock A, $500,

Time	Cash Market	Futures Market
0 days	Borrow $1250 for 90 days at 10% Interest owed will be $ 31.25 Buy 5 shares of stock A at $100 Buy 10 shares of stock B at $75	Sell 1 futures contract at 1285.00
40 days	Receive $2.00 dividend on each share of stock A, totaling $10 Invest proceeds for 50 days at 10%	
50 days	Receive $1.00 dividend on each share of stock B, totaling $10 Invest proceeds for 40 days at 10%	
90 days	Sell 5 shares of stock A at $100 Sell 10 shares of stock B at $75 Receive total proceeds from invested dividends of $10.14 and $10.11 Total proceeds are $1270.25 Repay debt plus interest of $1281.25	Buy 1 futures contract at fair value at expiration of 1250, which is the spot index value
P&L	Loss: $11.00	Profit: $35.00

Total profit of $35.00 − $11.00 = $24.00

Reverse Cash-and-Carry Arbitrage

A reverse cash-and-carry arbitrage opportunity involves selling the underlying stock and buying the futures contract in a similar but opposite fashion (Kolb, 1997, p. 343).

Time	Cash Market	Futures Market
0 days	Sell 5 shares of stock A at $100 Sell 10 shares of stock B at $75 Invest proceeds of $1250 for 90 days at 10% Interest earned will be $31.25	Buy 1 futures contract at 1255.00
40 days	Borrow $10.00 for 50 days at 10% Pay dividend on stock A Interest owed will be $0.14	
50 days	Borrow $10.00 for 40 days at 10% Pay dividend on stock B Interest owed will be $0.11	
90 days	Buy back 5 shares of stock A at $100 Buy back 10 shares of stock B at $75 Repay debt plus interest of $20.25 Receive interest of $31.25	Sell 1 futures contract at fair value at expiration of 1250, which is the spot index value
P&L	Profit: $11.00	Loss: $5.00.

Total Profit of $11.00 − $5.00 = $6.00

SUMMARY

In this chapter you have been exposed to all the different variable types available in Visual Basic.NET. Also, you should now understand how to declare variables using the Dim statement and the various identifiers and access modifiers as well as how to define them. Good programmers will also understand the importance of the Option Strict On, though for simplicity's sake we will neglect it in this book. Also, our variable naming convention requires that we add prefixes to our variable names that indicate the data type of the variable. Variable names should also describe something about the nature of the value, such as dblStockPrice.

Further, we investigated the different operators available to programmers in VB.NET and looked at how some of them could be used in the financial markets. Our example consisted of calculating the cash value of a stock index and the fair value of a futures contract on that index.

PROBLEMS

1. What is a variable, and what is a constant?
2. When should you use Option Strict?
3. Write a line of code that would declare a variable to hold the value of the gamma of an option.
4. Write a line of code that would calculate the average of five daily returns known as dblMonReturn, dblTuesReturn, dblWedReturn, dblThursReturn, and dblFriReturn.
5. What is a concatenation operator? What is the value of a string variable known as strOptionSymbol if strOptionSymbol = "INTC" & " " & "Sep" & " " & "50"?

PROJECT 4.1

Create a VB.NET console application that accepts five daily closing stock prices from the user and calculates the mean and standard deviation of the stock's log returns (see Figure 4.3). The formula for the log return is

$$r_i = \ln\left(\frac{S_i}{S_{i-1}}\right)$$

Of course, the equations for mean and standard deviation are

$$\mu_{r;t,T} = \frac{1}{n}\sum_{i=1}^{n} r_i \qquad \text{and} \qquad \sigma_{r;t,T} = \sqrt{\frac{1}{n-1}\sum_{i=1}^{n}(r_i - \bar{r})^2}$$

Since we won't cover functions until later in the book, here's a hint. We can calculate the natural log using VB.NET's built-in log function.

```
dblTuesReturn = Math.log( dblTuesPrice / dblMonPrice )
```

Also, the square root can be found by raising the value to the 0.5 power using the ^ operator.

Be sure to name your variables using the naming conventions.

FIGURE 4.3

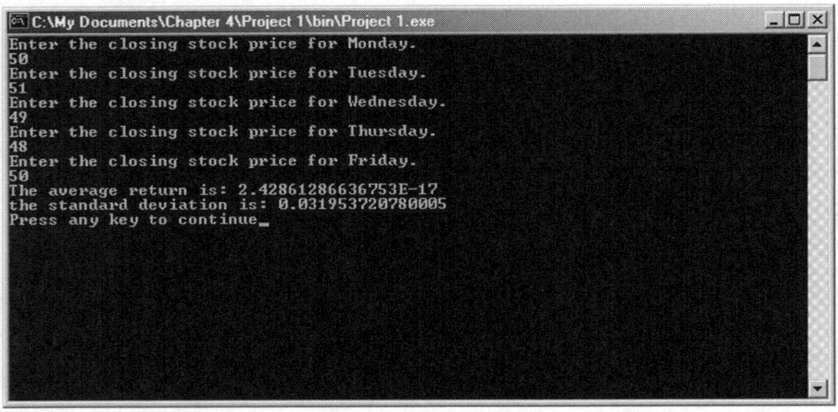

PROJECT 4.2

To calculate the value of the Dow Jones Industrial Average, a price-weighted index, the equation is

$$\text{DJIA} = \frac{\sum_{i=1}^{30} P_i}{\text{divisor}}$$

Futures contracts on the DJIA trade at the Chicago Board of Trade.

Create a console application that calculates the fair value of a two-stock, price-weighted index according to this formula. Assume that the two stocks, A and B, are priced at 100 and 75, respectively, and pay dividends in the amounts and times shown in the chapter (Kolb, 1997, p. 330).

Control Structures

The code we wrote in Chapter 4 was all linear, or sequential, in nature. That is, lines of code were executed in order, one after the other, till the end of the program. Although this is fine for very short tasks, to tackle more complex situations, we will need to employ control structures, which involve the use of program flow statements. Program flow statements fall into one of two categories:

- *Selection structures*. Conditional, or decision statements, in which code is executed based on whether or not a condition is met
- *Repetition structures*. Looping statements, in which code is executed repeatedly either a number of times or until a condition is met

SELECTION STRUCTURES

If ... Then ... Else Statement

The If ... Then ... Else statement lets us say, in effect, "If this is true, then do this; otherwise, do that." The logic couldn't be more intuitive. The following example illustrates the use of the If ... Then ... Else structure.

```
If dblStockPrice > 55 OrElse dblStockPrice < 40 Then
      Console.WriteLine("SELL!!!")
Else
      Console.WriteLine("HOLD")
End If
```

In the example, the statements following the If are executed only if the expression evaluates to True, that is if the stock price is greater than 55 or less than 40. The Else block of code executes if the expression evaluates to False. So in this case, if the stock price is between 40 and 55, we will hold. The expression used in If . . . Then is a Boolean expression, true or false. The use of the Else block in an If statement is optional.

The Select Case Statement

The Select Case structure is very similar to the If . . . Then . . . Else structure, but it is much more efficient and makes our code much more readable if there are several branches to the decision structure. In the Select Case structure we can include an unlimited number of clauses. Let's look at an example that not only illustrates the logic statements within a Select Case framework, but also demonstrates how to build a histogram of log returns:

```
Dim intBin1, intBin2, intBin3, intBin4, intBin5, intBin6 As Integer
Dim dblDailyReturn As Double = Math.Log( 51 / 50 )
Select Case dblDailyReturns
        Case Is < -.02
                intBin1 += 1
        Case -.02 To -.01
                intBin2 += 1
        Case -.01 To 0
                intBin3 += 1
        Case 0 To.01
                intBin4 += 1
        Case .01 To.02
                intBin5 += 1
        Case Is > .02
                intBin6 += 1
        Case Else
                MsgBox "Error."
    End Select
```

Since the natural log of (51 / 50) is 0.0198, the value of intBin5 will be incremented by 1. The Case Else clause at the end of the structure is optional. Also, multiple conditions are evaluated separately with a logical OR as opposed to an AND, so it's best to keep Select Case logic as simple as possible. Let's look at another example evaluating strings.

Call and put option symbols include a strike price and expiration month. The second-to-last letter in the symbol denotes the month of expiration, and the last term denotes the price. So, for example, GEKD would be the symbol for the General Electric November 20.00 calls. GERT would be the June 17.50 puts. We will have more examples using option symbols later in the book, but here is a Select Case structure using the char data type to determine the month of expiration:

```
Dim chrMonth As Char = "D"
Dim strMonth As String
Select Case chrMonth
      Case "A", "a", "M", "m"
            strMonth = "January"
      Case "B", "b", "N", "n"
            strMonth = "February"
      Case "C", "c", "O", "o"
            strMonth = "March"
      Case "D", "d", "P", "p"
            strMonth = "April"
      Case "E", "e", "Q", "q"
            strMonth = "May"
      Case "F", "f", "R", "r"
            strMonth = "June"
      Case "G", "g", "S", "s"
            strMonth = "July"
      Case "H", "h", "T", "t"
            strMonth = "August"
      Case "I", "i", "U", "u"
            strMonth = "September"
      Case "J", "j", "V", "v"
            strMonth = "October"
      Case "K", "k", "W", "w"
            strMonth = "November"
      Case "L", "l", "X", "x"
            strMonth = "December"
   End Select
```

Since the value of chrMonth is "D," the value of strMonth will be set to "April."

REPETITION STRUCTURES

Visual Basic.NET provides a number of different types of loops that you can use to implement repetitive operations.

The For . . . Next Loop

The For . . . Next loop executes a series of statements a specific number of times. The basic syntax is:

```
For x = 0 to 10 Step 2
      Console.Writeline("Your stock is down" & x & "points.")
Next x
```

Here, the program will loop through this code five times, starting with x=0. Each time it loops, x will be incremented by 2 until the maximum value of x, in this case 10, is reached. In the example above, the printout will show our stock fall by 2 points with each successive loop.

If the Step phrase is left out, your program will automatically increment the loop counter variable by $+1$. Let's take a look at this code:

```
For x = 1 to 5
      intSum += x
Next x
```

After completing the loop, the value of intSum $= 1 + 2 + 3 + 4 + 5 = 15$.

The For Each . . . Next Loop

The For Each . . . Next loop is a special type of loop designed to be used with data structures, such as an array. We will not discuss arrays until later in the book, so for right now, just note the structure of this type of loop. Here is an example:

```
Sub Main()
      Dim dblReturn, dblLowReturn As Double
      Dim dblIBM As Double() = New Double() {.01,.005, -.05, 0,.02}
      For Each dblReturn In dblIBM
            If dblReturn < dblLowReturn Then
                  dblLowReturn = dblReturn
```

```
        End If
    Next dblReturn
        Console.WriteLine("The lowest return is" & dblLowReturn)
    End Sub
```

The For Each ... Next loop cycles through each element in an array, or collection, without requiring specification of each element's index. Each time through the loop, the variable element, in this case dblReturn, is assigned the contents of the next item in the array.

For two-dimensional arrays, the For Each ... Next structure will iterate through all the elements by row. That is, it will increment the second index until it reaches the upper bound, then increment the first index, and then restart iterating through the second again.

As we will see later, For Each ... Next loops are also very useful for looping through collections of objects.

The Do ... While Loop

Here is an example of a Do ... While loop:

```
Sub Main()
    Dim dblStockPrice# = 35
    Do While dblStockPrice < 100
        dblStockPrice += 1
    Loop
    Console.WriteLine("The stock price is" & dblStockPrice)
End Sub
```

When this loop is finished, it prints out the price as 100. This routine evaluates dblStockPrice < 100 each time through the loop. When dblStockPrice = 99, the loop increments dblStockPrice to 100. The next evaluation of dblStockPrice = 100 is False, and so program execution exits the loop and continues with the line after the Loop statement, printing dblStockPrice as 100.

The Do ... Until Loop

Here is an example of a Do ... Until loop:

```
Sub Main()
    Dim dblSellPrice# = 95
    Dim dblStockPrice# = 45
    Do Until dblStockPrice >= dblSellPrice
```

```
        dblStockPrice *= Math.Exp(0.1)
        Console.WriteLine("We are still holding the stock.")
    Loop
    Console.WriteLine("We have sold the stock at" & dblStockPrice)
End Sub
```

As with the Do ... While loop, the Do ... Until is not necessarily executed at all since the program evaluates the exit condition before entering the loop. In this example, we sold the stock at 100.149.

The Do ... Loop While Loop

To make sure that a loop executes at least once, place the exit condition at the Loop statement, rather than at the Do statement, as in the following:

```
Sub Main()
    Dim dblStockPrice# = 35
    Do
        Console.WriteLine("Incrementing the stock price.")
        dblStockPrice -= 1
    Loop While dblStockPrice > 30
    Console.WriteLine("Sold the stock at" & dblStockPrice)
End Sub
```

In this program the stock is sold at 30.

The Do ... Loop Until Loop

You can similarly put the Until condition at the end of a loop. In the previous example you knew you wanted to go through the loop at least once. By putting the Until statement at the end, you don't need to worry about the initial value of the variable.

```
Sub Main()
    Dim dblStockPrice# = 35
    Do
        dblStockPrice -= 1
    Loop Until dblStockPrice = 25
    Console.WriteLine("We sold the stock at" & dblStockPrice)
End Sub
```

In this program, the stock is sold at 25.

The While ... End While Loop

Visual Basic.NET also provides another general-purpose Loop statement called the While ... End While loop. The While ... End While loop has the following syntax:

```
Sub Main()
    Dim dblStockPrice# = 35
    While dblStockPrice <= 50
        dblStockPrice += 1
        Console.WriteLine("Holding the stock.")
    End While
    Console.WriteLine("We sold the stock at" & dblStockPrice)
End Sub
```

In this program the stock is sold at 51.

THE EXIT COMMANDS

There are occasions where you need to break out of a loop. In such a case we can insert an Exit command. Depending on which type of loop structure you are using, you will use the Exit For command or the Exit Do command. We might generally do this inside an If ... Then statement inside a loop. Here is an example of an infinite loop. The Do While 1 statement will never evaluate to False, and so this program will loop forever until some event causes an exit from the loop. As you can imagine, it's best to be very careful with infinite loops.

```
Sub Main()
    Dim dblStockPrice# = 35
    Do While 1
        dblStockPrice += 1
        If dblStockPrice > 100 Then
            Exit Do
        End If
    Loop
    Console.WriteLine("We sold the stock at" & dblStockPrice)
End Sub
```

In this program, we sold the stock at 101.

NESTED LOOPS

You can put a For ... Next loop inside another For ... Next loop. Consider the following example showing nested For ... Next loops to transpose a matrix. Again, we haven't looked at arrays yet, so don't worry about the variable references. For now, just note the structure of embedded loops.

```
For x = 0 To intRows
        For y = 0 To intCols
                    outArray(y, x) = inArray(x, y)
        Next y
Next x
```

Although For . . . Next loops are useful when we know in advance how many times we want to execute the loop, there are occasions when we do not have this information in advance.

ESTIMATING AND FORECASTING VOLATILITY

When analyzing financial data, we often estimate volatility over a period of time in the past. This is easily done if we have a time series of price data, as was the case in Project 4.1 where we used four log returns to calculate the standard deviation of returns. If we have several years of historical data, we can estimate the daily volatility by simply calculating the standard deviation of daily log returns.

How though do we estimate volatility given only 1 day of data? Usually, we would use the same method. We estimate 1 day standard deviation using close-to-close data as follows:

$$\sigma_{CC} = \sqrt{\left[\ln\left(\frac{C_i}{C_{i-1}}\right)\right]^2}$$

However, this method certainly does not capture all the information of intraday volatility. A stock could close at 50 one day, gap open to 53 the following day, trade down to 44, and close back at 50. In this case, using this close-to-close calculation would not be a very good indicator of volatility since "0" is not a good description of what happened.

To better account for one-period volatility, several other, more efficient methods have been proposed that use intraperiod highs and lows to estimate volatility. These methods are often grouped under the term *extreme value estimators*. Since several models that we use in financial markets are based on the assumption of continuous time, it is more intuitive to examine the entire time period rather than simply the ends. The most well known of the extreme value estimators have been proposed by Parkinson (1980) and Garman and Klass (1980) (cited in Nelken, 1997, Chap. 1). The Parkinson's equation uses the intraperiod high and low thusly:

$$\sigma_P = 0.601\sqrt{\left(\ln\frac{H_i}{L_i}\right)^2}$$

The Garman-Klass estimator, which uses the intraperiod high and low as well as the open and close data, has the form

$$\sigma_{GK} = \sqrt{\left[\frac{1}{2}\left(\ln\frac{H_i}{L_i}\right)^2 - [2\ln(2) - 1]\left(\ln\frac{C_i}{O_i}\right)^2\right]}$$

Notice that these equations represent an estimate of the one-period historical volatility of the underlying symbol. You may notice, however, that neither of these models takes into account gaps, either up or down, from the previous day's close. Volatility that happens overnight will not be accounted for in either of these models. For this and other reasons there are dozens of derivatives of these two extreme value estimators currently in use. We will not examine any of them beyond the two standard models presented.

These Parkinson and Garman-Klass models estimate past volatility. They do not forecast future volatility. Forecasting volatility is its own subject and is the topic of literally hundreds of research papers and books. The most popular models for forecasting volatility are the GARCH (generalized autoregressive conditional heteroscedasticity) family.

Dozens of variations of GARCH models have been proposed for forecasting volatility based on the assumption that returns are generated by a random process with time-varying and mean-reverting volatility (Alexander, 2001, p. 65). That is, in financial markets, periods of low volatility tend to be followed by periods of low volatility, but are interspersed with periods of high volatility. The most commonly referenced GARCH model for forecasting variance is GARCH(1,1):

$$\hat{\sigma}^2_{t+1} = (1 - \alpha - \beta) \cdot V + \alpha r^2_t + \beta \hat{\sigma}^2_t \qquad (5.1)$$

and

$$\hat{\sigma}^2_{t+j} = V + (\alpha + \beta)^{j-1} \cdot (\hat{\sigma}^2_{t+1} - V) \qquad (5.2)$$

where α and β are optimized coefficients, r is the log return, and V is the sample variance over the entire data set. Determining the values of these coefficients, α and β, is in itself an art and a science called optimization. In a later chapter we will discuss how to employ an optimization engine to calculate the values of these coefficients using maximum-likelihood methods. For now, let's get familiar with forecasting variance, and therefore the volatility, of an underlying stock for use in option pricing.

Since the variance forecasts are additive, we can estimate the volatility between now, time t, and expiration h days in the future in the following way:

$$\hat{\sigma}^2_{t,t+h} = \sum_{j=1}^{h} \hat{\sigma}^2_{t+j} \qquad (5.3)$$

So if 10 days remain to expiration, we first calculate the forecast of variance for $t+1$, or tomorrow, using Equation (5.1). Then we can calculate the individual forecasts for the remaining 9 days using Equation (5.2). Summing them up, we get a forecast of variance from today until expiration 10 days from now. From there, we can easily calculate an annualized volatility, which may or may not differ from a market-implied volatility in an option.

Let's create a Windows application that uses a For ... Next loop to forecast volatility for a user-defined number of days ahead.

Step 1 Open VB.NET and select New Project. In the New Project window, select Windows Application, and give your project the name GARCH and a location of C:\ModelingFM.

Step 2 Now that the GUI designer is on your screen, from the Toolbox add to your form a button, named Button1, a text box, named TextBox1, and a label, named Label1. In the Properties window for Button1, change the text property to "Calculate." You should also clear the text property for the TextBox1 and Label1.

Step 3 In the Solution Explorer window, click on the View Code icon to view the Form1 code window.

In this project, we will demonstrate the use of a user-defined value type, called QuoteData, as well as other data types. You may remember the discussion of a QuoteData type in the previous chapter. In any case, we need a construct to hold price data, and the QuoteData type works nicely. Before we can use the QuoteData type, we need to define it for the compiler. Then we can declare some variables, known as qdMonday and qdTuesday, as QuoteDatas.

Step 4 In the code window, change the code to the following:

```
Public Class Form1
     Inherits System.Windows.Forms.Form
Windows Form Designer generated code
     Structure QuoteData
        Public dblOpen As Double
        Public dblHigh As Double
        Public dblLow As Double
        Public dblClose As Double
     End Structure
     Dim qdMonday As QuoteData
     Dim qdTuesday As QuoteData
End Class
```

Step 5 In the Class Name combo box at the top left of your code window, select Form1. In the Method Name combo box at the top right of your code window, select Form1_Load. A code stub for the Form1_Load event handler will appear. Within this subroutine add the following code to define the contents of qdMonday and qdTuesday:

```
Private Sub Form1_Load(ByVal sender ...) Handles MyBase.Load
     qdMonday.dblOpen = 50
     qdMonday.dblHigh = 51.25
     qdMonday.dblLow = 49.75
     qdMonday.dblClose = 50.5
```

```
    qdTuesday.dblOpen = 50.5
    qdTuesday.dblHigh = 51.0
    qdTuesday.dblLow = 48.5
    qdTuesday.dblClose = 49.5
End Sub
```

We have now defined two daily bars for a stock. From here we can add code to forecast volatility.

Step 6   In the same way as in Step 5, select the Button1_Click event. Within this subroutine add the following code to declare and define some variables and calculate the volatility forecast according to the GARCH(1,1) formula:

```
Private Sub Button1_Click(ByVal sender...) Handles Button1.Click
    Dim dblSampleVariance# = 0.0002441      ' V is the equation
    Dim dblAlpha# = 0.0607                  ' Optimized coefficient
    Dim dblBeta# = 0.899                    ' Optimized coefficient
    Dim dblPrevForecast# = 0.0004152
    Dim dblTotalForecast, x As Double
    Dim dblOneDayAheadForecast# = (1 - dblAlpha - dblBeta) * _
        dblSampleVariance + dblAlpha * Math.Log(qdTuesday.dblClose _
        / qdMonday.dblClose) ^ 2 + dblBeta * dblPrevForecast
    For x = 1 To TextBox1.Text
        dblTotalForecast += (dblSampleVariance + (dblAlpha + _
        dblBeta)  ^ (x - 1) * (dblOneDayAheadForecast - _
        dblSampleVariance))
    Next x
    ' Calculate the annualized volatility forecast.
    Label1.Text = dblTotalForecast ^ 0.5 * (256/10) ^ 0.5
End Sub
```

The GARCH(1,1) equation forecasts variance. The square root of this 10-day variance forecast will give us a 10-day volatility forecast. Multiplying this by the square root of 256 trading days divided by 10 gives us an annualized volatility number.

Step 7   Run the program. The result will appear as shown in Figure 5.1.

F I G U R E 5.1

Chapter 5, GARCH Example	_ □ ×
Number of Days to Forecast:	10
Calculate	
Annualized Volatility Forecast:	0.312201156178445

SUMMARY

In this chapter we learned how to use If . . . Then . . . Else statements, Select Case statements, and many different kinds of loops to control program flow. Loops will become more important in future chapters about arrays and data structures. We also looked at how to use a loop to forecast volatility using the GARCH(1,1) equation.

PROBLEMS

1. What are the two types of structures discussed in this chapter?

2. Assume you bought stock in MMZR at 50. Write an If ... Then ... Else structure to sell the stock if it goes up by 10 percent or down by 5 percent.

3. What is the difference between the following two loops:

```
Do While x < 10
      x += 1
Loop
```

and

```
Do
      x += 1
Loop While x < 10
```

4. What are the different repetition structures available in VB.NET?

5. Take a look at the following piece of code:

```
For x = 0 To 2
      For y = 0 To 3
            Console.WriteLine(x * y)
      Next y
Next x
```

What would be printed out to the screen?

PROJECT 5.1

The GARCH(1,1) equation forecasts volatility using two optimized coefficients, alpha and beta, and three values—an estimate of the previous day's variance, r^2; the long-run variance, V; and the previous day's forecast, σ_t^2. The estimate of the previous day's variance uses the log of the close-to-close method discussed in the chapter. However, as we saw, close-to-close may not be a good representation of intraperiod volatility.

Create a VB.NET Windows application that calculates three forecasts for volatility for a user-defined number of days ahead. This time make the GARCH(1,1) forecast using the close-to-close, the Parkinson, and the Garman-Klass estimators of one-period volatility. Print out the three forecasts in three labels.

PROJECT 5.2: MONTE CARLO SIMULATION

Visual Basic.NET has a built-in random number generator, rnd(), which draws uniformly distributed deviates (random numbers) between 0 and 1. In finance, we often wish to use a normal distribution for Monte Carlo simulation. Here is the code to generate a random number drawn from the standard normal distribution using the rnd() function:

```
Dim dblNormRand As Double
Randomize()
dblNormRand = rnd() + rnd() + rnd() + rnd() + rnd() + rnd() +
rnd() + rnd() + rnd() + rnd() + rnd() + rnd() - 6
```

Create a VB.NET Windows application that will use a For ... Next loop and a Select Case structure to generate a user-defined number of normally distributed random deviates and put the deviates into 10 bins as shown in the Select Case explanation in the chapter. Your result should look similar to Figure 5.2.

To initialize the VB's random number generator, place Randomize() in the Form1_Load event before calling rnd().

F I G U R E 5.2

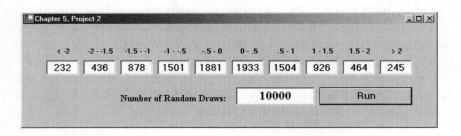

CHAPTER 6

Procedures

A procedure is a generic term that refers to the two types of routines—subroutines and functions. Procedures are packaged pieces of code that perform specific operations. Visual Basic.NET has hundreds of procedures that we can use in our programs to perform common tasks such as string manipulation, error checking, and even a few mathematical and financial calculations. What's more, we can create our own, user-defined procedures to accomplish specific tasks in our programs.

When we call a procedure in our program, we are telling Visual Basic.NET to execute the code associated with that procedure. Furthermore, we may specify input arguments, or parameters, that we want to pass into the procedure—that is, the value or values we want the routine to work on. When we define a procedure, we must specify four things: a name for the procedure; a comma-separated list of parameters the procedure accepts, if any; the data type of the return value, if any; and the procedure definition, which is the code that executes when the routine is called.

The only difference between a subroutine and a function is that a function returns a value, aptly named the *return value* or *return argument*, whereas a subroutine does not. A return value gets sent back from the function to the code that called it. In general, functions are preferred to subroutines, and they will be used whenever possible. The distinction between functions and subroutines will become clear when we use them later.

We programmers use procedures to better organize code by breaking it up into smaller tasks. This makes the program code easier to read and debug. Also, procedures that perform common tasks can be called over and over from different sections of the program, reducing duplication of code and making the program easier to maintain. For example, if we wanted to calculate the mean returns for 100 stocks, we could write one function called Average() and use it a hundred times over, rather than making the calculation in code for each of the 100 stocks. Let's look at the code for an Average() function:

```
Public Function Average(ByVal dblReturn1 As Double, _
                        ByVal dblReturn2 As Double ) As Double
      Return ( dblReturn1 + dblReturn2 )/2
End Function
```

Now let's review the four elements of a function. One, the name of this function is Average(). Two, this function accepts two input arguments, both of type Double, that will have the names dblReturn1 and dblReturn2 within the function definition. Three, this function returns a value of type Double. And, four, the function definition is the code between the function header, the Public Function Average line, and the function footer, End Function. We could call this function from somewhere else in our program this way:

```
Sub Main()
        Dim dblAverageReturn# = Average(.015,.005)
        Console.WriteLine( dblAverageReturn )
End Sub
```

Here the value of dblAverageReturn is set equal to the return value of the function Average(). Of course, this program prints out .01.

One way to describe a function is to think about a black box that processes input, much like a mathematical function. In algebra we may use an expression like this:

$$y = f(x_1, x_2, x_3)$$

$f(x)$ is, of course, a function. This function has a name, f. The function accepts input arguments, namely x_1, x_2, and x_3. The function named f has a return value to which y is then set equal. The definition of f exists somewhere else and is, say, $f(x_1, x_2, x_3) = 2x_1 + 3x_2 + 4x_3$. Functions in programming are no different.

INPUT ARGUMENTS

Both functions and subroutines can take input arguments. The input argument list, often called the parameters, has its own syntax that requires separate consideration.

We can declare as many input arguments with their respective data types as are needed, provided we separate each parameter with a comma. The basic syntax is to specify a local name for the value and a data type. For example, here is a simple subroutine that prints out two numbers in the console window:

```
Private Sub PrintPrices(ByVal dblPrice1 As Double, _
                        ByVal dblPrice2 As Double)
     Console.WriteLine( dblPrice1 )
     Console.WriteLine( dblPrice2 )
End Sub
```

We then call the PrintNumbers subroutine. We specify the parameters after the name as follows:

```
Sub Main()
     PrintPrices( 45.23, 65.54 )
End Sub
```

In this example, the values 45.23 and 65.54 are passed to the variables dblPrice1 and dblPrice2. Within the subroutine definition, the values passed in will be known by the local names dblPrice1 and dblPrice2. Since this is a subroutine, there is no return value as was the case in the Average() function. The output of this simple program will be:

```
45.23
65.54
```

There are times when we may not be required to pass all the arguments in a parameter list to a procedure. This is typically the case when parameters later in the list are dependent on specific values of variables earlier in the list. To declare a parameter as optional, we include the Optional keyword in the parameter declaration. When we declare a parameter as optional, all subsequent parameters in the list must also be optional. Here is an example:

```
Public Function PV( ByVal Rate As Double, _
                    ByVal NPer As Double, _
                    ByVal Pmt As Double, _
                    Optional ByVal FV As Double, _
                    Optional ByVal Due As Date) _
                    As Double
```

Here values for FV and Due are not required by the function definition to perform the calculation and return the PV, present value.

ByRef and ByVal

Let's take a look at the important distinction between ByRef and ByVal, the two methods for passing input arguments to functions.

Passing an input argument ByVal means that the original variable, which is being passed as an input argument, will not be changed by the function definition. That is to say, the procedure makes a copy of the value and performs the operations within the procedure definition on the copy, as opposed to the original variable. This is demonstrated by the following example:

```
Sub Main()
    Dim dblStockPrice# = 52.78
    Increment(dblStockPrice)
    Console.WriteLine("Stock price after increment is: " _
                      & dblStockPrice)
End Sub
Private Sub Increment(ByVal dblNum As Double)
    Console.WriteLine("Increment subroutine was passed: " & dblNum)
    dblNum += 1
    Console.WriteLine("New value is: " & dblNum)
End Sub
```

This program outputs:

```
Increment function was passed: 52.78
New value is: 53.78
Stock price after increment is: 52.78
```

The dblStockPrice variable is unaffected by the addition within the Increment subroutine. This is because only the value of dblStockPrice has been passed to dblNum. dblNum is a completely separate variable. ByVal is the default method for passing values into functions. Now try this example again, but change ByVal in Increment() to ByRef as follows:

```
Private Sub Increment(ByRef dblNum As Double)
```

This time the output is:

```
Increment was passed: 52.78
New value is: 53.78
Stock price after increment is: 53.78
```

Here a reference to the location of dblStockPrice in memory is passed to dblNum, not the value of dblStockPrice. Therefore, as far as the computer is concerned, both dblNum and dblStockPrice are referring to the same physical space, or location, in memory. Hence, when dblNum is incremented, the value of dblStockPrice changes since they are both the same variable.

ParamArray

There is one additional keyword we can use in procedure declarations—ParamArray. ParamArray enables us to pass an arbitrary number of arguments into function. That is, ParamArray allows an indeterminate number of input arguments passed as either a one-dimensional list or an array of the type specified. Within the function definition, the parameter array is treated as an array of its declared type. To use a ParamArray, just specify the last parameter in a parameter list as a ParamArray:

```
Sub Main()
    Dim dblPrices As Double() = New Double() {52.34, 35.34, 0.15}
    PrintPrices(dblPrices)                    ' Pass as an array
    PrintPrices(10.5, 95.34, 31.22, 74.23)   ' Pass as a list
End Sub

Private Sub PrintPrices(ByVal ParamArray dblStockPrices As Double())
    Dim i As Double
    Console.WriteLine("Portfolio of stocks contains " & _
            dblStockPrices.Length & " stocks. _
            The prices are: ")
    For Each i In dblStockPrices
        Console.WriteLine(" " & i)
    Next i
End Sub
```

This program calls the function twice: The first time the array, dblPrices, is passed with three prices; the second time a list of four prices is passed. In Chapter 8, we will take an in-depth look at arrays. Also, notice the use of the For Each . . . Next loop structure, which we discussed in the previous chapter.

RETURN VALUES

As we said, functions have return values, which do not necessarily have to be numbers; they can return any data type. We can set the return value of a function by using the Return keyword. Here is a function that returns a Boolean, expressing whether or not our stock has hit a support level:

```
Public Function SupportLevel( dblStockPrice As Double, _
                   dblStrongSupport As Double ) As Boolean
        If dblStockPrice > dblStrongSupport
            Return True
        Else
            Return False
        End If
End Function
```

Functions can return any value type, such as doubles, integers, Booleans, or strings. As we will learn in later chapters, functions can also return reference types like arrays and objects.

BLACK-SCHOLES OPTION PRICING FORMULA

In programming VB.NET, and all other languages for that matter, the process of creating our own user-defined procedures is exactly the same as in algebra. However, as you may have noticed, we like to give our procedures and input variables more descriptive names than just f and x's and y's. Programmers prefer to use names like Command1_Click() or BlackScholesCall() that describe the nature of the operations performed within the procedure definition.

The Black-Scholes price of a call option is a function of several input values, namely S, the price of the underlying stock; X, the strike price; t, the time to expiration; r, the interest rate; and σ, the volatility; so that

```
y = BlackScholesCall( S, X, t, r, σ )
```

The mathematical definition of the Black-Scholes equation for the price of a call option is

$$\text{BlackScholesCall} = SN(d_1) - Xe^{-rt}N(d_2)$$

where

$$d_1 = \frac{\ln(S/X) + (r + (\sigma^2/2))T}{\sigma\sqrt{T}}$$

and

$$d_2 = d_1 - \sigma\sqrt{T}$$

To make a VB.NET function that calculates the price of a call option according to the Black-Scholes formula, we need four things: a function name, a list of input arguments with their respective data types, a return type, and a function definition.

```
Public Function BlackScholesCall(ByVal dblStock As Double, _
                                 ByVal dblStrike As Double, _
                                 ByVal dblTime As Double, _
                                 ByVal dblInterestRate As Double, _
                                 ByVal dblSigma As Double) _
                                 As Double
    Dim d1, d2, Nd1, Nd2 As Double
    ' Calculate d1 and d2
    d1 = (Math.Log(dblStock / dblStrike) + (dblInterestRate + _
        (dblSigma ^ 2) / 2) * dblTime) / _
        (dblSigma * Math.Sqrt(dblTime))
    d2 = d1 - dblSigma * Math.Sqrt(dblTime)
    ' Calculate N(d1) and N(d2)
    Nd1 = NormCDF(d1)
    Nd2 = NormCDF(d2)
    ' Calculate the price of the call
    Return dblStock * Nd1 - dblStrike * Math.Exp(-dblInterestRate _
        * dblTime) * Nd2
End Function
```

The code that calls the BlackScholesCall() function then doesn't need to know how the function calculates the result. It just takes the output it needs and goes on its merry way. This definition of the function will be somewhere else. We could call the function in this fashion:

```
Sub Main()
    Dim dblOptionPrice As Double
    dblOptionPrice = BlackScholesCall( 42, 40, .5, .1, .2 )
    Console.WriteLine(dblOptionPrice)
End Sub
```

The variable dblOptionPrice then will be set equal to the return value of the function called BlackScholesCall(), which of course calculates the price of a call option according to the parameters, or input arguments, it receives.

The Black-Scholes formula is just one of several methods to calculate the price of an option. We will not, however, cover option pricing theory in depth in this book, although we will briefly cover binomial trees in Chapter 8. We refer you to one of several other books on the topic, especially *The Complete Guide to Option Pricing Formulas* by Espen Gaarder Haug (New York: McGraw-Hill, 1998), which contains particularly complete coverage of option pricing methods.

Let's create a short Windows application that calculates the price of a call option using the BlackScholesCall() function.

Step 1   Open a new Windows application in Visual Basic.NET and name it BlackScholes.

Step 2   Once the IDE for your new program is ready, in the Project menu, click on Add Module to add a code module.

Step 3   In the module, type in the BlackScholesCall() function code as shown previously, or copy it from the file named BlackScholesCall.txt from the CD and paste it in. Your module should look like this:

```
Module BlackScholes
    Public Function BlackScholesCall(ByVal dblStock ...) As Double
            ' Function definition in here.
    End Function
End Module
```

Step 4   Since the BlackScholesCall() function itself calls another function named NormCDF(), we will have to add this function, which is an approximation of the cumulative normal distribution function. Again, in the Project menu, click on Add Module. Add the following code to the new module:

```
Module NormalCDF
    Public Function NormCDF(ByVal X As Double) As Double
        ' Calculate the cumulative probability distribution
        ' function for standard normal at X
        Dim a, b, c, d, prob As Double
        a = 0.4361836
        b = -0.1201676
        c = 0.937298
        d = 1 / (1 + 0.33267 * Math.Abs(X))
        prob = 1 - 1 / Math.Sqrt(2 * 3.1415926) * Math.Exp(-0.5 *
            X * _ X) * (a * d + b * d * d + c * d * d * d)
        If X < 0 Then prob = 1 - prob
        Return prob
    End Function
End Module
```

Step 5 At the top of your code window, click on the Form1.vb [Design] tab to return to the GUI development window. From the Toolbox, add a label, named Label1, and a command button, named Button1, to your form.

Step 6 Double-click on the command button to bring up the code stub for the Button1_Click event. To this event subroutine, add the following code:

```
Private Sub Button1_Click(ByVal sender ...) Handles Button1.Click
        Dim dblCallPrice As Double
        dblCallPrice = BlackScholesCall(42, 40, 0.5, 0.1, 0.2)
        Label1.Text = Str(dblCallPrice)
End Sub
```

Step 7 Run the program (see Figure 6.1).

The program you have just created illustrates the use of two functions: the BlackScholesCall() and the NormCDF(). It also illustrates the use of a subroutine, Button1_Click(). Again, notice that the two functions accept input arguments and have a return value, whereas the subroutine does not have a return value.

To review, the BlackScholesCall() function header shows that the values passed into the function will be known as dblStock, dblStrike, dblTime, dblInterestRate, and dblSigma within the function definition. Also, the return value of the function will be of type double as indicated at the tail end of the function header:

FIGURE 6.1

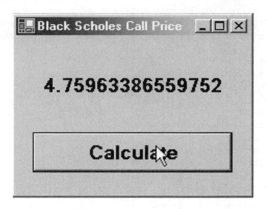

```
Public Function BlackScholesCall(ByVal dblStock As Double, _
                                 ByVal dblStrike As Double, _
                                 ByVal dblTime As Double, _
                                 ByVal dblInterestRate As Double, _
                                 ByVal dblSigma As Double) _
                                 As Double
```

The function definition exists between the header and the footer, End Function. The return value is set using the Return keyword. Notice that within both the BlackScholesCall() and NormCDF() functions, we call other functions from the Math library, including Math.Exp(), Math.Log(), and Math.Sqrt(). These are prebuilt functions in VB.NET that we can call in our programs without having to provide function definitions for them.

MATH FUNCTIONS

If you program in Excel, you should be well versed in prebuilt mathematical functions. Visual Basic.NET too has numerous built-in mathematical functions that we can call in our programs. The following table summarizes the available functions found in the Math namespace that may be important in quantitative finance. To call these functions, we need to precede the function name with the class name Math and a dot (.). That is, the fully qualified function name for the Max() function, for example, is Math.Max().

Math Functions	Description	Example
Abs()	Returns the absolute value of x	dblError = Math.abs (dblForecast - dblActual)
Ceiling()	Returns the integer greater than or equal to the input argument	dblSell = Math.ceiling (dblStockPrice)
Exp()	Returns e (the base of natural logarithms) raised to the power of x	dblFV = dblPV * Math.exp(dblR * dblTime)
Floor()	Returns the integer less than or equal to the input argument	dblBuy = Math.floor (dblStockPrice)
Log()	Returns the natural logarithm of x	dblRate = Math.log (dblTuesday/dblMonday)
Max()	Returns the maximum of two input arguments	DblPrice = Math.max(0, x)
Min()	Returns the minimum of two input arguments	DblPrice = Math.min(0, x)
Sign()	Returns: 1 if x is greater than 0; 0 if x equals 0; − 1 if x is less than 0	blnBUYSELL = Math.sign (dblMoonphase)
Sqrt()	Returns the square root of x	dblStDev = Math.sqrt(myVariance)

STRING FUNCTIONS

A string is oftentimes just a thing that we print out or pass from one part of our program to another without regard for its contents. Other times, however, we need to know what's inside. We might need to verify its contents, modify it in some way, or extract a specific piece of information from it. When dealing with options quotes, for example, we sometimes need to parse out the stock symbol, the expiration month, and the strike price, which are all strung together in one long option symbol. The string functions we will need to know, but certainly not all that are available, are summarized below. As you will see, some of the functions are in the Microsoft.VisualBasic.Strings class.

String Functions	Description	Example
Chr()	Returns the character associated with a specific character code	myChar = Chr(65)

(continues)

String Functions	Description	Example
GetChar()	Returns a char value type representing the character from a specific index in a string	myChar = GetChar("IBMDP", 4)
Join()	Concatenates an array of strings into a delimited string	myString = Join(myArray, Optional delimiter)
Len()	Returns the integer length of String	myInt = Len(string)
InStr()	Returns an integer specifying the starting position of the first occurrence of a string within another string	myInt = InStr(1, string, "D")
Left()	Returns the leftmost length of characters of a string	strTicker = Microsoft.VisualBasic. Left(strOptionsSymbol, 3)
Right()	Returns the rightmost length of characters of a string	strStrike = Microsoft.VisualBasic.Right (strOptionsSymbol, 1)
Mid()	Returns length characters from String, starting at position Start	myString = Mid(string, start, length)
Split()	Returns an array of strings consisting of the delimited strings (or words) of an input argument string	myString = "IBM April 80 Call" myArray = Split(myString)
StrComp()	Returns − 1, 0, or 1, depending upon the result of a string comparison	myInt = StrComp(myStringA, myStringB)

Many of these functions are helpful in parsing strings. Parsing is the process of extracting smaller pieces or substrings from a string. Here are some examples showing how to parse strings using the string functions in the table.

The Split Function

The Split function accepts a string as an input argument and returns an array consisting of the parsed values of the array.

```
Sub Main()
      Dim strMyString As String
      Dim strReturnArray As String()
```

```
        strMyString = "INTC Jun 25 Call"
        strReturnArray = Split(strMyString)
        Console.WriteLine(strReturnArray(0))
    End Sub
```

After running this code, the values in the strReturnArray will look like this:

```
strReturnArray(0)  =  INTC
strReturnArray(1)  =  Jun
strReturnArray(2)  =  25
strReturnArray(3)  =  Call
```

The Left, Right, and Mid Functions

The Left and Right functions are very similar to each other. The Left and Right functions accept two input arguments—a string and a length. The Left function returns a string containing the leftmost "length" number of characters in the string. The Right function returns the rightmost "length" number of characters. Here is an example:

```
Sub Main()
    Dim strTicker, strOptionsSymbol, strStrike As String
    strOptionsSymbol = "IBMDP"
    strTicker = Microsoft.VisualBasic.Left(strOptionsSymbol, 3)
    strStrike = Microsoft.VisualBasic.Right(strOptionsSymbol, 1)
    Console.WriteLine(strTicker)
    Console.WriteLine(strStrike)
End Sub
```

The variable strTicker then will be equal to just IBM. strStrike will equal P.

The Mid function accepts a string, a starting number, and a length. It returns a string of length with a given string. So

```
Dim strMonth$ = Mid(strOptionsSymbol, 4, 1)
```

strMonth will equal D.

FORMATTING NUMBERS FOR OUTPUT

The Format() function converts and formats dates and numbers into strings. Format() gives us a much greater degree of control over how our data is presented for either screen or printer output. In VB.NET, we can choose from predefined named formats or create our own user-defined format for finer control. Numeric data, regardless of type, can be formatted using the Format() function. The following table explains some of the predefined formats and some user-defined formats with their associated outputs:

Predefined Format Function Names	Example	Output
Assume that dblVolatility = 0.1234567		
General Number	Format(dblVolatility, "General Number")	0.1234567
Currency	Format(dblVolatility, "Currency")	$0.12
Fixed	Format(dblVolatility, "Fixed")	0.12
Standard	Format(dblVolatility, "Standard")	0.12
Percent	Format(dblVolatility, "Percent")	12.34%
Scientific	Format(dblVolatility, "Scientific")	1.23E-01

User-Defined Format Function	Example	Output
	Format(dblVolatility, "#.####")	.12345
	Format(dblVolatility, "0.####")	0.12345
	Format(dblVolatility, "00000")	00000
	Format(dblVolatility, "#####")	[nothing]
	Format(dblVolatility, "###%")	12%
	Format(dblVolatility, "###,###,##0.000")	0.123
	Format(dblVolatility, "\$###,###,##0.00")	$0.12

Note the use of the backslash in the final line of code. It allows the computer to interpret the next character literally instead of as a format character. Here is a quick code example that will print out the value of dblVolatility as 0.1235:

```
Sub Main()
    Dim dblVolatility# = 0.1234567
    Console.WriteLine(Format(dblVolatility, "0.####"))
End Sub
```

CONVERSION FUNCTIONS

As mentioned in Chapter 4, Option Strict On requires explicit conversion of data types in cases where data loss could occur. This includes any conversion between numeric types and string types. For example, data loss may occur when a string variable is converted to a double or any other data type with less precision or smaller capacity. If Option Strict is set to On, an error will occur if an implicit conversion exists in our program. VB.NET provides several functions for explicit conversion. Also, as we mentioned earlier, in order to clarify and simplify the algorithms and logic in our example programs, we have almost always left Option Strict by default set to Off. However, production applications you create should include Option Strict On and explicit type conversions through the use of these conversion functions.

Conversion Functions	Description	Example
Str()	Converts a number to a string	strPrice = str(dblStockPrice)
Val()	Converts a string to a number	dblStockPrice = val(strPrice)
CBool()	Converts a value to a Boolean	myBool = CBool(myVal)
CChar()	Converts a value to a char	myChar = CChar(myVal)
CDate()	Converts a value to a date	myDate = CDate(myVal)
CDbl()	Converts a value to a double	myDbl = CDbl(myVal)
CDec()	Converts a value to a decimal	myDec = CDec(myVal)
CInt()	Converts a value to an integer	myInt = CInt(myVal)
CLng()	Converts a value to a long	myLng = CLng(myVal)
CShort()	Converts a value to a short	myShort = CShort(myVal)
CSng()	Converts a value to a single	mySng = CSng(myVal)
CStr()	Converts a value to a string	myStr = CStr(myVal)
CType()	Converts a value into a specified type	myDbl = CType(myValue, Double)

As you can probably imagine, not all conversions are possible. We clearly cannot convert IBMDP into a double. Here is a short program illustrating the use of a conversion function:

```
Option Strict On
Module Module1
    Sub Main()
        Dim dblVolatility# = 0.1234567
        Dim sglVolatility As Single
        sglVolatility = CSng(dblVolatility)
        Console.WriteLine(sglVolatility)
    End Sub
End Module
```

This program prints out the value of sglVolatility as .1234567 since no data is lost in the conversion.

VALIDATION FUNCTIONS

As shown in the table below, VB.NET's validation functions allow us to check the data type of a value before we perform an operation. You may have noticed in previous programs that errors occur if the user enters a bad value. If, for example, instead of entering 1000, a number to be used in a calculation, the user enters XYZ, the program will end with an error since the calculation requires a number, not a string. Validation functions allow us to check first to see that the user-inputted values are correct. If not, we can prompt the user with a message box to reenter the values properly.

Validation Function	Description	Example
IsArray()	Returns True or False indicating whether a value is a reference to an array	myBool = IsArray(myArray)
IsConstant()	Returns True or False indicating whether a value is a constant	myBool = IsConstant(myConstant)
IsDate()	Returns True or False indicating whether a value is a date	myBool = IsDate(myDate)
IsNumeric()	Returns True or False indicating whether a value is a number	myBool = IsNumeric(myNumber)
IsReference()	Returns True or False indicating whether a value is a reference	myBool = IsReference(myRef)

Here is a short program that will keep prompting the user to enter a valid numeric value until it gets the value.

```
Sub Main()
        Do While 1
            Console.WriteLine("Please enter a volatility:")
            If IsNumeric(Console.ReadLine()) Then
                Console.WriteLine("Thank you for the valid input.")
                Exit Do
            Else
                MsgBox("Please enter a valid value.")
            End If
        Loop
    End Sub
```

DATE FUNCTIONS

Visual Basic.NET provides a wealth of date functions that can be used to manipulate dates, which, as you can probably imagine, become very valuable in modeling fixed-income securities, futures, and options. Here are several of the date functions:

Date Function	Description	Example
DateAdd()	Returns a date to which a specific time interval has been added	dtMyDate = ("d", Now, 30)
DateDiff()	Returns the number of time intervals between two dates	lngMyDays = DateDiff("d", Now, dtMyExpiration)
DateSerial()	Returns a date from a year, month, and day	dtMyDate = DateSerial(1,1,2003)
DateValue()	Returns a date from a string representation of a date	dtMyDate = DateValue("January 1, 2003")
Day()	Returns an integer representing the day of the month from 1 to 31	intMyDay = Day(Now)
Hour()	Returns an integer representing the hour of the day from 0 to 23	intMyHour = Hour(Now)
Minute()	Returns an integer representing the minute of the hour from 0 to 59	intMyMinute = Minute(Now)
Month()	Returns an integer representing the month of the year from 1 to 12	intMyMonth = Month(Now)
Now	Returns the current date and time from the computer's built-in clock	dtMyNow = Now
Second()	Returns an integer representing the minute of the hour from 0 to 59	intMySecond = Second(Now)
TimeOfDay	Reads or sets the time from your computer's clock	dtMyTime = TimeOfDay
Today	Reads or sets the date from your computer's clock	dtMyDate = Today
Weekday()	Returns an integer representing the day of the week from 1 to 7 starting on Sunday	intMyDay = Weekday(Now)
Year()	Returns an integer representing the year from 1 to 9999	intMyYear = Year(Now)

Here is a short program illustrating the use of the DateDiff() function.

```
Sub Main()
      Dim intMyDays As Integer
      intMyDays = DateDiff("d", #1/7/2003#, #4/23/2003#)
      Console.WriteLine(intMyDays)
End Sub
```

This program calculates the number of days between these two dates, 106. We can convert calendar days to trading days using the formula:

```
Trading days = Calendar days - 2(Int(Calendar days / 7))
```

FINANCIAL FUNCTIONS

VB.NET also has several built-in financial functions, which we will rarely, if ever, use in this book. They are, however, worth noting, and some are listed in the table below. In Chapter 10 we will look at how to create our own library of financial classes and functions.

Financial Function	Description
FV()	Returns the future value of an annuity given the interest rate, number of payments, payment, optional present value, and optional flag specifying when payments are due
Ipmt()	Returns the interest payment for a given period of an annuity given the interest rate, payment period, number of payments, present value, optional future value, and optional flag specifying when payments are due
IRR()	Returns the internal rate of return for a series of cash flows as an array
MIRR()	Returns the modified internal rate of return for a series of cash flows given the interest rate paid and interest rate received
NPer()	Returns the number of periods for an annuity given the interest rate, payment, present value, optional future value at maturity, and optional flag specifying when payments are due
NPV()	Returns the net present value of an investment given the interest rate and cash flow values
Pmt()	Returns the payment for an annuity given the interest rate, number of payments, present value, optional future value, and optional flag specifying when payments are due

Financial Function	Description
PPmt()	Returns the principal payment for a given period of an annuity given the interest rate, payment period, number of payments, present value, optional future value, and optional flag specifying when payments are due
PV()	Returns the present value of an annuity given the interest rate, number of payments, payment, optional future value, and optional flag specifying when payments are due
Rate()	Returns the interest rate per period for an annuity given the number of payments, payment, present value, optional future value, and optional flag specifying when payments are due
FV()	Returns the future value of an annuity given the interest rate, number of payments, payment, optional present value, and optional flag specifying when payments are due

MsgBox FUNCTION

The MsgBox procedure displays a dialog box with a message, an OK button, an optional icon, and a title. MsgBox can also return the value of the button pressed by the user.

The title parameter is simply the text that appears across the title bar of the message box. This defaults to your application's name. The MsgBox function can have one, two, or three buttons. The function returns the value of the button your user pressed. Before we talk about these values, however, we need to take a quick detour and talk about VB.NET's predefined constants.

The following is an example call to MsgBox:

```
Sub Main()
    Dim myResponse As MsgBoxResult
    myResponse = MsgBox("Continue?", vbYesNo + vbQuestion, "Continue")
End Sub
```

Or more simply,

```
MsgBox("Please enter valid data.",, "Option Calculator")
```

RANDOM NUMBER FUNCTIONS

The Rnd() function in VB.NET returns a random number from a uniform distribution between 0 and 1. For example,

```
Sub Main()
      Randomize()
      Dim myRnd As Double = Rnd()
      Console.WriteLine(myRnd)
End Sub
```

Make sure to call the Randomize() function to initialize, or "seed," the random number generator. You only need to call Randomize() once, and so if your program needs random numbers, just include the call in the form load event.

Several mathematical methods have been developed for accomplishing the task of generating standard normal deviates, including the well-known rejection method with the Box-Muller transformation, which can be converted into program code. However, we prefer a much simpler method, as shown here:

```
Function StdNormRnd() As Double
      Return Rnd() + Rnd() + Rnd() + Rnd() + Rnd() + Rnd() + Rnd() + Rnd() + _
             Rnd() + Rnd() + Rnd() + Rnd() - 6
End Function
```

In all cases, this method will suffice, and the StdNormRand() function above will be used in this book. Here are two other functions for random numbers from distributions other than the standard normal. First, normal distribution with mean and standard deviation:

```
Function NormRnd(dblMean As Double, dblStdDev As Double) As Double
      Return StdNormRnd() * dblStdDev + dblMean
End Function
```

And second, the lognormal:

```
Function LogNormalRnd(dblMean As Double, dblStdDev As Double) As Double
      Return Exp(dblMean + dblStdDev * StdNormRnd())
End Function
```

IMPLIED VOLATILITY

Most often in financial markets, we are interested in calculating the volatility implied by an option's price as opposed to the price itself, since the price can be observed in the market. Rather than passing the stock price, strike, time, interest rate, and volatility into a function to get the price, we would rather pass the option price, stock price, strike, time, and interest rate into a function and get the volatility.

Analyzing and forecasting volatility is an important facet of automated derivatives trading. In Chapter 5 we looked at some ways of forecasting volatility based upon estimates of past, or historical, volatility. If the implied volatility of an option, as observed from its market price, deviates substantially from our forecast of volatility between now and expiration, there may be a trading opportunity. That is, if the implied volatility is substantially higher than our forecast, we may consider selling the option. Alternatively, if the implied volatility is substantially lower than our forecast, we may consider buying the option.

Let's augment the program we started earlier in this chapter to calculate the implied volatility of a call option given an options symbol, a price for the underlying stock, and the price of the call option. We will use some of the string manipulation functions to determine the month of expiration and the strike price from an option symbol according to the following tables:

Expiration Month Codes

	Jan	Feb	Mar	Apr	May	Jun	Jul	Aug	Sep	Oct	Nov	Dec
Calls	A	B	C	D	E	F	G	H	I	J	K	L
Puts	M	N	O	P	Q	R	S	T	U	V	W	X

Strike Price Codes (Abbr.)

A	B	C	D	E	F	G	H	I	J	K	L	M
5	10	15	20	25	30	35	40	45	50	55	60	65
N	**O**	**P**	**Q**	**R**	**S**	**T**	**U**	**V**	**W**	**X**	**Y**	**Z**
70	75	80	85	90	95	100	7.5	12.5	17.5	22.5	27.5	32.5

Step 8 Add three more modules to your program to hold the TimeTillExp(), ImpliedVolatilityCall(), and StrikePrice() functions. Type in the function

definitions for the three functions as follows. Alternatively you can copy and paste in the code from the CD. Here is the code for the TimeTillExp() function:

```
Module ExpirationTime
    Public Function TimeTillExp(ByVal strOptionSym As String) As Double
        ' Find the second to last character in the string.
        Dim strMonthStrike As String = Right(strOptionSym, 2)
        Dim chrMonth As Char = Left(strMonthStrike, 1)
        Dim strMonth As String
        Dim dtExpDate As Date
        Select Case chrMonth
            Case "A", "a", "M", "m"          'Use a Select...Case structure to
                strMonth = "January"         ' transform the month character
            Case "B", "b", "N", "n"          ' into the appropriate string.
                strMonth = "February"
            Case "C", "c", "O", "o"
                strMonth = "March"
            Case "D", "d", "P", "p"
                strMonth = "April"
            Case "E", "e", "Q", "q"
                strMonth = "May"
            Case "F", "f", "R", "r"
                strMonth = "June"
            Case "G", "g", "S", "s"
                strMonth = "July"
            Case "H", "h", "T", "t"
                strMonth = "August"
            Case "I", "i", "U", "u"
                strMonth = "September"
            Case "J", "j", "V", "v"
                strMonth = "October"
            Case "K", "k", "W", "w"          ' Assume all options expire on
                strMonth = "November"        ' the 15th of the month. If the
            Case "L", "l", "X", "x"          ' date has passed for the
                strMonth = "December"        ' current year, find the date
        End Select                           ' for the following year.
        dtExpDate = DateValue(strMonth & "15," & Year(Today()))
        If Today() > dtExpDate Then _
        dtExpDate = DateValue(strMonth & "15," & (Year(Today()) + 1))
        Return (DateDiff(DateInterval.Day, Today(), dtExpDate)) / 365
    End Function
End Module
```

Notice that the TimeTillExp() function makes use of several functions we have looked at in this chapter, including Right() and Left() to find the second-to-last character in the option symbol string, DateValue() to convert a string representation of a date into a variable of data type Date, Year() to determine the year corresponding to the date returned by Today(), and DateDiff() to calculate the number of days between Today() and the expiration date, assuming options always expire on the fifteenth of the month, which simplifies this example. Here is the code for the ImpliedVolatilityCall() function:

```
Module ImpliedVol
    Public Function ImpliedVolatilityCall(ByVal dblMarketPrice As Double,
                                ByVal dblStock As Double, _
                                ByVal dblStrike As Double, _
                                ByVal dblTime As Double, _
                                ByVal dblInterestRate As Double) _
                                As Double
        Dim ImpliedVol, LowVol, HighVol, epsilon, mu, _
            TheoreticalPrice, PreviousPrice As Double
        HighVol = 10
        ImpliedVol = HighVol
        TheoreticalPrice = BlackScholesCall(dblStock, dblStrike, _
                            dblTime, dblInterestRate, HighVol)
        epsilon = TheoreticalPrice - dblMarketPrice
        mu = TheoreticalPrice - PreviousPrice
        Do While (Math.Abs(epsilon) > 0.0000001)
            If Math.Abs(mu) < 0.0000001 Then Exit Do
            If epsilon > 0 Then
                ImpliedVol = HighVol
                HighVol = HighVol - (HighVol - LowVol) / 2
            Else
                LowVol = HighVol
                HighVol = LowVol + (ImpliedVol - LowVol) / 2
            End If
            PreviousPrice = TheoreticalPrice
            TheoreticalPrice = BlackScholesCall(dblStock, dblStrike, _
                                dblTime, dblInterestRate, HighVol)
            epsilon = TheoreticalPrice - dblMarketPrice
            mu = TheoreticalPrice - PreviousPrice
        Loop
        Return HighVol
    End Function
End Module
```

And finally, here is the code for the StrikePrice() function:

```
Module Strike
    Public Function StrikePrice(ByVal strOptionSym As String) As Double
        Dim chrStrike = Right(strOptionSym, 1)
        Select Case chrStrike
            Case "A", "a"
                Return 5
            Case "B", "b"
                Return 10
            Case "C", "c"
                Return 15
            Case "D", "d"
                Return 20
            Case "E", "e"
```

```
                        Return 25
                Case "F", "f"
                        Return 30
                Case "G", "g"
                        Return 35
                Case "H", "h"
                        Return 40
                Case "I", "i"
                        Return 45
                Case "J", "j"
                        Return 50
                Case "K", "k"
                        Return 55
                Case "L", "l"
                        Return 60
                Case "M", "m"
                        Return 65
                Case "N", "n"
                        Return 70
                Case "O", "o"
                        Return 75
                Case "P", "p"
                        Return 80
                Case "Q", "q"
                        Return 85
                Case "R", "r"
                        Return 90
                Case "S", "s"
                        Return 95
                Case "T", "t"
                        Return 100
                Case "U", "u"
                        Return 7.5
                Case "V", "v"
                        Return 12.5
                Case "W", "w"
                        Return 17.5
                Case "X", "x"
                        Return 22.5
                Case "Y", "y"
                        Return 27.5
                Case "Z", "z"
                        Return 32.5
            End Select
        End Function
End Module
```

Step 9   On your form, place four text boxes named txtStockPrice, txtOptionSymbol, txtOptionPrice, and txtImpliedVol. In the Button1_Click event, change the code to the following:

```
Private Sub Button1_Click(ByVal sender ...) Handles Button1.Click
        Dim dblImpVol As Double
        Dim strOptionSymbol$ = txtOptionSymbol.Text
        Dim dblStockPrice# = txtStockPrice.Text
        Dim dblOptionPrice# = txtOptionPrice.Text
        Dim dblTimeTillExp# = TimeTillExp(strOptionSymbol)
        Dim dblStrike# = StrikePrice(strOptionSymbol)
        Dim dblRate# = 0.1
        dblImpVol = ImpliedVolatilityCall(dblOptionPrice, _
                    dblStockPrice, dblStrike, dblTimeTillExp, dblRate)
        txtImpliedVol.Text = Format(dblImpVol, 0.#####")
End Sub
```

Notice that our code employs several function calls to our user-defined functions as well as to the Format() function.

Step 10   Run the program (see Figure 6.2). The results you obtain will be different from the one shown in Figure 6.2 since the time to expiration is always changing. However, if you pick an expiration around 6 months in the future, a strike price of 40, a stock price of 42, and an option price of 4.76, your implied volatility should be around 20 percent.

F I G U R E 6.2

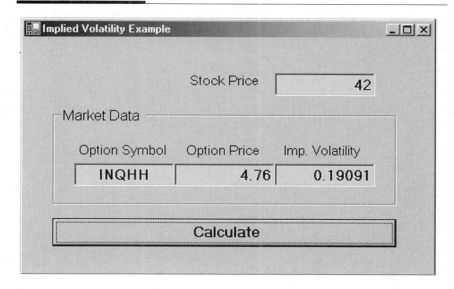

SUMMARY

A procedure is a piece of code that performs a specific task. Functions return a value to the calling statement. Subroutines are exactly the same as functions except that they do not return a value. In general, functions are preferred.

Procedures are the building blocks of VB.NET programs. Modularizing our code into separate procedures, or blocks of code, enables reusability and cuts down on errors and debugging time.

PROBLEMS

1. What is a subroutine? What is a function? What is the difference between a subroutine and a function?
2. Write a line of code that calculates the number of days between January 7, 2003, and November 9, 2002, and assigns the value to a variable named intNumDays.
3. What function would we use to find the date 37 days from today?
4. Write a line of code that assigns the value of the log of 1.05 to a variable named dblReturn.
5. What function could we use to make sure that a user-entered value is actually a number?
6. How could we print out a randomly drawn number from the standard normal distribution to five decimal places?

PROJECT 6.1

Create a Visual Basic.NET Windows application that calculates the
price and Greeks of a call option using the BlackScholesCall()
function and the functions for the Greeks found on the CD included
with this book. Allow the user to input an option symbol and parse
it as in the chapter example.

The project should allow the user to input the stock price and
the volatility. You can simply set the value of the interest rate in
your code. Your program should calculate the other two input
arguments necessary to calculate the prices and Greeks of an
option—the expiration and the strike—from the option symbol
using the functions discussed in the chapter.

PROJECT 6.2

The lognormal distribution assumes that the natural logarithm of
the price-relative from time t to $t + h$ is drawn from a normal
distribution with mean μ and standard deviation σ. The volatility
of a stock then is the sample standard deviation of the logs of the
price-relatives.

To simulate the price path of a stock, we need to first draw a
random number, Z, from the standard normal distribution. Using
the following equation, we can then derive a random stock price at
time $t + h$.

$$S_{t+h} = S_t e^{[\mu(h)+\sigma Z \sqrt{h}]}$$

Create a VB program that will allow the user to enter the initial
stock price, the mean and standard deviation, and the change in
time, h, and will generate a random series of 10 successive prices so
that each new price depends on the previous one. Remember that
volatility is an annualized number based on 256 trading days, and
so a change in time of 1 day would be $1/256 = 0.0039$. Be sure to
include this in your calculations. Also, use the Format() function so
that your random prices print out in a readable fashion. Try using
the MsgBox and the IsNumeric() function to validate user inputs.

CHAPTER 7

Objects

Thus far, we have looked at procedural programming in Chapter 4 and event-driven programming in Chapters 5 and 6 using control structures and procedures. Event-driven programming focuses on the use of events, such as—among others—button clicks and form loads, to control the execution of code. In event-driven programming, different procedures run when different events happen. For the remainder of the book, we will use things called objects and object-oriented programming (OOP), although we will still use events to illustrate code execution. OOP focuses on the use of objects to control program flow. As you will see, OOP enables us to perform very large and complex tasks with just a few lines of code.

OBJECTS AND CLASSES

In previous chapters, we have looked at several classes and objects in our programs. The buttons that we put on our forms are objects. The button objects, known by default names like Button1, are actually instances of the button class. So we say that an object is an instance of a class. Microsoft's .NET Framework gives us hundreds of premade classes, like buttons and text boxes as well as other nonvisible classes, that we can instantiate and use in our programs.

VB.NET is an object-oriented programming language and as such uses reference types to encapsulate things. These things, called classes, have both data and functionality tied together within their definitions. Classes have "member variables" that store data and functionalities, or behaviors, held in procedures known as *methods* or *member functions*. Classes may also have events associated with them in the way a button has a click event. In a working program, different objects, which again are instances of classes, work together, or talk to each other, through their respective public interfaces. That is to say, private data within an object, which is not accessible from the outside world, is available to the outside programming environment through the object's public interface.

For example, your name is a private piece of data about you. No individuals can know your name unless they interact with your public interface, your ears and your voice. They can get the value of your name by asking you what your name is, and then you will tell them the value of your private name data using your public voice interface. To extend the analogy, when you were born, your parents set the value of your name much like we can set the text property of a button at design time. If you wanted to change, or set, your name during your lifetime, that is at run time, you would say You.Name = "Gordon Gekko."

In VB.NET, we can create our own user-defined classes and create objects based on them. For example, we could create a class called StockOption. In a program, an IBM April 80 call would be an object, that is, an instance of the StockOption class.

The organization of a class can be difficult to envision to programmers not used to thinking in terms of classes and objects. Here are the elements that make up a class:

Member Variables	Description
Variable	Simple data
Constant	Read-only values shared by all objects in the class
Nested types	Other types—classes, structures, interfaces, enums, etc.

Properties	Description
Property	Values of member variables are defined and retrieved through public Get and Set methods of a property

Member Functions	Description
Methods	Procedure that provides the object with functionality
Constructor	New() method runs when an object is instantiated
Finalization	Method that runs just before an object is destroyed

Events	Description
Event	Message sent from an event source to listener objects, called an event receiver

In order to use OOP in VB.NET, we need to understand four main concepts of object-oriented programming: abstraction, encapsulation, inheritance, and polymorphism.

ABSTRACTION

Abstraction is the process of creating an abstract model of a real-world object or thing. The process consists of taking the attributes, or properties, and functionalities, or methods, of an object and turning them into logical pieces of data and functionality.

Again, let's look at a stock option. To turn a stock option into a class in VB.NET, we need to think about the properties of a stock option—that is, what nouns are associated with a stock option, like the option symbol, the strike price, and the expiration date, as well as the verbs, or functionalities, or behaviors, of a stock option, like calculating implied volatility or calculating and returning the price. When we come up with a list of nouns, the "what it is" of an object, and verbs, the "what it does," we say that the object has been abstracted. So let's assume for a minute we have fully abstracted a StockOption class into the following nouns and verbs:

Nouns	Description
Option symbol	The option symbol consists of a symbol for the underlying symbol, a symbol for the month, and a symbol for the strike price
Expiration month	Derived from the option symbol
Strike price	Derived from the option symbol
Underlying symbol	Derived from the option symbol
Price of the option	We will use the Black-Scholes model to set the price
Market price	The option's price observed in the marketplace
Volatility of the option	We will need to set the volatility
Interest rate	We will need to set the interest rate
Greeks	We will need to calculate the Greeks
Time till expiration	Calculated from the expiration month
Days till expiration	Calculated from the expiration month
Calculated from the market price	

Verbs	Description
Derive expiration month	Symbol for month is found in the option symbol
Derive strike price	Symbol for strike price is found in the option symbol
Derive underlying symbol	Symbol for the underlying symbol is found in the option symbol
Calculate price	Need a procedure to calculate Black-Scholes price
Calculate Greeks	Need procedures to calculate the Greeks
Calculate trading days and time till expiration	Need a procedure to calculate the days and time till expiration using trading days
Calculate the implied volatility	Need a procedure to calculate the implied volatility

ENCAPSULATION

Encapsulation refers to the process of containing the abstracted properties and methods into a class, exposing to the outside world only those methods that absolutely must be exposed, which are then known collectively as the class's public interface. So classes hide the implementation of their properties and methods and communicate with the external programming environment through the public interface. In this way encapsulation protects the object from being tampered with and frees the programmer from having to know the details of the object's implementation.

In our StockOption example the outside programming environment does not need to be exposed to the method of calculating the price, and so this functionality is encapsulated and made unavailable to the outside world. This idea will become clearer as we go along. For right now let's look at the code to encapsulate just the private variable named strOptionSym to hold the option symbol in the StockOption class, along with a public property called Symbol to get the value of the strOptionSym.

Let's create a StockOption class.

Step 1   Open a new Windows application named OptionObject and add a single label, named Label1, to Form1.

Step 2   Under the Project menu item, select Add Class. A new class code window will appear.

Step 3   Add the following code to the StockOption class:

```
Public Class StockOption
      Private strOptionSym As String
      Public Sub New (ByVal strSymbol As String)
            strOptionSym = strSymbol
      End Sub
      Public ReadOnly Property Symbol()
            Get
                    Return strOptionSym
            End Get
      End Property
End Class
```

Notice that the class name is StockOption. Be careful. StockOption is a class, not an object. In this example, strOptionSym is private, and so we will not be able to get or set the value of it from outside the object itself. We can, however, set the value of strOptionSym through the constructor method known as the New() subroutine.

So New() is called the constructor method. Any time an object is instantiated, or born, using the New keyword, the object's constructor method executes. In this case the public subroutine New() accepts a string and sets the value of strOptionSym, our private member variable, equal to it. By requiring that an option symbol be passed to the constructor method, we prevent ourselves, or any other programmer using this class, from creating a new option object without a symbol.

Also notice that we can get the value of strOptionSym through the public property Symbol, which has a Get method within it. Public properties provide us with access to private member variables through Get and Set methods. Notice, however, that our Symbol property is ReadOnly, implying that once the strOptionSym member variable is set via the New() method, it cannot be changed.

Creating a reference type, such as an object, out of a class is a two-stage process. First, we declare the name of the object, which will actually then be a variable that holds a reference to the location of the object in memory. Second, we create an instance of a class using the New keyword. This is when the constructor method will run. Here is an example of showing the two-stage process:

```
Dim myOption As StockOption
myOption = New StockOption("IBMDP")
```

Alternatively, we can accomplish the process using one line of code:

```
Dim myOption As New StockOption("IBMDP")
```

In different situations it will be advantageous to use one or the other of these two methods. We will use both methods over the course of the book. As with variables, it is important to pay close attention to the scope of your reference types, which will dictate in many cases the method of instantiation.

Step 4   In the Form1 code window, add the following code to
the Form1_Load event:

```
Private Sub Form1_Load(ByVal sender As...) Handles MyBase.Load
        Dim myOption As New StockOption("IBMDP")
        Label1.Text = myOption.Symbol
End Sub
```

Now when the program is running, myOption is the object,
whereas StockOption is the class. We set the value of strOption-
Symbol by passing a string into the constructor, New(), as shown.

Step 5   Run the program (see Figure 7.1).

The content of this program is not earth-shattering of course,
but congratulate yourself nonetheless; you have just created your
first class, your first object, and your first object-oriented program.
Of course, a stock option consists of a lot more data and
functionality than just a symbol. Also, as we saw in our abstraction
of a stock option, some of this other data might not be set from the
outside, but rather calculated internally. For example, we would
obviously prefer to have the option object derive the strike price
internally from the option symbol rather than require that we set it
explicitly from the outside. Let's take a look at the fully developed
StockOption class found on the CD.

Step 6   Clear the StockOption class of the previous definition
and paste in the full StockOption class code from the
StockOption.txt file found on the CD.

F I G U R E 7.1

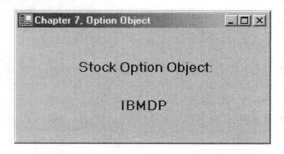

Step 7   Add three labels to your form and change the
            Form_Load event code to:

```
Private Sub Form1_Load(ByVal sender As ...) Handles MyBase.Load
    Dim MyOption As StockOption = New StockOption("IBMDP")
    Label1.Text = MyOption.Underlying
    Label2.Text = MyOption.ExpMonth
    Label3.Text = MyOption.Strike
    Label4.Text = MyOption.BSPrice
End Sub
```

Step 8   Run the program (see Figure 7.2).

F I G U R E 7.2

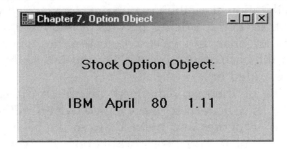

Once we have completely turned our model into computer
code, we say that the class has been encapsulated. A major benefit
of OOP is that because the data and methods encapsulated in
classes are so closely tied together, we do not need to pass
arguments back and forth as inputs to procedures. Rather, member
functions can access member variables directly within their
definitions. In the StockOption class code, notice that the member
methods, such as SetStrikePrice, are able to access the member
variables directly. Also notice that the BlackScholesPrice() method,
which contains a method definition setting the price of all
StockOption objects to 1.11, is overridable. This means that method
definitions in classes that inherit from the StockOption class may
override the definition in the base, or parent, StockOption class.

INHERITANCE

The best way to understand inheritance is to continue the StockOption object example. A stock option, through abstraction and encapsulation into a class and then instantiation, can be an object in VB.NET. This object built on the StockOption class contains only those properties and methods that are common to all stock options. Certainly the method of calculating the price is not common to all stock options. We calculate the price of a call differently than we calculate the price of a put.

A call option is a stock option. As such, it has methods that are not common to all stock options, such as calculation of its price. So rather than create a whole new CallOption class, we can create a derived, or child, class, called CallOption, that inherits all the properties and methods from the base, or parent, StockOption class. The CallOption class then may have some added properties or functionalities, such as pricing algorithms that are unique to call options on stocks. Likewise, we could create a PutOption class that inherits from the base StockOption class and has its own specific functionalities added on.

Continuing on then, an American call option is a call option. So we could create a derived class called AmerCallOption that inherits all the properties and methods from the base CallOption class and so on. For the purposes of this book, however, we will stop with the CallOption class.

A derived class can add functionality beyond that of the base class, and it can also override methods of its base class. That is, a derived class may replace a member function definition of the base class with its own new definition. In such cases, the base class definition should indicate which if any methods may be overridden in derived classes using the Overridable inheritance modifier. Here is a table of the inheritance modifiers:

Inheritance Modifier	Description
MustInherit	Indicates an abstract class that cannot be instantiated, only inherited
MustOverride	Must be overridden in the derived class. Necessitates a MustInherit class
Overridable	May be overridden in the derived class
NotOverridable	Prevents overriding in derived classes
Overrides	Indicates overriding a base class definition
Shadows	Has the same name as a method in the base class

In our program, let's create a derived class CallOption that will inherit all the member variables and methods from the base, StockOption class.

Step 9 In your program, add another class module and to it add the following code:

```
Public Class CallOption
    Inherits StockOption

    Public Sub New(ByVal strSymbol As String)
        MyBase.New(strSymbol)
    End Sub

    Protected Overrides Sub BlackScholesPrice()
        Dim d1 As Double, d2 As Double, Nd1 As Double, Nd2 As Double
        d1 = (Math.Log(dblStock / dblStrike) + (dblInterestRate + _
            (dblSigma ^ 2) / 2) * dblTimeTillExp) / _
            (dblSigma * Math.Sqrt(dblTimeTillExp))
        d2 = d1 - dblSigma * Math.Sqrt(dblTimeTillExp)
        Nd1 = NormCDF(d1)
        Nd2 = NormCDF(d2)
        dblBSPrice = dblStock * Nd1 - dblStrike * _
                Math.Exp(-dblInterestRate * dblTimeTillExp) * Nd2
    End Sub
End Class
```

In the derived class CallOption, the BlackScholesCall() method definition overrides the definition in the base StockOption class. Again, notice that the procedure in the CallOption class called BlackScholesPrice() is a member function and, therefore, has direct access to the member variables.

Also, because constructor methods are not inherited, we needed to add a New() method to our derived CallOption class that explicitly calls the constructor of the base class using the MyBase keyword. The MyBase keyword always references the base class within any derived class.

Step 10 Change the Form_Load event code to:

```
Private Sub Form1_Load(ByVal sender As ...) Handles MyBase.Load
        Dim MyCallOption As CallOption = New CallOption("IBMDP")
        Label1.Text = MyCallOption.Underlying
        Label2.Text = MyCallOption.ExpMonth
        Label3.Text = MyCallOption.Strike
        MyCallOption.IntRate=0.1            ' default IntRate = .1
```

F I G U R E 7.3

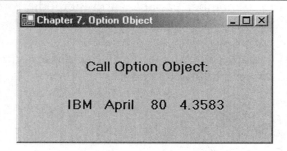

```
        MyCallOption.StockPrice = 80
        MyCallOption.Volatility = 0.25
        Label4.Text = Format(MyCallOption.BSPrice, "#.0000")
    End Sub
```

Step 11   Run the program (see Figure 7.3).

As we mentioned before, your program will have a different price from the one shown in Figure 7.3 since the time till expiration changes as time moves forward. Also, the StockOption class sets the IntRate = .1 by default, and so in future programs we will not need to set it explicitly.

POLYMORPHISM

Polymorphism allows us to have one method name, or function name, used in different derived classes, but yet have different implementations, or functionalities, associated with that name depending on the class. In our CallOption class above, and the PutOption class also found on the CD, for example, we have inherited a BlackScholesPrice() method from the parent Stock-Option class, but yet each of the derived classes has its own method for calculation since the equations for Black-Scholes call and put pricing are different.

EVENTS

Events allow an object, called the publisher or source, to notify other objects, called the subscribers or receivers, when something happens. The most intuitive event is the button Click event. When the user clicks a button, the Click event fires, and as we have seen, we can write code that will execute when this happens. Creating events in VB.NET is really quite easy. Here are the four steps to create an event:

1. Create an event member in the publisher class.
2. Within the subscriber class, create an instance of the publisher using the WithEvents keyword.
3. Fire the event in the publisher using the RaiseEvent keyword.
4. Create a method in the subscriber that will run when the event is fired using the Handles keyword.

We will not review events further. So for more information on events, we refer you to the VB.NET help files.

ACCESS MODIFIERS

In the complete StockOption class, we have changed all the Private access modifiers to Protected, because Private member variables and Private methods are not accessible in derived classes. Take a look at the BlackScholesPrice() method:

```
Protected Overridable Sub BlackScholesPrice()
```

Protected member variables and methods are accessible in derived classes. So since we intended to create a derived class, CallOption, from our base class StockOption, we needed to use the Protected access modifier. Here are the access modifiers for classes:

Access Modifier	Scope
Public	Accessible anywhere
Private	Accessible only by methods of the class. Derived class methods cannot access Private properties or methods
Protected	Accessible by base class and derived class methods
Friend	Accessible by base class methods, derived class methods, and certain other classes
Shared	Shared members are callable directly from the class without requiring an instance of the class

OVERLOADING

The complete StockOption class also contains two New() methods. This is an example of method overloading. We can create as many methods with the same name in a single class as are needed as long as the lists of input arguments are different from one another, either in number of arguments or in the data types of the arguments.

Methods other than New() that are overloaded must include the Overloads keyword. Although not illustrated in the code for StockOption, an example would be:

```
Public Overloads Function NormCDF(ByVal x As Integer) As Double
```

where this function overloads the original NormCDF() function because it differs in its parameter list.

```
Public Overloads Function NormCDF(ByVal x As Double) As Double
```

NOTHING

Because the name of an object is really a variable holding a reference to the location of the object in memory, we can assign a value of Nothing to the object, which allows the .NET garbage collector to dispose of the unused memory. This method disposes of the instance of the object, but not the name of the object.

```
MyOption = Nothing
```

CALCULATING AT-THE-MONEY VOLATILITY

Very rarely, if ever, in financial markets can we look at an at-the-money (ATM) option and calculate its implied volatility. Yet in our discussions about markets, we often talk in terms of ATM volatility. Quantitative research papers frequently use time series of ATM volatility, and what's more, many mathematical models assume the reader understands that volatility means at-the-money volatility. But what is ATM volatility if it cannot be observed in the marketplace? The answer is that ATM volatility is a value we must calculate from the implied volatilities of the puts and calls with the strikes surrounding the ATM value—those

nearest, above and below, the price of the underlying symbol. Furthermore, since time is always moving forward and expirations are continuously drawing nearer, we have to include volatilities for the nearby and second nearby expirations to come up with a constant-maturity ATM volatility. That is, if we wish to refer to an ATM volatility that is, for example, 30 calendar days out (which is somewhat difficult to envision since only on 1 day a month will an expiration be exactly 30 days away), we need a mathematical construct to interpolate between options in the nearby and second nearby expirations.

In this section we will use the Chicago Board Options Exchange's market volatility index (VIX) methodology for calculating ATM volatility. As described by Robert Whaley in his paper "The Investor Fear Gauge" (2000), the VIX represents the ATM volatility for the S&P 100 (OEX) index. The CBOE computes the value of the VIX from the prices of eight puts and calls with the strikes nearest, above and below, the price of the underlying security for the nearby and second nearby expirations (Whaley, 2000, p. 1). The implied volatilities derived from these eight options are then weighted to form a 30-calendar-day, 22-trading-day, constant-maturity, ATM implied volatility for the OEX index. The prices used for these eight options will be the midpoints between the respective bids and offers.

While the implied volatilities for these eight options should be calculated using a cash dividend–adjusted binomial method to account for the facts that OEX index options are American style and that the underlying index portfolio pays discrete cash dividends, we will use the traditional Black-Scholes model for European options to derive all required implied volatilities. Forecasting dividends for the 100 stocks that make up the index is beyond the scope of this book. As you can imagine, this will, of course, lead to small deviations from the value of the actual VIX.

If it happens that the implied volatilities for these eight options are calculated using calendar days, then each must be converted to a trading-day implied volatility. If the number of calendar days to expiration is $Days_C$ and the number of trading days till expiration is $Days_T$, then $Days_T$ is calculated as follows:

$$\text{Days}_T = \text{Days}_C - 2 \cdot \text{int}(\text{Days}_C/7)$$

To convert calendar-day volatilities to trading-day volatilities, we multiply the eight by the square root of the ratio of the number of calendar days to the number of trading days thusly:

$$\sigma_T = \sigma_C\left(\sqrt{\frac{N_C}{N_T}}\right)$$

Fortunately, the StockOption class already assumes trading days for time to expiration, and so we will not need to make this adjustment.

In practice, the risk-free interest rate we should use in the calculation is the continuous yield of the T-bill with the maturity most closely matching the option's expiration. If the time till expiration is shorter than 30 days, however, the 30 day T-bill rate is used. The StockOption class sets the default interest rate to .1, and we will just use that.

The calculations will be clearer if we look at an example. Let's assume today is February 3 and the OEX index is at 435.70. The options with the nearest strikes above and below would be the 435s and 440s. If we take the midpoints of the bids and asks of the puts and calls for the next two expirations, February 16 and March 16, for both these strikes, we will have eight option prices and eight trading-day volatilities, as shown in Figure 7.4.

Now we need to average the eight implied volatilities to arrive at a single ATM volatility 22 days hence, denoted by the gray X in Figure 7.5. First we average the call and put volatilities in each of the quadrants, respectively, to reduce the number of volatilities to four.

In Figure 7.5, the subscript N refers to the nearby expiration and S to the second nearby, and subscript A and B mean above and below the current price of the underlying. In the upcoming formulas, P stands for the price of the underlying, and X means the strike price, so that X_A refers to the strike price above the price of the underlying security and X_B to the strike price below. Also in upcoming formulas, N refers to the number of trading days, so that

F I G U R E   7.4

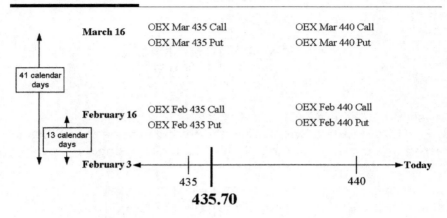

N_N and N_S refer to the number of trading days till the nearby and second nearby expirations, respectively.

Second we average the two volatilities across each of the two expirations. The average of the two nearby volatilities to arrive at the ATM volatility for the nearby expiration is found using

$$\sigma_N = \sigma_{N,B}\left[\frac{X_A - P}{X_A - X_B}\right] + \sigma_{N,A}\left[\frac{P - X_B}{X_A - X_B}\right]$$

F I G U R E   7.5

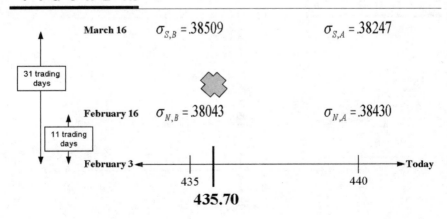

and the ATM volatility for the second nearby expiration is found using

$$\sigma_S = \sigma_{S,B}\left[\frac{X_A - P}{X_A - X_B}\right] + \sigma_{S,A}\left[\frac{P - X_B}{X_A - X_B}\right]$$

as shown in Figure 7.6.

Third and last, we average the two remaining volatilities to arrive at a constant-maturity 22 trading hence, using

$$\text{VIX} = \sigma_N\left[\frac{N_S - 22}{N_S - N_N}\right] + \sigma_S\left[\frac{22 - N_N}{N_S - N_N}\right]$$

as shown in Figure 7.7. (These calculations are all taken from Whaley, 2000, p. 12ff.)

Now let's create a VB.NET Windows application that uses option objects to calculate the constant-maturity ATM volatility for IBM using the VIX methodology, again assuming no dividends.

Step 1   Open a new VB.NET Windows application called ATMExample.

F I G U R E   7.6

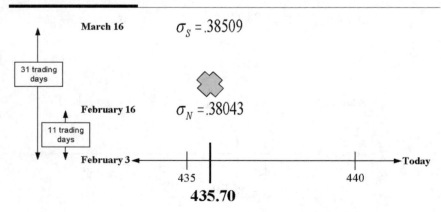

F I G U R E 7.7

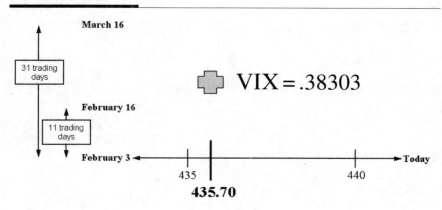

$$VIX = .38303$$

435.70

Step 2   On the menu bar, select Project, Add Class three times and paste in the code for the StockOption, CallOption, and PutOption classes.

Step 3   Now we will need eight put and call objects and eight corresponding prices. This will require 16 text boxes laid out in a pattern similar to that shown in Figure 7.4 for the two expirations. Name the text boxes with the following scheme: The name of the text box for the nearby call option with the strike below the underlying price should be txtCallNB for Call, Nearby, Below. The text box for the second nearby put with the strike price above the underlying price should be txtPutSA for Put, Second, Above. Figure 7.8 shows the respective names for the text box controls.

Step 4   Add the following code to the Button1_Click event to read in the price of the underlying IBM stock and create eight put and call objects and set their MarketPrices and StockPrices.

```
Dim UnderlyingPrice As Double = txtUnderlyingPrice.Text

Dim CallNB As New CallOption(txtCallNB.Text)
CallNB.MarketPrice = txtCallNBprice.Text
CallNB.StockPrice = UnderlyingPrice
```

F I G U R E 7.8

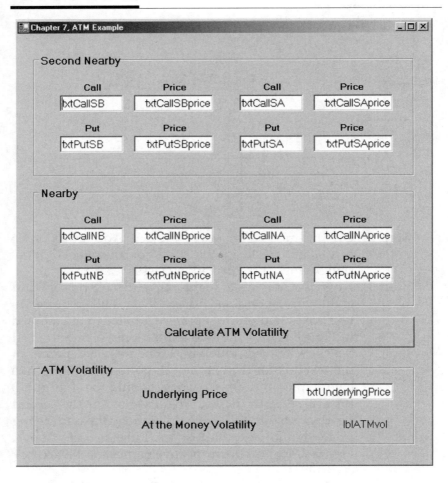

```
Dim PutNB As New PutOption(txtPutNB.Text)
PutNB.MarketPrice = txtPutNBprice.Text
PutNB.StockPrice = UnderlyingPrice

Dim CallNA As New CallOption(txtCallNA.Text)
CallNA.MarketPrice = txtCallNAprice.Text
CallNA.StockPrice = UnderlyingPrice

Dim PutNA As New PutOption(txtPutNA.Text)
PutNA.MarketPrice = txtPutNAprice.Text
PutNA.StockPrice = UnderlyingPrice
```

```
Dim CallSB As New CallOption(txtCallSB.Text)
CallSB.MarketPrice = txtCallSBprice.Text
CallSB.StockPrice = UnderlyingPrice

Dim PutSB As New PutOption(txtPutSB.Text)
PutSB.MarketPrice = txtPutSBprice.Text
PutSB.StockPrice = UnderlyingPrice

Dim CallSA As New CallOption(txtCallSA.Text)
CallSA.MarketPrice = txtCallSAprice.Text
CallSA.StockPrice = UnderlyingPrice

Dim PutSA As New PutOption(txtPutSA.Text)
PutSA.MarketPrice = txtPutSAprice.Text
PutSA.StockPrice = UnderlyingPrice
```

As mentioned earlier, the StockOption class already calculates the time till expiration using trading days as opposed to calendar days, and so no conversion of the volatilities will be necessary.

Step 5 Once these eight option objects are created, we need to average the call and put volatilities in each of the quadrants, respectively, to reduce the number of volatilities to four. For this we will need four new variables of type double. Add the following code to the Button1_Click event:

```
Dim dblVolNB, dblVolNA, dblVolSB, dblVolSA As Double

dblVolNB = (CallNB.ImpliedVol + PutNB.ImpliedVol) / 2
dblVolNA = (CallNA.ImpliedVol + PutNA.ImpliedVol) / 2
dblVolSB = (CallSB.ImpliedVol + PutSB.ImpliedVol) / 2
dblVolSA = (CallSA.ImpliedVol + PutSA.ImpliedVol) / 2
```

Step 6 Now we will need to weight the above and below volatilities to arrive at an average volatility for each of the two expirations, nearby and second nearby.

```
Dim dblNearbyVol, dblSecondVol As Double
dblNearbyVol = dblVolNB *((CallNA.Strike - UnderlyingPrice) / _
    (CallNA.Strike - CallNB.Strike)) + dblVolNA * ((UnderlyingPrice- _
    CallNB.Strike) / (CallNA.Strike - CallNB.Strike))
dblSecondVol = dblVolSB * ((CallSA.Strike - UnderlyingPrice) / _
    (CallSA.Strike - CallSB.Strike)) + dblVolSA * ((UnderlyingPrice - _
    CallSB.Strike) / (CallSA.Strike - CallSB.Strike))
```

Step 7 And, finally, we can calculate the ATM constant maturity volatility:

```
Dim ATMVol As Double = dblNearbyVol * ((CallSA.DaysTillExp - 22) / _
    CallSA.DaysTillExp - CallNA.DaysTillExp)) + dblSecondVol * ((22 - _
    CallNA.DaysTillExp) / (CallSA.DaysTillExp - CallNA.DaysTillExp))
lblATMvol.Text = Format(ATMVol, "0.#####")
```

Step 8   Run the program (see Figure 7.9).

The results you get will be different from the results shown in Figure 7.9 since the time-to-expiration calculations are continuously changing. Thus on the CD we have included a spreadsheet called ATMs.xls, against which you can check your answers.

F I G U R E 7.9

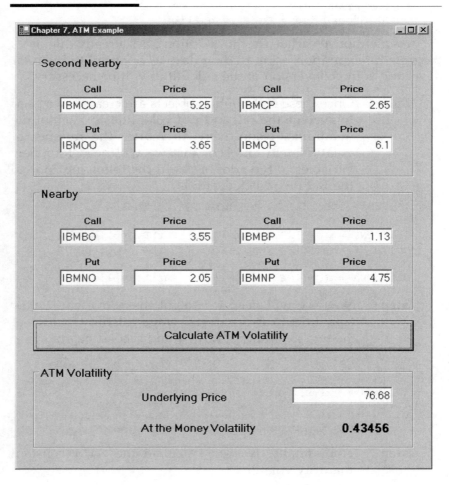

As you can see, creating and managing multiple objects can be quite a difficult task codewise. Suppose, for example, we had a portfolio of 100 options. How much coding would we have to do then? Obviously we will need a superior method for dealing with this situation. In the following chapter we will discuss arrays, which are a convenient way to hold multiple value types, that is, variables. In later chapters we will look at data structures, which provide convenient methods for dealing with groups of objects such as portfolios of options.

SUMMARY

In this chapter we introduced the concepts of classes and objects. Object-oriented programming necessitates that we understand the ideas of abstraction, encapsulation, polymorphism, and inheritance. Further we used the StockOption and CallOption classes to illustrate these concepts as well as access modifiers and method overloading. Lastly we built a complex model using eight put and call objects to calculate the ATM volatility for IBM. This was a complex program!

PROBLEMS

1. In OOP, what is meant by the term *abstraction*?
2. What is encapsulation?
3. What is polymorphism?
4. What is inheritance?
5. What are the differences between the access modifiers Public, Private, and Protected?

PROJECT 7.1

To the CallOption and PutOption classes, add methods for the Greeks. Build a Windows application that accepts user inputs for an options symbol, a stock price, and a volatility, and calculates the Black-Scholes price and Greeks for either a call or a put. Your program should print out in labels all the necessary information including the price and all the Greeks.

PROJECT 7.2

Create a Stock class. Although this class will be comparatively simple, you should add Private member variables for, at least, the ticker, price, dividend, and dividend date, along with Public properties for each of them. You should set the ticker in the constructor function New(). Then create a VB.NET Windows application that creates an object based upon the Stock class using user-entered values. Override the ToString() method to print out the ticker and the price in a label.

In VB.NET, the overridable ToString() method is inherited by every class by default. ToString() allows us to simply print out a string representation of an object. Within your Stock class, you can implement this method in the following way:

```
Public Overrides Function ToString() As String
    Return strTicker & " " & str(dblStockPrice)
End Function
```

Arrays

In VB.NET, arrays are objects that essentially group identical value types together contiguously in memory in one or more dimensions—hence, the Dim keyword. We can access any one element in an array by referencing the array name and the element's index, or position or address, within the array. When doing financial modeling, we use arrays frequently, and so a good understanding of them and how they work is very important. Arrays come in particularly handy when dealing with data, doing matrix algebra, and creating binomial and trinomial trees.

ONE-DIMENSIONAL ARRAYS

Although arrays occupy space in memory, simply declaring an array does not create the space. Rather, because an array is a reference type, an array declaration creates a variable that stores a reference to the space in memory occupied by an array. So creating an array object is again a two-stage process. Here is a sample declaration for an array of doubles:

```
Dim dblClosingPrices As Double()
```

Then the New keyword is necessary to create an actual array object. The value in parentheses defines the upper bound for the array. The lower bound is always 0.

```
dblClosingPrices = New Double(2) {}
```

A simple way to populate an array is to use the initializer list, like this:

```
dblClosingPrices = New Double(2) {52.5, 51.4, 45.24}
```

Alternatively, the two statements could be combined:

```
Dim dblClosingPrices As Double() = New Double(2) {}
```

or using the initializer:

```
Dim dblClosingPrices As Double() = New Double(2) {52.5, 51.4, 45.24}
```

Since the index of the first element is always 0, the upper bound, in this case 2, will always be 1 less than the number of elements in the array, in this case 3. We can access any element in a one-dimensional array by referencing its index, or address, within the array.

```
dblClosingPrices(0) = 52.5
dblClosingPrices(1) = 51.4
dblClosingPrices(2) = 45.24
```

If we attempt to access an array element outside the upper bound, say dblClosingPrices(53), we will get an error message saying that the index was outside the bounds of the array. Should the situation arise, we could also declare an array of the user-defined data type QuoteData.

```
Dim qdPriceData As QuoteData() = New QuoteData(10) {}
```

And we could reference the individual elements of a QuoteData array in the following way:

```
qdPriceData(3).dblClose = 43.45
```

TWO-DIMENSIONAL ARRAYS

A two-dimensional array object could be instantiated in one line this way:

```
Dim dblCovariance As Double(,) = New Double(1,1) {}
```

We could declare and populate a two-dimensional array using the two-line method and the initializer in this way:

```
Dim dblCovariance As Double(,)
dblCovariance = New Double(1,1) {{.057, .83}, {.192, -.12}}
```

We can access any element in a two-dimensional array by referencing its index, or address, in the array.

```
Sub Main()
     Dim dblCovariance As Double(,)
     dblCovariance = New Double(1, 1) {{0.057, 0.83}, _
                                       {0.192, -0.12}}
     Console.WriteLine(dblCovariance(0, 0))
     Console.WriteLine(dblCovariance(1, 0))
     Console.WriteLine(dblCovariance(0, 1))
     Console.WriteLine(dblCovariance(1, 1))
End Sub
```

This program prints out the elements of the dblCovariance array as:

```
.057
.192
.083
-0.12
```

As discussed in Chapter 5, we can access each element in a two-dimensional array in VB.NET by writing a nested For ... Next loop structure, such as:

```
For Rows = 0 To 1
     For Cols = 0 To 1
          ' Do something with dblCovariance(Rows, Cols)
     Next Cols
Next Rows
```

JAGGED ARRAYS

On occasion, the structure of the data in a program may be two-dimensional, but not rectangular. That is, not every row will be the same length. In such cases it may be advantageous from a memory savings standpoint to use a jagged array. A jagged array is an array that has rows of different lengths. In memory a jagged array is really stored as an array of arrays. Here is how to declare a jagged array in one line:

```
Dim dblBinomTree As Double()() = New Double(2)() {}
```

Binomial trees are valuable tools in derivatives pricing, and there are several methods for building binomial trees in code using arrays. Some methods only require a single-dimensional array. However, in cases where the entire tree must be maintained in memory, jagged arrays work quite well. In fact, binomial trees fit rather elegantly into jagged arrays and waste no memory space. Figure 8.1 shows different potential price paths of a stock.

The initial value in the tree, 100, is calculated using the formula

$$100 = S_0 \cdot D^0 \cdot U^0$$

The two prices after one step forward, 107.43 and 93.09, are found using

$$107.48 = S_0 \cdot D^0 \cdot U^1$$

$$93.04 = S_0 \cdot D^1 \cdot U^0$$

As you can see, we calculate individual nodes on the tree by incrementing the exponents of U and D. We can make these calculations and populate a jagged array very easily since the exponents map to the indexes of the array elements. Figure 8.2 shows the array elements with their values and indexes.

F I G U R E   8.1

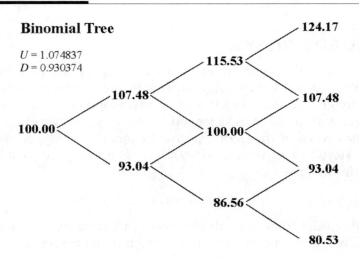

Binomial Tree

$U = 1.074837$
$D = 0.930374$

100.00	107.48	115.53	124.17
(0, 0)	(0, 1)	(0, 2)	(0, 3)
93.04	100.00	107.48	
(1, 0)	(1, 1)	(1, 2)	
86.56	93.04		
(2, 0)	(2, 1)		
80.53			
(3, 0)			

We can initialize the elements of a binomial tree into a jagged array as per Figure 8.2 in this fashion:

```
Sub Main()
    Dim x, y As Integer
    Dim dblStockPrice As Double = 100
    Dim U As Double = 1.074837
    Dim D As Double = 0.930374
    Dim dblBinomTree As Double()() = New Double(3)() {}
    For x = 0 To 3
        dblBinomTree(x) = New Double(3 - x) {}
        For y = 0 To 3 - x
            dblBinomTree(x)(y) = dblStockPrice * D ^ x * U ^ y
            Console.WriteLine("(" & x & ", " & y & " ) = " & _
                              dblBinomTree(x)(y))
        Next y
    Next x
End Sub
```

Jagged arrays are held in memory and require that we declare the upper bound of the first dimension first. That is, we first declare the number of rows, and then we can go through row by row and declare the upper bound of each particular row as in the line of code above.

```
dblBinomTree(x) = New Double(3 - x) {}
```

ARRAY METHODS

Because arrays in VB.NET are instances of the Array class, and therefore are objects, they have properties and methods associated with them. Here are some of the properties and methods as well as several functions found in the System.Array namespace. To use these functions we should include an Imports System.Array statement above all the other code in a module.

Array Properties	Description	Example
Length	Returns the total number of elements in the array	intA = myArray.Length
Rank	Returns the number of dimensions in the array	intA = myArray.Rank

Array Methods	Description	Example
GetLength	Returns the number of elements in a given dimension	intA = myArray.GetLength(0)
GetUpperBound	Returns the upper bound of a given dimension	intA = myArray. GetUpperBound(0)

System.Array Functions	Description	Example
Clear	Sets a range of elements within the array equal to 0	Clear(SourceArray, 0, 3)
Copy	Makes a copy of all or part of an array given a length	Copy(SourceArray, TargetArray, 5)
IndexOf	Finds the index number associated with the first occurrence of a value	intA = IndexOf(SourceArray, "IBM")
Reverse	Reverses some or all of the elements in an array given a starting and ending index	Reverse(SourceArray, 1, 10)
Sort	Sorts some or all of a one-dimensional array in ascending order	Sort(SourceArray)

Here is a short console application illustrating some of these methods:

```
Imports System.Array
Module Module1
    Sub Main()
        Dim x As Integer
        Dim dblReturns As Double() = New Double(4) {0.0176, 0.0083, _
                                     0.0232, -0.0241, 0.0077}
        Sort(dblReturns)
        For x = 0 To dblReturns.GetUpperBound(0)
            Console.WriteLine(dblReturns(x))
        Next x
    End Sub
End Module
```

This program declares and populates a one-dimensional array named dblReturns. The Sort() function puts the elements in the order from lowest to highest. The GetUpperBound() member function returns the upper bound, 4, so that the For ... Next loop will run five times. Also notice the inclusion of the Imports statement at the top. The function definition for Sort() is found in the System.Array namespace. We will discuss namespaces in greater detail in Chapter 10. This program prints out:

```
-.0241
.0077
.0083
.0176
.0232
```

DYNAMIC ARRAY SIZING

In situations where the number of elements in an array either is unknown or will not be fixed, we use the Dim statement along with the ReDim() procedure.

```
Dim dblCovariance As Double(,)
```

Before we can use this array, we must dimension bounds using the ReDim statement. For example:

```
ReDim dblCovariance(4, 4)
```

All arrays in VB.NET are dynamic, and the ReDim() function can be called as many times as is necessary. Be aware, though, that VB.NET does not allow you to change the number of dimensions in an array.

Also be careful because each time you ReDim an array, the contents of the array are destroyed unless you use the Preserve keyword. Preserve will keep the existing data intact and grow the size of the array.

```
ReDim Preserve dblCovariance(5, 5)
```

As another example, say we want to read some historical price data from a file, but we do not know how many items of information are in the file. We could read through the file, count how many items there are, and then use a single ReDim statement to allocate an array of sufficient size.

What if the information was coming from a live data connection? In that situation we would not have the opportunity to determine the number of items ahead of time. The solution is to use the Preserve keyword in conjunction with ReDim, as shown below:

```
Dim dblPriceData As Double()
Dim intNumElements As Integer
Dim blnMoreData As Boolean
Do While blnMoreData
        intNumElements += 1
        ReDim Preserve dblPriceData(intNumElements)
' Read data feed and set blnMoreData to True if more data was read.
        End While
```

PASSING ARRAYS TO FUNCTIONS

Visual Basic.NET allows us to pass arrays to functions as input arguments and also return them from functions as output arguments, or return values. Here is an example of the basic syntax for passing arrays to and from functions:

```
Sub Main()
 Dim dblReturns As Double() = New Double(9) {0.0203, -0.0136, 0.0012, _
                              0.0266, -0.0063, -0.0601, _
                              0.0307, 0.0123, 0.0055, _
                              0.0441}

 Console.WriteLine(Average(dblReturns))
 End Sub
```

Here, we have created an array of doubles and populated the array, using the initializer, with 10 values representing daily returns. Then we have passed the array to a function called Average() that accepts an array of doubles as an input argument and returns a double, which is the average of the elements in the array:

```
Public Function Average(ByRef InArray As Double()) As Double
        Dim dblTotalReturn As Double
        Dim x As Integer
        Dim dblLength# = UBound(InArray, 1)
        For x = 0 To dblLength
```

```
                    dblTotalReturn += InArray(x)
          Next x
          Return dblTotalReturn / (dblLength + 1)
     End Function
```

Because arrays are always passed to functions by reference, it is important to remember that certain operations performed on those arrays, such as matrix transposition and inversion, will actually destroy the original matrix. To avoid this situation, it may be necessary to first make a copy of the array within the function definition and then proceed by making calculations on the new copy of the original array.

THE ERASE STATEMENT

The Erase statement clears an array and releases the memory used by the array object. To reuse the array after Erase, we can use the ReDim statement.

```
     Erase dblReturns
```

UBOUND FUNCTION

The Ubound() function returns the upper bound of a dimension of the array. It works the same as the array class member function GetUpperBound() except that the array dimensions are 1 and 2 for a two-dimensional array. For example:

```
     Dim dblPriceData As Double(,) = New Double(10,5)
     Dim intUpperBound As Integer
     intUpperBound = UBound(dblPriceData,1)
```

intUpperBound will equal 10.

USING ARRAYS FOR DATA

When modeling returns, we often determine average rates of return and volatilities. In this case, we need to use continuous rates of return, such that

$$R_i = \ln\left(\frac{S_i}{S_{i-1}}\right)$$

Given historical returns, we can calculate the average return:

$$\mu_{R;t,T} = \frac{1}{n}\sum_{i=1}^{n} R_i$$

We can calculate the variance of returns:

$$\sigma_{t,T}^2 = \frac{1}{n}\sum_{i=1}^{n} (R_i - \bar{R})^2$$

We can calculate the skew:

$$\text{Skew} = \frac{n}{(n-1)(n-2)}\sum_{i=1}^{n}\left(\frac{R_i - \bar{R}}{s}\right)^3$$

The skewness of a distribution characterizes the degree of asymmetry around its mean. Positive skewness indicates an asymmetric tail extending toward more positive values. Negative skewness indicates an asymmetric tail extending toward negative values.

   We can calculate the kurtosis:

$$\text{Kurtosis} = \left\{\frac{n(n+1)}{(n-1)(n-2)(n-3)}\sum_{i=1}^{n}\left(\frac{R_i - \bar{R}}{s}\right)^4\right\} - \frac{3(n-1)^2}{(n-2)(n-3)}$$

This returns the kurtosis of a data set. Kurtosis characterizes the relative peakedness or flatness of a distribution compared with the normal distribution. Positive kurtosis indicates a relatively peaked distribution. Negative kurtosis indicates a relatively flat distribution.

Step 1   In VB.NET, open a new Windows application called DataArray.

Step 2   Add five labels to the form.

Step 3 Add five modules and in them, place the functions for Average(), Var(), VarP(), Skew(), and Kurtosis() from the CD.

Step 4 In the form load event, add the following code to pass an array of return data into each of the functions:

```
Private Sub Form1_Load(ByVal sender As ...) Handles MyBase.Load
  Dim dblReturns As Double() = New Double(9) {0.0203, -0.0136, 0.0012, _
                                              0.0266, -0.0063, -0.0601, _
                                              0.0307, 0.0123, 0.0055, _
                                              0.0441}
        Label1.Text = Format(Average(dblReturns), "#.#####")
        Label2.Text = Format(Var(dblReturns), "#.#####")
        Label3.Text = Format(VarP(dblReturns), "#.#####")
        Label4.Text = Format(Skew(dblReturns), "#.#####")
        Label5.Text = Format(Kurtosis(dblReturns), "#.#####")
End Sub
```

Step 5 Run the program (see Figure 8.3). As with any calculations you make in code, be sure to verify them against Excel's built-in functions—Average(), Var(), VarP(), Skew(), and Kurt().

F I G U R E 8.3

Chapter 8, Data Array Example	
Average	.00607
Variance	.00085
Pop Variance	.00077
Skew	-1.21773
Kurtosis	2.29979

USING ARRAYS FOR MATRIX ALGEBRA

We often use matrix algebra when doing financial research. For example, modern portfolio management techniques frequently make use of covariance matrices. Using matrix notation, we can calculate the variance of a portfolio in the following manner:

$$\sigma_P^2 = \omega'\Omega\omega$$

where Ω is the covariance matrix and ω is the vector of portfolio weights. A covariance matrix, of course, exists in two dimensions, where:

$$\Omega = \mathrm{Cov}(r_A, r_B) = \frac{1}{n}\sum [r_{A,i} - E(r_A)][r_{B,i} - E(r_B)]$$

So that, for example, a covariance matrix for a three-asset portfolio is

$$\Omega = \begin{bmatrix} 0.0025 & -0.0011 & -0.001 \\ -0.0011 & 0.0058 & 0.0003 \\ -0.001 & 0.0003 & 0.0048 \end{bmatrix}$$

and

$$\omega = \begin{bmatrix} 0.3 \\ 0.5 \\ 0.2 \end{bmatrix}$$

To calculate the portfolio variance, σ_P^2, we need to employ some specialized matrix math functions that handle the algorithms using two-dimensional arrays. Fortunately the CD contains several math functions that manipulate two-dimensional arrays.

Step 1 In VB.NET, open a new Windows application called MatrixArray.

Step 2 Add at least one label to the form.

Step 3 Add two modules and paste in the code for the MMult2by1() and MMult1by1() functions.

Step 4 Add the following code to the Form1_Load event:

```
Private Sub Form1_Load(ByVal sender As ...) Handles MyBase.Load
    Dim dblCovar As Double(,) = New Double(2, 2) { _
                    {0.0025, -0.0011, -0.001}, _
                    {-0.0011, 0.0058, 0.0003}, _
```

```
                              {−0.001, 0.0003, 0.0048}}
      Dim dblWeights As Double() = New Double(2) {0.3, 0.5, 0.2}
      Dim dblPortVar As Double
      dblPortVar = MMult1by1(MMult2by1(dblCovar, dblWeights), dblWeights)
      Label1.Text = Val(dblPortVar)
   End Sub
```

Step 5   Run your program (see Figure 8.4). Again, be sure to
verify your calculations against Excel's built-in
function MMult().

F I G U R E   8.4

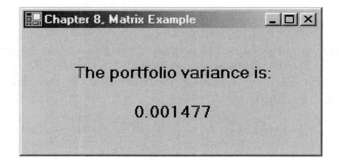

USING ARRAYS FOR TREES

Here we will show a simple example using a jagged array to price
an American call option using a binomial tree. The call option has
the following attributes: stock price, S, is 100, strike price, X, is 100,
time till expiration is 3 months, interest rate, I, is 0.1, and the
annualized volatility, sigma, is 0.25. The binomial tree will consist
of three steps, as in the example using a jagged array previously in
the chapter. Each step in the tree then will be 3 calendar months or
21 trading days, 0.25 of a year, divided by 3, so that the change in
time for each step is $t = 0.25/3 = 0.083333$. This option will expire
in a total of three steps, one for each of the 3 months. So $N = 3$. We
calculate U and D thusly:

$$U = e^{\sigma\sqrt{t}} = e^{0.25\sqrt{08333}} = 1.074837$$

$$D = e^{-\sigma\sqrt{t}} = e^{-0.25\sqrt{08333}} = 0.930374$$

We will add a variable A to shorten the calculations:

$$A = e^{-I \cdot t} = e^{-0.1 \cdot 0.083333} = 0.991701$$

Also, the probability of an up move is found, such that

$$P = \frac{(e^{I \cdot t} - D)}{U - D} = \frac{e^{0.1 \cdot 0.083333} - 0.930374}{1.074837 - 0.930374} = 0.5399892$$

Once we have declared and defined the necessary variables, we can calculate the terminal payoffs for the option for each outcome by calculating the intrinsic value in this way:

$$\text{Tree}_{x,N-x} = \max(S_0 \cdot D^x \cdot U^{N-x} - X, 0)$$

American-style options require that a decision be made at each node about whether to exercise the option. So we must compare the intrinsic value of the option with the risk-neutral valuation at each node:

$$\text{Tree}_{x,y-x} = \max[S_0 \cdot D^x \cdot U^{y-x} - X, A \cdot (P \cdot \text{Tree}_{x,y-x+1} + (1 - P)$$

$$\cdot \text{Tree}_{x+1,y-x}]$$

where $y = N - 1$.

The value of the call option will then be Tree(0)(0).

Step 1   In VB.NET open a new console application.
Step 2   Add the following code:

```
Imports System.Math
Module Module1
Sub Main()
    Dim x, y As Integer
    Dim N As Integer = 3
    Dim dblStockPrice As Double = 100
    Dim dblStrike As Double = 100
    Dim dblTimeStep As Double = .25 / N
    Dim dblIntRate = 0.1
    Dim dblSigma = 0.25

    Dim U As Double = Exp(dblSigma * dblTimeStep ^ 0.5)
    Dim D As Double = Exp(-dblSigma * dblTimeStep ^ 0.5)
    Dim A As Double = Exp(-dblIntRate * dblTimeStep)
    Dim P As Double = (Exp(dblIntRate * dblTimeStep) - D) / (U - D)
```

```
Dim dblBinomTree As Double()() = New Double(N)() {}
For x = 0 To N
    dblBinomTree(x) = New Double(N - x) {}
    dblBinomTree(x)(N - x) = Max((dblStockPrice * D ^ x * _
                            U ^ (N - x)) - dblStrike, 0)
Next x
For y = N - 1 To 0 Step -1
    For x = 0 To y
        dblBinomTree(x)(y - x) = Max((dblStockPrice * D ^ (x) * _
                            U ^ (y - x)) - dblStrike, A * (P * _
                            dblBinomTree(x)(y - x + 1) + (1 - P) * _
                            dblBinomTree(x + 1)(y - x)))
    Next x
Next y
Console.WriteLine("The price of the call option is: " & _
                    dblBinomTree(0)(0))
End Sub
End Module
```

Step 3   Run the program by selecting Start Without Debugging from the Debug menu item.

The value of the call option using this method is 6.6468, which rounds to 6.65. Figure 8.5 shows a map of the values of dblBinomTree()(). We can increase the accuracy of our pricing model by increasing the number of steps, N. For example, if we change N to 20, so that $t = 0.25/20 = 0.0125$, the value of the call option is 6.19.

F I G U R E 8.5

6.65	10.59	16.36	24.17
(0, 0)	(0, 1)	(0, 2)	(0, 3)
2.15	**4.01**	**7.48**	
(1, 0)	(1, 1)	(1, 2)	
0	**0**		
(2, 0)	(2, 1)		
0			
(3, 0)			

SUMMARY

In this chapter, we have looked at how to create and manipulate arrays of variables. We use arrays often in finance to hold data, do matrix math, and build trees for pricing derivatives. Important things to take note of are how to employ dynamic array sizing and how to pass and return arrays to and from functions.

PROBLEMS

1. What is a jagged array?
2. How do we pass an array to a function?
3. Why is declaring an array a two-stage process?
4. Because arrays are reference types, what is the danger with passing arrays to functions?
5. What is dynamic array sizing, and how is it accomplished?

PROJECT 8.1

Create a Windows application that creates a two-dimensional covariance matrix given three one-dimensional arrays of returns for three stocks. The covariance matrix should look like the following:

$$
\begin{bmatrix}
\sigma_{a,a} & \sigma_{a,b} & \sigma_{a,c} \\
\sigma_{b,a} & \sigma_{b,b} & \sigma_{b,c} \\
\sigma_{c,a} & \sigma_{c,b} & \sigma_{c,c}
\end{bmatrix}
$$

Hard-code the three arrays of returns and use the Covariance() function on the CD to make the calculations. Print out the matrix in labels on the form.

PROJECT 8.2

Create a Windows application that sorts an array of 20 returns. Then print out the fifth lowest return in a text box. Hard-code the returns in a one-dimensional array.

CHAPTER 9

Problem Solving

Up to this point we have ignored program errors and debugging, and we will do so again after this chapter. The reason for this is simple: Intermingling program logic with error-handling logic makes computer code very difficult to read and understand. This book is primarily concerned with teaching the logic of modeling derivative instruments and building automated trading systems. However, problem solving is an extremely important topic to consider when creating production software, and so we will address it on its own in this chapter.

Unfortunately, exceptions or problems, in the form of syntax errors and logic errors, inevitably creep into our programs. Very rarely, if ever, do our programs run correctly the first time. More often, several mistakes are present in the syntax or logic of our programs that we must correct before the program will run smoothly. If you haven't already noticed, the longer and more complex our programs become, the longer it takes to debug them—in fact, exponentially longer. For these reasons, programming is really a series of problems to be solved. We call the process of finding and fixing errors in our applications *debugging*, and learning to debug quickly is one of the most important skills you can gain as a financial engineer. Fear not, however—the more experience and knowledge you gain, the faster you will become at solving problems.

In this chapter we will look at syntax, logic, and run-time errors in a program, and we will explore some helpful techniques for finding and correcting them. Furthermore, we will show you how to write blocks of code called exception handlers that will properly react to error conditions that occur while a program is running and will prevent the program from crashing.

SYNTAX ERRORS

Syntax errors occur when our program code violates the rules of Visual Basic.NET, and they will be caught when we attempt to compile the program. Often syntax errors are misspelled variables or keywords, improper use of VB.NET language elements, or simple things like unmatched parentheses. Since VB.NET requires variable declaration by default, misspelled variables are caught immediately and can be fixed. This is because VB.NET IDE recognizes syntax errors prior to compilation and puts squiggly blue lines underneath them even while we are writing our code. We're guessing you've probably had significant experience with syntax errors over the course of the previous chapters. If we happen to miss a few syntax errors before compiling the program, the compiler will catch and list them in the Task List window along with a full description of the error.

LOGIC ERRORS

Logic errors are those that arise from incorrect results. In financial engineering, our programs frequently make dozens or even hundreds of mathematical calculations. Quite often our first attempt at a mathematical algorithm will produce incorrect results, for example, when a Black-Scholes calculator gives an incorrect option price. The only way to avoid these types of logic errors is to plan our programs carefully before writing code and to prototype our algorithms in Excel so that we have something against which to verify our results. Again, as you no doubt have found, logic errors are the hardest type to find and fix since it may not always be clear exactly where they originate. In the worst-case scenario, a logic error can turn into a run-time error and crash our program.

RUN-TIME ERRORS

Run-time errors are those that often cause our programs to terminate. Examples of logic errors that can turn into run-time errors are divide-by-zero exceptions and array index out-of-range exceptions. Other run-time errors may arise when we attempt to connect to a database, open a file, or send an XML message, where errors beyond our control disrupt the flow of our program.

What can be especially annoying about run-time errors is that they may not show up the first time, or even the first ten times, we execute a program—but only on the eleventh time. That is to say, a specific run-time error may occur only when a certain sequence of events takes place.

To deal with some potentially unavoidable run-time errors, we can create exception handlers (blocks of code) to resolve or handle errors in our programs and allow it to continue.

In order to demonstrate these different types of errors, we will need an example program.

FORECASTING COVARIANCE

Covariances between assets play an important part of many automated trading and risk management systems. As shown in Chapter 8, correlations and covariances are calculated using historical price data. But covariances can also be updated and forecast using GARCH methodologies since covariance rates often exhibit mean reversion. One GARCH approach forecasts covariances thusly:

$$\hat{\sigma}_{t+1,i,j} = (1 - \alpha - \beta) \cdot C + \alpha r_{t,i} r_{t,j} + \beta \hat{\sigma}_{t,i,j}$$

and

$$\hat{\sigma}_{t+n,i,j} = C + (\alpha + \beta)^{j-1} \cdot (\hat{\sigma}_{t+1,i,j} - C)$$

where C is the long-run covariance.

Now let's create a short program to forecast the covariance between two stocks over the next 20 days.

Step 1 In VB.NET start a new Windows application named CovarForecast.

Step 2   On Form1, add a single text box with the multiline
property changed to True.

Step 3   In the Project menu bar item, select Add Class. You
can leave the file name as the default Class1.vb.

Step 4   In the Class1 code window, change the class name to
CovarForecast and add the following code:

```
Public Class CovarForecast
    Private dblForecasts As Double()
    Private dblAlpha As Double
    Private dblBeta As Double
    Private dblPrevForecast As Double
    Private dblCovariance As Double
    Public Sub New()
        dblForecasts = New Double(20) { }
        dblPrevForecast = 0.00022627
        dblCovariance = 0.000205927        ' Long Run Covariance
        dblAlpha = 0.1943                  ' Optimized coefficient
        dblBeta = 0.5274                   ' Optimized coefficient
        CalcForecasts()
    End Sub

    Private Sub CalcForecasts()
        Dim j As Integer
        Dim newIBMreturn# = 0.0232
        Dim newMSFTreturn# = 0.0352
        dblForecasts(1) = (1 - dblAlpha - dblBeta) * dblCovariance + _
                        dblAlpha * newIBMreturn * newMSFTreturn + _
                        dblBeta * dblPrevForecast
        For j = 2 To 20
            dblForecasts(j) = dblCovariance + dblAlpha + dblBeta ^ _
                    (j - 1) * (dblForecasts(1) - dblCovariance)
        Next j
    End Sub
    Public Function GetForecasts() As Double()
        Return dblForecasts
    End Function
End Class
End Sub
```

As with most classes, our CovarForecast class has several
Private member variables and a constructor function. Also the
CovarForecast class has a Private subroutine CalcForecasts() and a
Public method GetForecasts().

In the constructor method, we set the values of the appropriate
variables including the long run covariance, the optimized values
of alpha and beta, and the previous 1-day-ahead forecast. Within
the CalcForecasts() subroutine, we receive new data about our two
stocks, IBM and MSFT. Namely, a big up day in the market has

raised both boats significantly, and consequently the historical correlation will increase. However, over the long term, we expect the correlation to revert to the mean, as we will see in our forecasts.

Step 5   Back in the Form1 code window, add the following code in the Form1_Load event:

```
Private Sub Form1_Load(ByVal sender As ...) Handles MyBase.Load
        Dim x As Integer
        Dim myForecasts As Double()
        Dim myCovars As CovarForecast
        myCovars = New CovarForecast()
        myForecasts = myCovars.GetForecasts()
        For x = 1 To myForecasts.GetUpperBound(0)
            TextBox1.Text &= x & " day ahead forecast: " & vbTab & _
                Format(myForecasts(x), "0.0000000") & vbCrLf
        Next x
    End Sub
```

In the Form1_Load event, we have created a CovarForecast object named myCovars. Once we instantiate an object based upon the CovarForecast class, the constructor method performs all the calculations and places the forecasted values into an array. We call the GetForecasts method to retrieve this array and loop through the elements to print the values in the text box.

Step 6   Run the program (see Figure 9.1).

If you copied the code correctly, your program will run. However, the results you got were not the same as shown in Figure 9.1. We have devilishly hidden a logic error in the code. But first let's examine the syntax. The program code above contains no syntax errors. So we will create one and see what happens.

Step 7   In the first line of the Form1_Load event, purposely misspell myCovars as myCobars.

```
Dim myCobars As New CovarForecast()
```

Notice that in your code the reference to the correctly spelled object myCovars is now underlined in blue. If we attempt to compile the program, a build error will occur which will be described in the Task List window. Double-clicking on this error message in the Task List window will take you right to the line of

F I G U R E 9.1

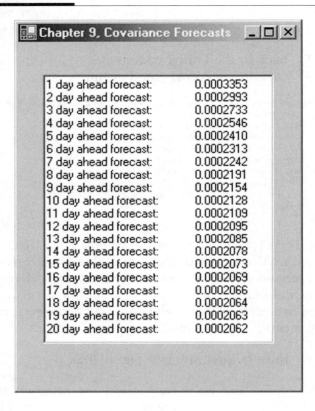

code containing the error, as shown in Figure 9.2. Syntax errors such as this are common and easily fixed. Logic errors are much more difficult to root out.

If we had not provided a picture showing the correct results, how would we know there is a problem in the program? With no method for verifying our calculations, we are lost.

As discussed in the methodology presented in Chapter 2, all complex calculations should first be modeled in Excel before conversion to programming code. Figure 9.3 demonstrates the prototyping of this model in spreadsheet format. If we know that the spreadsheet calculations were done properly, it is clear that our coded formulas are incorrect. Focusing on the lines containing the

F I G U R E 9.2

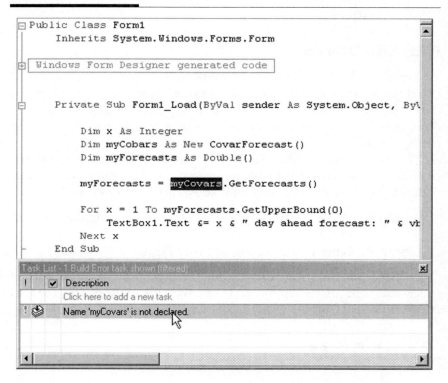

F I G U R E 9.3

PreviousForecast	0.00022627		Covariance	0.000205927
1	0.00033532			
2	0.00029931		Alpha	0.1943
3	0.00027332		Beta	0.52740
4	0.00025456			
5	0.00024103		IBM	MSFT
6	0.00023126		0.0232	0.0352
7	0.00022421			
8	0.00021912			
9	0.00021545			
10	0.00021280			

math, we can use breakpoints and the Locals window to watch the values of variables.

BREAKPOINTS

We can set breakpoints at different lines of code to suspend program execution. Then we can examine the value of variables currently in scope. To enable the debugging features such as breakpoints, we must compile the program using the debug configuration.

To set a breakpoint, we click the gray area to the left of the line of code where we want to pause execution. Alternatively, we can right-click over a line of code and select Insert Breakpoint.

Step 8 Set a breakpoint on the forecast calculation line within the For ... Next loop.

Step 9 Now run the program (see Figure 9.4).

When the program reaches our breakpoint, execution will be suspended. In this suspended state, we can explore the current values of our variables.

F I G U R E 9.4

```
Private Sub CalcForecasts()

    Dim j As Integer

    Dim newIBMreturn# = 0.0232
    Dim newMSFTreturn# = 0.0352

    dblForecasts(1) = (1 - dblAlpha - dblBeta) * dblCovarianc

    For j = 2 To 20
        dblForecasts(j) = dblCovariance + dblAlpha + dblBeta
    Next j

End Sub

Public Function GetForecasts() As Double()
    Return dblForecasts
End Function

End Class
```

F I G U R E 9.5

Name	Value	Type
Me	{CovarForecast.CovarForecast}	CovarForecast.CovarForecast
Object	{CovarForecast.CovarForecast}	Object
dblForecasts	{Length=21}	Double()
(0)	0.0	Double
(1)	0.0003353174341	Double
(2)	0.0	Double
(3)	0.0	Double
(4)	0.0	Double
(5)	0.0	Double
(6)	0.0	Double
(7)	0.0	Double
(8)	0.0	Double
(9)	0.0	Double
(10)	0.0	Double
(11)	0.0	Double
(12)	0.0	Double
(13)	0.0	Double
(14)	0.0	Double
(15)	0.0	Double
(16)	0.0	Double
(17)	0.0	Double
(18)	0.0	Double
(19)	0.0	Double
(20)	0.0	Double
dblAlpha	0.1993	Double
dblBeta	0.5274	Double
dblPrevForecast	0.00022627	Double
dblCovariance	0.00205927	Double
i	2	Integer
newIBMreturn	0.0232	Double
newMSFTreturn	0.0352	Double

Step 10 On the Debug menu bar, open the Locals window. The Locals window shows the current value of 0.0003353174341, which is consistent with our spreadsheet model, so clearly the bug is not in the line that defines the value of dblForecasts(1) (see Figure 9.5).

Step 11 Press the F5 key to restart execution. The program will proceed through the loop one time and repause when it again hits our breakpoint. This time the Locals window shows the value of dblForecasts(2) to be 0.19457416751494433. This is not right.

Step 12 Stop execution of the program altogether.

A quick inspection of the calculations line within the For . . . Next loop shows that a pair of parentheses around dblAlpha plus dblBeta was left out. Add them in so that the corrected line reads as follows:

```
dblForecasts(j) = dblCovariance + (dblAlpha + dblBeta) ^ _
                     (j - 1)*(dblForecasts(1) - dblCovariance)
```

Now run the program again and verify your answers against the Excel model. This time the numbers should be correct.

In addition to the Locals window, there are several other windows and commands that we will look at briefly.

OTHER DEBUGGING WINDOWS AND COMMANDS

The Autos, Watch, and Me windows all enable us to examine the current value of variables or objects currently within scope. In the Watch window, we can examine current variable values by typing the variable name into the Name field and pressing Enter. We can also change the value of variables listed in the Watch window for testing and debugging purposes. To alter a variable's value, enter the new value in the Value field.

Clicking the Continue button on the Debug menu bar will resume execution of a program that we have paused. The Stop Debugging button will stop the program. The Step Over button, as its name implies, will cause execution of the next line of code. If the next line of code is a function or subroutine call, the function will execute in its entirety in that one step. The Step Into button, on the other hand, executes only the next line. If the line contains a function call, control will transfer to the function definition for line-by-line debugging. And finally, the Step Out will cause a procedure to finish and then will return control to the calling line of code.

Up to this point, we have briefly examined ways to quickly fix syntax and logic errors in our programs. Often, however, other run-time errors beyond our control may arise that cause our programs to crash. We can actually write code that will handle run-time errors on the fly and allow our program to continue.

EXCEPTION HANDLING

Exception handling is the process of catching and dealing with run-time errors as they occur, according to a prescribed set of instructions. Although we often use the terms *exception* and *error* interchangeably, an exception is actually an object, which can subsequently become an error and break our program if it does not handle the exception properly. VB.NET supports two methods of exception handling—structured and unstructured. Both methods allow us to plan for exceptions and thereby prevent them from disrupting the flow of our programs and potentially crashing them. If you intend to create production software, you should consider using exception handlers in any method that may itself generate an error or that calls procedures that may generate them.

Exceptions that occur in procedures that are not able to handle them are transmitted back to the calling procedure. If that calling method is unable to handle it, it is then again transmitted back to the method calling it and so on. In this way, the common language run-time (CLR) searches for an exception handler and will continue up the series of procedure calls till it finds one. If no handler is ever found, the CLR displays an error message and shuts the program down. We can build into our programs structured or unstructured exception handlers to catch exceptions before they become errors.

Of course, implementing an exception-handling strategy into our software projects requires a fair amount of effort. As with everything else in software development, planning pays off. Be sure to build your strategy into the design process from the get-go. It is very difficult to add exception-handling systems later on down the road. You can be assured, though, that once a software system has been designed and implemented properly, the exception handling should not hinder performance.

Structured Exception Handlers

Structured exception handlers consist of Try ... Catch ... Finally ... End Try blocks of code that detect and respond to errors during run time. (In the future, we will refer to these as simply Try ... Catch blocks.) The point in a program at which an exception occurs is called the throw point. When something is "tried" and creates an exception, the CLR throws the exception. If no exception occurs, however, the program continues execution with the statement following the End Try. In this way, structured exception handlers help us create robust applications that rarely crash.

```
Try
      [Some code in here that may generate an error.]
Catch exp as Exception
      [Code to execute when a problem occurs.]
Finally
      [Code that will always run.]
End Try
```

Within a Try . . . Catch block, the Try block will usually contain some code we are wary of, that is, some code that may generate an error. For example, if we are trying to connect to a database or send a message over the Internet, a problem beyond our control may occur and create an error. When an exception occurs, the Try block terminates immediately, and the CLR searches the available Catch statements and executes the first one that is able to handle an exception of that type. Within a Try . . . Catch block, there are one or more Catch statements, each specifying an optional exception parameter, which represents a unique exception type. A parameterless Catch will catch all exception types. In fact, exceptions of any kind are actually Exception objects that inherit from the System.Exception class. The Try . . . Catch mechanism allows Exception objects and derived class objects to be thrown and caught. Once caught, the Catch handler interacts with the Exception object in a way that we can control.

The optional Finally block can contain code that will always execute, regardless of whether an exception is thrown. Because it will always run immediately before the Try . . . Catch block loses scope, the Finally block is usually an excellent location in which to place deallocation code, for example, close files or connections or release objects.

Let's add a Try . . . Catch block to our program.

Step 13 In the Form1_Load event, change the code to instantiate a CovarForecast object to include the following:

```
Dim myCovars As CovarForecast
Try
    myCovars = New CovarForecast()
Catch exp As Exception
    MsgBox(exp.Message)
    Exit Sub
End Try
```

This Try ... Catch block will catch any exceptions thrown during the execution of the constructor method of the myCovars object, which will propagate back up to our calling function. As it stands now, all exceptions will be caught by the one and only Catch statement, which will show a MessageBox with the Exception object's message property. The Exception.Message property contains a default message associated with the specific Exception object. This message can be customized by passing a message to the Exception object's constructor function.

At this point, however, no exceptions will be thrown by our program. So let's create one.

Step 14 In the constructor method of the CovarForecast class, lower the number of elements in the dblForecasts array to 10, which will cause an array out-of-bounds exception.

```
dblForecasts = New Double(10) { }
```

Step 15 Run the program (see Figure 9.6).

Again, our Catch handler, which specifies Exception, will catch all exceptions types.

Step 16 Change the Try ... Catch block to the following:

```
Try
    myCovars = New CovarForecast()
Catch exp As IndexOutOfRangeException
    MsgBox(exp.Message)
    Exit Sub
Catch exp As InvalidCastException
    MsgBox(exp.Message)
```

F I G U R E 9.6

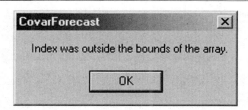

```
    Exit Sub
Finally
    MsgBox("Finally block exectuing.")
End Try
```

This time, we have defined two specific exception types—IndexOutOfRangeException and InvalidCastException. Further, we have added a Finally block, which will execute whether or not we encounter an error.

Step 17 In the constructor method of the CovarForecast class, change the dblPrevForecast to some string value.

```
dblPrevForecast = "IBM"
```

Step 18 Run the program (see Figure 9.7).

In this case, the exception will first be thrown by the invalid cast from "IBM" to a double. Once the exception has been handled, the Finally block will run and also show a message box. Notice also that in the current set of Catch handlers, exceptions other than the IndexOutOfRangeException or the InvalidCastException class will not be handled and will cause the program to terminate.

Speaking of specific error types, be aware that .NET's CLR allows division by zero. Division by zero will produce a special value "not a number," written in string form as "NaN." Our programs can be made to test for NaN results by using constants for positive or negative infinity.

Unstructured Exception Handling

In unstructured exception handling, we place an On Error GoTo statement at the beginning of a block of code. The On Error GoTo will then handle any and all exceptions occurring within that

F I G U R E 9.7

particular block regardless of class. When an exception is raised after the On Error GoTo statement, the program execution will go to the line specified in the On Error statement. As with structured error handling, if a call is made to another function, and an exception occurs within that function, it will propagate back to the calling method if it is not handled within the function. Here is the basic layout of the On Error GoTo error handler:

```
Sub mySub()
    On Error GoTo ErrorHandler
        [Some code in here that may generate an error.]
    Exit Sub
ErrorHandler
        [Code to execute when a problem occurs.]
        Resume
End Sub
```

If an error occurs within mySub(), program execution will automatically jump to the ErrorHandler label. The Resume statement included in the ErrorHandler will then resume execution back at the line where the error occurred. Of course, the Exit Sub statement is mandatory, or else program execution will run into ErrorHandler when it comes to the end of the subroutine code. Let's look at an example:

Step 19   Change the Form1_Load event code to the following:

```
Private Sub Form1_Load(ByVal sender As ...) Handles MyBase.Load
        On Error GoTo ErrorHandler
        Dim x As Integer
        Dim myForecasts As Double()
        Dim myCovars As CovarForecast
        myCovars = New CovarForecast()
        myForecasts = myCovars.GetForecasts()
        For x = 1 To myForecasts.GetUpperBound(0)
            TextBox1.Text &= x & " day ahead forecast: " & vbTab & _
                    Format(myForecasts(x), "0.0000000") & vbCrLf
        Next x
        Exit Sub
ErrorHandler:
        MsgBox(Err.Description)
End Sub
```

Step 20   Run the program (see Figure 9.8).

F I G U R E   9.8

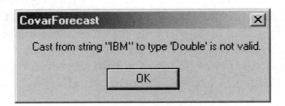

The Err object, which is used only with the On Error GoTo statement, contains properties that are set by the most recent exception. The Number property holds a value corresponding to the cause of the error. The Description property holds a text message that describes the nature of the error. Unstructured error-handling routines rely on the Err.Number property to determine the error's cause. If exceptions of multiple types may occur, our error-handling routine should test the Number value for proper handling.

An alternative to the On Error GoTo structure is On Error Resume Next, which will cause program execution to continue with the line of code immediately following the one that generated the exception. In this way, On Error Resume Next allows our program to continue despite an exception. In fact, the On Error Resume Next structure may in some cases be preferable to On Error GoTo, especially when accessing objects. On Error Resume Next allows us to place error-handling code specifically where errors will occur, as opposed to shifting to another line in the procedure.

While we have touched only briefly on unstructured error handling, be aware that, in general, use of the On Error GoTo structure will degrade performance. Furthermore, unstructured error handling is often difficult to debug. So in most cases, structured error-handling techniques are preferable.

THE THROW STATEMENT

In VB.NET we can use the Throw statement to purposely throw an exception. Throw creates an exception object that we can manipulate with either structured or unstructured exception-

F I G U R E 9.9

handling code. We often use Throw to trap errors within our code, because as we have seen, VB.NET will move up the hierarchy of procedures till it encounters an appropriate exception handler. Whenever an exception is thrown with a Throw statement, the Err object is set and a new Exception object is instantiated.

Step 21 In the CovarForecast class code, correct the previous errors and add a Throw statement to raise a DllNotFoundException.

```
dblForecasts = New Double(20) { }
dblPrevForecast = 0.00022627
Throw New DllNotFoundException("Error, error, error.")
```

Step 22 Run the program (see Figure 9.9).

In the next chapter we will look at how to create .dll files.

SUMMARY

In this chapter we have addressed solving problems in our program that occur during design time and run time. Further, we showed some techniques for finding logic errors in our programs. VB.NET has a wealth of tools for helping financial engineers debug production programs before implementation. Although for readability's sake, we will often skip error-handling routines in this book, real software development necessitates that we include runtime error-handling routines in the designs of our programs. In general, it is preferable to take advantage of VB.NET's structured error-handling model and its inherent efficiency as opposed to the unstructured On Error GoTo model.

PROBLEMS

1. What do the terms *syntax, logic,* and *run-time errors* mean?
2. What do breakpoints allow us to do?
3. What window in the Debug menu bar lets us change the value of a variable during run time?
4. What is structured exception handling? What is unstructured exception handling?
5. What is the System.Exception class?

PROJECT 9.1

Several errors may occur when a user enters a value to be used in calculations. For example, a user may enter "IBM" for a stock price or some invalid symbol in the txtTicker text box. Create a simple VB.NET Windows application that will accept a stock ticker, a stock price, and a number of shares to calculate a market capitalization. Use a structured error-handling mechanism with multiple Catch statements to prompt the user to reenter correct data based upon the specific exception type.

PROJECT 9.2

Create a Windows application that accepts user inputs for an options symbol, a stock price, and a volatility and that calculates the Black-Scholes price and Greeks for either a call or a put. Add a structured error-handling mechanism to ensure the program will never break, regardless of what the user enters. Also, your program should recognize specific exception types and prompt the user to reenter valid values. Print out the calculated values in text boxes on the screen.

.NET Type System

In Chapter 7 we looked at classes and objects. Yet in fact, classes are only one of many mechanisms we can use to describe the functionality of objects in our programs. What we really create in VB.NET code are types. The term *type* represents a broader description of any combination of data storage and functionality. Classes are but one example of a type, as are variables and functions.

Instances of types allocate space for data storage and provide us with the behaviors we require. Deciding what types to use— classes, modules, subroutines, functions, structures, etc.—in our programs for data manipulation will be the focus of the remainder of the technology portions of the book.

TYPES

A type is a generic term used to describe a representation of a value. Instances of types, in their various forms, encapsulate all the logic in our programs, and so fully understanding types is fundamental to higher-level .NET programming, not just VB.NET. Through the .NET Framework's common language specification and common type system, it is easy to use several different languages to create a single application, although this book is only concerned with Visual Basic.NET. This common type system looks like this:

VB.NET Common Type System	Example
Interfaces	
Value types	Variables, constants, structures, et al.
Reference types	Classes, arrays, etc.

Interfaces

An interface specifies a group of methods that can only be implemented by another class or structure. We cannot then instantiate interfaces by themselves. As a practical matter, predefined .NET interfaces start with the letter I, as in ICollection, IList, and IComparable. In the VB.NET help files, we can survey the different interfaces and their respective members. In addition, we can declare our own, user-defined interfaces. Here is an example:

```
Interface ITradable
        Function Buy(ByVal Price As String) As Double
        Function Sell(ByVal Price As String) As Double
End Interface
```

The ITradable interface indicates that we can buy or sell something, but does not define how it happens. So different financial instruments have the ability to be traded electronically, and therefore, as objects, they should implement the ITradable interface. We have not though specified exactly how they will be traded, since the implementation of a trade for different instruments may be very different. For example, routing a buy order to the ISE may require a much different implementation than, say, routing a buy order to the CME.

So we have deferred the implementation of the interface to the definition of the class, which implements the interface. Nonetheless, the "stub" is there.

We may at some point then implement an interface like this:

```
Class InstrObj
        Implements ITradable
        ...
        Public Function Buy(ByVal Price As String) As Double _
                Implements ITradable.Buy
            ...
        End Function
End Class
```

Classes may implement multiple interfaces although interfaces do not support multiple inheritance in derived classes. If a class definition includes that of ITradable (the buy and sell interfaces) and an object is instantiated, we can call the sell method:

```
Dim myInstr As New InstrObj()
myInstr.Sell("Market")
```

ASSEMBLIES

Assemblies are the fundamental building blocks of VB.NET applications and are held in executable files (EXEs) or dynamic link library files (DLLs). An assembly is a collection of types, which can be modules, interfaces, classes, delegates, enumerations, structures, and other units of functionality. When we create a VB.NET application, the most common assemblies are already referenced for us. However, if we need to use an assembly that is not already referenced, we need to add a reference to the corresponding DLL file and use the Imports statement for the appropriate namespace. Once we have added a reference to the assembly and imported the namespace, all the classes, properties, methods, and other types in the namespace are available to our application as if the assembly's code were part of it Be aware that a single assembly might contain multiple namespaces, and each namespace might contain multiple types.

NAMESPACES

The VB.NET Framework class library is made up of namespaces, which contain and organize types, which are defined in an assembly. If two classes have the same name, we can still use them both as long as they are in different namespaces and we qualify the class names using the namespace. "Fully qualified" object names are prefixed with the name of the namespace where the object is defined. So, for example, System.Windows.Forms.ListBox is the fully qualified name of the Listbox class since we have included the namespace. All namespaces in VB.NET begin with either System or Microsoft.

IMPORTS STATEMENT

The Imports statement does not itself provide access to assemblies, but rather simplifies access to them by eliminating the need to fully qualify named references. That is, we can use types defined within the imported namespace of the assembly without qualification. A module may contain any number of references and Imports statements, as long as the Imports statements appear after any Option statements and before any other code. For example,

```
Imports System.Data.OleDb
```

BUILDING AN OPTIONS LIBRARY

Creating an assembly with namespaces and types in VB.NET is very simple. We simply need to create a new class library, build it, and add a reference to the .dll file in future programs.

Step 1 In VB.NET, create a new project.

Step 2 In the New Project window, select Class Library and name your project Options.

Step 3 Within the class definition add the code for the StockOption class from the CD, the same one discussed in Chapter 7.

Step 4 Add a new class module, name the class CallOption, and paste in the code for the CallOption class from the CD. Also add a class module for the PutOption class, the same one discussed in Chapter 7.

Step 5 On the menu bar, select Build and Build Options. Close VB.NET.

Now a DLL file has been created, and we can add a reference to it in subsequent programs that we write and use these classes without having to copy and paste over and over again. Let's take a look.

Step 1 Create a new Windows application named LibraryExample.

Step 2   In the Project menu, click on Add Reference. When the Add Reference window shows up, click on Browse. In the Browse window, find the Options project folder, and within the bin subfolder double-click on the FinMath.dll file. Click OK.

Step 3   Add four labels to your form.

Step 4   In the Form1_Load event add the following code:

```
Imports Options
Public Class Form1
    Inherits System.Windows.Forms.Form
    Private Sub Form1_Load(ByVal sender As ...) Handles MyBase.Load
        Dim myOption As New CallOption("IBMDP")
        myOption.StockPrice = 80
        myOption.IntRate = 0.1
        myOption.Volatility = 0.25
        Label1.Text = myOption.Underlying
        Label2.Text = myOption.ExpMonth
        Label3.Text = myOption.Strike
        Label4.Text = Format(myOption.BSPrice, "#.####")
    End Sub
End Class
```

Notice the use of the Imports Options syntax at the top of the coding. This informs the compiler that we will be using classes located in the Options name-space.

Step 5   Run the program (see Figure 10.1).

F I G U R E   10.1

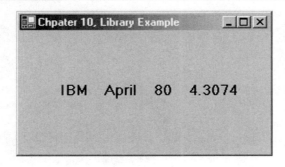

IBM   April   80   4.3074

VOLATILITY SMILES

On an options exchange, dozens of option contracts trade on each stock. All the options with a given expiration month create a strike structure of implied volatility, which usually has the shape of a smile. All the options with a given strike form a term structure of implied volatility. Together the strike and term structures create an implied volatility surface. That is, any given stock has several implied volatilities—though, as we saw in a previous chapter, we can use four sets of near-the-money (nearby and second nearby) puts and calls to calculate a single at-the-money volatility.

As a matter of practice, options with nearby expirations have prices determined more by supply and demand as opposed to volatility forecasts, whereas longer dated options have prices more greatly influenced by historical volatility. That is to say, near-term options tend to have implied volatilities greater than historical volatilities would imply, and longer-term options tend to have volatilities more in line with past movements of the underlying security. The graph in Figure 10.2 illustrates a volatility surface where across any given expiration there is a volatility smile.

F I G U R E 10.2

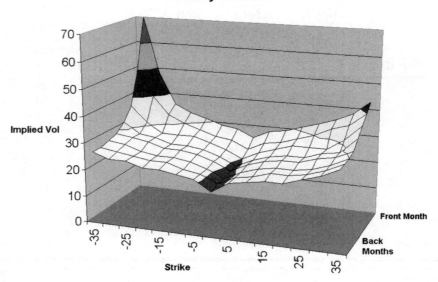

Models of the volatility smile, or skew, enable us to examine how the out-of-the-money volatilities are related to at-the-money volatility and how this relationship behaves as price, time, and volatility itself change. There are a wide range of methods for modeling this relationship between option strikes and volatility, including linear and nonlinear regression models and interpolation and cubic spline models. Many of these models require the use of matrix algebra and regression.

Included on the CD with this book is the MatrixMath assembly. Save this .dll file to your hard drive before you begin the next project. The MatrixMath.dll contains the following shared functions:

Matrix Function	Description	Example
MMult()	Matrix multiplication for two 2-dimensional matrices	dblArray = Matrix.MMult(Aarray, Barray)
MInverse()	Matrix inversion	dblArray = Matrix.Minverse (myArray)
MTranspose()	Matrix transposition	dblArray = Matrix.MTranspose (myArray)
MDeterm()	Matrix determinant	dblDouble = Matrix.MDeterm (myArray)
MMult2by1 ()	Matrix multiplication for a 2-dimensional matrix by a vector	dblVector = Matrix.MMult2by1 (AArray, BVector)
MultRegression()	Multiple linear regression	dblArray = Matrix.MultRegression (Aarray, Bvector)

In the case of the MatrixMath.dll, we will not instantiate any objects based upon the class in this namespace. Rather we will simply use the Public Shared class functions as you will see. Here is an abbreviated code snippet from the MatrixMath.dll to illustrate the use of Public Shared class functions:

```
Public Class Matrix
     Public Shared Function MTranspose(ByRef...) As Double(,)
          ' Matrix transpose code in here.
     End Function
End Class
```

In all other ways, creating a .dll with class functions is the same as previously discussed for class libraries.

In the next project we will parameterize one arm, or half, of the front-month volatility smile using a linear structure with level (L), slope (S), and curvature (C) parameters. This model is closely related to the yield curve models proposed by Nelson and Siegel (1987) and Wilmer (1996).

$$\hat{\sigma}_i = L \cdot x_1 + S \cdot x_2 + C \cdot x_3$$

where:

$$x_1 = 1 \qquad x_2 = \left[\exp\left(\frac{X_i - P}{\tau}\right) \right]$$

$$x_3 = \left[\frac{(X_i - P)^2}{\tau} \cdot \exp\left(\frac{-(X_i - P)}{\tau}\right) \right]$$

and:

$L =$ the level of the smile, denoting the at-the-money volatility
$S =$ the slope of the smile
$C =$ the curvature of the smile
$X_i =$ the strike price i
$P =$ the price of the underlying stock
$\tau =$ the optimized location parameter

In this model, the parameters L, S, and C are found using a multiple-regression algorithm along with a simple iterative process to find the optimal location parameter τ. So the method is to increase τ by 1 and repeat the regression until the sum of the squared errors is minimized. Let's start by getting the multiple regression set up properly. As always, we should first model the algorithm using Excel before we code to ensure the correctness of our algorithms. The Excel spreadsheet file LSCforVol.xls, which models this method, is included on the CD.

Step 1 Open a new Windows application named LSCforVol.
Step 2 Add a single text box to Form1, and leave the default name, Textbox1.Text. Also, change the Multiline property of Textbox1 to True. You should now be able to increase the size of Textbox1 on your form.

Step 3 On the menu bar, select Project and Add Reference. Browse to find the MatrixMath.dll file on your hard drive and click OK.

Step 4 In the Form1 code window, add the following code:

```
Imports MatrixMath
Public Class Form1
    Inherits System.Windows.Forms.Form

Private Sub Form1_Load(ByVal sender As ...) Handles MyBase.Load
    Dim x As Integer
    Dim Tau As Integer = 10
    Dim AMatrix As Double(,) = New Double(7, 2) { }
    Dim dblStrikes As Double() = New Double() _
                        {0, 5, 10, 15, 20, 25, 30, 35}
    Dim dblVolatilities As Double() = New Double() _
                        {25, 26, 29, 35, 37, 43, 50, 65}
    Dim LSCparams As Double() = New Double(2) { }
    For x = 0 To 7
        AMatrix(x, 0) = 1
        AMatrix(x, 1) = Math.Exp(dblStrikes(x) / Tau) * _
                    dblStrikes(x)
        AMatrix(x, 2) = (dblStrikes(x) / Tau) * _
                    Math.Exp(-dblStrikes(x) / Tau) * dblStrikes(x)
    Next x
    LSCparams = Matrix.MultRegression(AMatrix, dblVolatilities)
    TextBox1.Text = "Level:   " & Format(LSCparams(0), "##.0000") & _
        vbCrLf & "Slope:   " & Format(LSCparams(1), "##.0000") & _
        vbCrLf & "Curvature:   " & Format(LSCparams(2), "##.0000") & _
        vbCrLf & "Tau:   " & Str(Tau)
End Sub
End Class
```

Step 5 Run the program (see Figure 10.3).

This model runs the LSC model for one arm of the volatility skew with a hard-coded value of $\tau = 10$. However, this is not the value of τ that minimizes the sum of the squared errors. The Windows application LSCforVol included on the CD contains the full code for calculating the optimized parameters for the above model. In the optimized version the correct value for τ is 12, giving new values to the parameters L, S, and C as shown in Figure 10.4.

Another method for modeling volatility smiles is to use a fourth-order polynomial such that

$$\hat{\sigma}_i = \beta_1 + \beta_2 m + \beta_3 m^2 + \beta_4 m^3 + \beta_5 m^4$$

where m = the strike price minus the price of the underlying stock. Let's create a VB.NET program to model a volatility smile using

F I G U R E 10.3

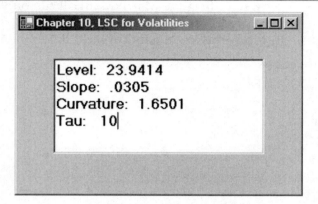

this algorithm. We have already created this model in Excel, which can be found in the spreadsheet PolynomialForVol.xls on the CD.

Step 1 Open a new Windows application and name it PolynomialForVol.

Step 2 Add a reference to the MatrixMath.dll file.

Step 3 Add a single text box to Form1, and leave the default name, Textbox1.Text. Also, change the Multiline property of Textbox1 to True. You should now be able to increase the size of Textbox1 on your form.

F I G U R E 10.4

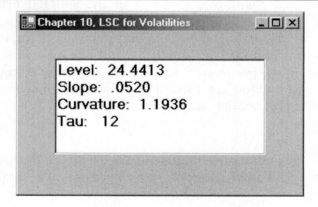

Step 4   Add the following code:

```
Imports MatrixMath
Public Class Form1
    Inherits System.Windows.Forms.Form

        Private Sub Form1_Load(ByVal sender As ...) Handles MyBase.Load
        Dim x As Integer
        Dim AMatrix As Double(,) = New Double(6, 4) { }
        Dim dblStrikes As Double() = New Double() _
                            {-15, -10, -5, 0, 5, 10, 15}
        Dim dblVolatilities As Double() = New Double() _
                            {47, 35, 20, 17, 19, 21, 28}
        Dim PolyParams As Double() = New Double(4) { }

        For x = 0 To 6
            AMatrix(x, 0) = 1
            AMatrix(x, 1) = dblStrikes(x)
            AMatrix(x, 2) = dblStrikes(x) ^ 2
            AMatrix(x, 3) = dblStrikes(x) ^ 3
            AMatrix(x, 4) = dblStrikes(x) ^ 4
        Next x
      PolyParams = Matrix.MultRegression(AMatrix, dblVolatilities)
      TextBox1.Text = "Beta1:  " & Format(PolyParams(0), "##.00000") _
            & vbCrLf & "Beta2:  " & Format(PolyParams(1), "##.00000") _
            & vbCrLf & "Beta3:  " & Format(PolyParams(2), "##.00000") _
            & vbCrLf & "Beta4:  " & Format(PolyParams(3), "##.00000") _
            & vbCrLf & "Beta5:  " & Format(PolyParams(4), "##.00000")
    End Sub
End Class
```

Step 5   Run the program (see Figure 10.5).

F I G U R E   10.5

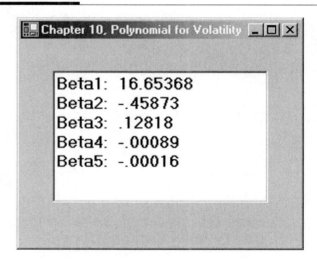

SUMMARY

In this chapter we examined in some depth the VB.NET Type System to gain a greater understanding about types, assemblies, namespaces, and interfaces. Further, we looked at how to create our own namespaces using the .NET Class Library template to create Options.dll. We determined that we can add a .dll file to a program we create by adding a reference to it and using an Imports statement. We then looked at volatility smiles and explored how to model them using the MatrixMath.dll file.

PROBLEMS

1. What are types?
2. What is a namespace?
3. What is an assembly?
4. How do we add a reference to a .dll file in VB.NET?
5. What is this Imports statement all about?

PROJECT 10.1

Create a .dll file using the StockOption, PutOption, and CallOption classes adding in methods to the appropriate classes for the option Greeks. Also, create a simple Windows application to test out your .dll.

PROJECT 10.2

Create a .dll file called Statistics.dll. Include in the class library Public Shared methods for the four moments of a distribution—mean, variance, skew, and kurtosis—as well as any other statistical functions you might want to use in the future. Again, make sure to build a simple Windows application to test the functions in the .dll file.

Database Programming

Back Testing

In times of change, it is the learners who will inherit
the earth while the learned will find themselves
beautifully equipped for a world that no longer exists.

Eric Hoffer

CHAPTER 11

Relational Databases

Financial analysis requires data. Furthermore, when doing quantitative financial analysis, we often find that the data, such as historical price or fundamental data, comes in a very simple database structure such as a flat file, or worse, a spreadsheet. Flat files are a primitive database design and often contain redundant and inconsistent data. Those who understand the elements of good database design certainly avoid the flat-file structure for all but the simplest data, such as historical price data.

Financial analysts are almost always experienced in Excel. And they should be. Excel is the most rapid development environment for building and testing financial models. But Excel is not a relational database, and it should not be used as such. Data in Excel is easily corrupted, and too much data in a spreadsheet has been known to overflow memory and cause crashes. Furthermore, production systems run in Excel almost always suffer from quality problems. If you are collecting and/or analyzing data on financial markets, we suggest you use the right tool for the job—a relational database.

It is difficult, however, to break away from Mother Excel. Using Excel, it's easy to paint a range of returns, for example, and pass it to the covariance function. Being able to see the data and the function calls is very comforting. If we use a database, however, we cannot see it, and this can be somewhat scary. But fear not. In the long run, we are much better off. There are far more advantages to using a database than disadvantages. Using databases and VB.NET programs gives us much more control and security when building production systems.

Visual Basic.NET is an efficient platform for creating financial applications that interact with data and databases. The front-end applications insulate the user from the back-end complexities and inner workings of the relational database management system and protect the data from accidental alteration or deletion.

Just remember, in very general terms, a database stores information and provides methods for managing the data, including methods to retrieve existing data, add new data, and edit data. As in the case of a flat file, a database may be a very simple construct, consisting of a single file. But as we grow in our understanding of databases, we will see that they can become very powerful, full-scale client-server relational database management systems. So it is important that we learn how relational databases work in order to accomplish more advanced analysis. As with other topics discussed in this book, we cannot hope to cover all the topics relating to relational databases. There are hundreds of books on the market that deal with this topic alone. But we will be able to discuss several relatively advanced topics and build three or four models that demonstrate relational database design and connectivity as used in quantitative research.

Let's consider a financial markets example using a relational database in the front office. On a trading desk, we may want to attribute trading profits and losses to different factors so as to assess the success of an automated trading system. But profit and loss analysis and risk management require combining data in a relational way with historical trade and price data along with profit and loss information. This scenario requires the use of a relational database management system.

In general there are two types of databases used in financial markets: operational databases and analytical databases. Operational databases store dynamic data such as portfolio and position information. Analytical databases hold static data such as historical price or trade history data, often in a flat file. Regardless of the brand of database software, both these types of databases will be managed using the relational database model (RDM) (Hernandez, 1997, p. 3).

In the RDM, data is held in tables, which are made up of columns, called *fields*, and rows, called *records*. Connections between different tables are defined in relationships. These relationships between tables are established through shared fields. The RDM has the advantage that, through its use of tables and relationships between them, data integrity is ensured and consistency and accuracy of data is guaranteed. Furthermore, changes in the design of the database will not adversely affect the VB.NET applications that we build to access it (Hernandez, 1997, p. 16).

Programs that we create in VB.NET can interact with databases through a set of objects known as MS ActiveX Data Objects (ADO) and a specialized language called Structured Query Language (SQL). SQL enables us to talk to a database from a VB.NET application. SQL is the industrywide standard for interacting with databases for everything from simple data retrieval, called queries, to modification and updating of data, and even to database creation. Regardless of which relational database management system you are using, SQL will be the language you will use to carry on a conversation in code. Relational database management systems (RDBMSs) are software applications for building, managing, and modifying relational databases. The most popular large-scale RDBMSs are from Microsoft, Oracle, and Sybase. This may be a lot of new information if you are not familiar with databases, but don't worry—in Chapters 12 and 13 we will look at ADO and SQL in greater depth.

In order to fully understand the RDM and the following chapters in this book, it is imperative that you become familiar with "database-speak," the terms and phrases used in the database industry. We have used some of the terms already—*tables, columns, rows, relationships*. Over the next few pages, we will define and briefly discuss some of the more important terms. Afterward, we will look at the three databases included on the CD that will illustrate most of these terms.

TABLES

A table is the primary structure in a relational database. It consists of columns and rows, often called fields and records. Tables represent items, such as historical data for IBM, and events, such as trades. Tables should then have names that describe the data they hold, like IBMData, or just IBM, or OptionTrades. Further, tables can be either data tables, which supply information such as historical prices, or validation tables, which implement data integrity. For example, we may have a table that contains a list of options' expiration dates.

FIELDS

A field, or column, represents a characteristic of a record. For example, our IBMData table would probably have a ClosePrice field. Fields then have names, data types, and lengths. Data in databases can be alphanumeric, numeric, or date/time. Also, fields can contain distinct or multipart values and may have values that are calculated.

RECORDS

A record, or row, holds the actual data in a table. A single record in a table is made up of one row containing all the columns in the table including a primary key that uniquely identifies a record. So January 21, 2003, identifies a unique record, or data point, of IBMData. The full record contains the date, open, high, low, and closing prices and the volume.

PRIMARY KEYS

Primary keys are special fields that uniquely identify a record in a table. So, as in the previous example, the Date field represents a unique record in a table of historical prices. Every table in a database must have a primary key, and no two tables should have the same primary key. Primary keys ensure that each record in a table is uniquely identifiable. Therefore, each element of the primary key field must be unique and cannot be null. So no duplicate dates would be allowed in our example.

FOREIGN KEYS

Foreign keys establish relationships between pairs of tables. Relationships between two tables arise when the primary key column in one table is identical to the foreign key column in the other. In a later example, we will see a graphic depiction of a relational database showing the primary and foreign keys for different tables along with arrows representing the relationships between them.

RELATIONSHIPS

As we have seen, relationships are connections between pairs of tables, through the use of primary and foreign keys. There are three different types of relationships: one to one, one to many, and many to many.

One-to-One Relationships

A relationship is said to be one to one if a single record in the first table is related to a single record in the second table, and vice versa.

One-to-Many Relationships

A relationship is said to be one to many if a single record in the first table can be related to several records in the second table, but at the same time a single record in the second table can only be related to a single record in the first table. It may seem a little confusing right now, but a later example will make this idea quite clear.

Many-to-Many Relationships

A relationship is said to be many to many if a single record in the first table is related to many records in the second table, and vice versa. In the case of a many-to-many relationship, we need to create a linking table by copying the primary key from each table into the new table. We suggest you find a good book on database design before you attempt to build complex databases that include many-to-many relationships.

QUERIES

A query is an SQL statement used to retrieve rows of information from one or more tables. Queries will often also contain search criteria to limit the amount of data returned from the tables. For example, we may create a query that retrieves the trade data only for the month of March 2001.

SQL queries also allow us to join tables. Joining tables enables use of data from several tables in a relational database for a single purpose. For example, we could display a single column from one table or several columns from multiple tables in a single query. From this, you may begin to see the flexibility and power of relational databases.

NORMALIZATION

Often you will hear database professionals talk about normalization or normal forms. Normalization is the process of breaking down a large table or tables into smaller tables in order to eliminate duplication of data and to prevent certain problems that commonly arise with database interaction. A normal form is a set of rules that test a table structure to ensure it is sound and free of errors. There are at least five normal forms—first through fifth—used to test for specific sets of problems. Tables we will use are in at least third normal form since each one has a primary key that uniquely identifies each record.

DATABASE DESIGN

Creating proprietary databases from scratch is no small task. It necessitates examinations of the business purposes of the database as well as the technical means to implement them. In short, designing relational databases requires a process or methodology. Doing so without one can lead to disaster. Again, several good books on relational database design have already been written, and so we will quickly review the process. Michael Hernandez in his book *Database Design for Mere Mortals* (1997) outlines a seven-phase process for database design:

1. Define the purpose of the database and the tasks that users will perform against it.
2. Analyze current database solutions.
3. Create tables, fields, and primary keys that characterize the subjects the database will track.
4. Determine the relationships that exist between tables.
5. Define the constraints or business rules for the data.
6. Develop ways to look at or view the data.
7. Review the integrity of the data, including checking the field specifications, testing the validity of relationships, and reviewing the business rules.

A well-designed database is easy to modify structurally, allows for efficient retrieval of data, and makes it easy for developers to build applications to connect to it (Hernandez, 1997, p. 28).

ACCESS DATABASES

MS Access databases are relational databases supported by all Microsoft Windows environments. You do not need to have MS Access software installed on your computer to interface with Access databases through VB.NET. In an Access database, all the various parts of the database are stored in a single file, which has an .mdb extension. The CD contains three Access databases—Finance.mdb, DirtyFinance.mdb, and Options.mdb—that we will use over the course of the remainder of the book. If you have MS Access software on your computer, feel free to open these databases in Access and examine their structures. Let's take a look at each of them.

The Finance.mdb Database

Finance.mdb is an MS Access database included on the CD with this book that uses flat files to hold daily historical price data for 13 stocks and the S&P 500. The individual data tables in Finance.mdb are named AXP, GE, GM, IBM, INTC, JNJ, KO, MCD, MO, MRK, MSFT, SUNW, WMT, and SPX. In addition, there is a validation table named Tickers, which contains the 13 stock ticker symbols shown.

The 14 data tables consist of the primary key column, labeled Date, and five other columns named OpenPrice, HighPrice, LowPrice, ClosePrice, and Volume. Each table holds 12 years of daily price data from January 2, 1990, to December 31, 2002. Table 11.1 is a sample of the IBM table showing the structure.

T A B L E 11.1

Date	OpenPrice	HighPrice	LowPrice	ClosePrice	Volume
2-Jan-90	23.54	24.38	23.48	24.35	1760600
3-Jan-90	24.53	24.72	24.44	24.56	2369400
4-Jan-90	24.62	24.94	24.56	24.84	2423600
5-Jan-90	24.81	25.25	24.72	24.78	1893900
8-Jan-90	24.66	25.06	24.66	24.94	1159800
2-Jan-90	23.54	24.38	23.48	24.35	1760600

The Tickers validation table consists of a single column named Symbols, which holds the ticker symbols for each of the 13 stocks. Table 11.2 is a sample of the Tickers table.

T A B L E 11.2

Symbols
AXP
GE
GM
IBM

We have made every attempt to ensure that the data in the Finance.mdb database is clean and free from errors. This is not the case with the DirtyFinance.mdb database.

The DirtyFinance.mdb Database

The DirtyFinance.mdb Access database included on the CD purposely contains dirty data. It is identical in every way structurally to the Finance.mdb data. The only difference is that we have gone through and corrupted the data using all kinds of sly and malicious techniques. But the errors we have created are typical of those you will encounter in real data purchased from data vendors. In Chapter 14 it will be your job to build a VB.NET program that finds the dirty data and to cleanse it.

The Options.mdb Database

The Options.mdb Access database uses a relational database structure to hold information about stocks and options as well as stock trades and option trades. In fact, there are four tables in the Options.mdb database representing each of these things—Stocks, OptionContracts, StockTrades, and OptionTrades. As we saw earlier, the relationships between two tables in a relational database are made possible by common primary and foreign keys. In Options.mdb, for example, the Stock and StockTrades tables are related through a StockSymbol primary key in the Stock table and the foreign key StockSymbol column in the StockTrades table. Figure 11.1 shows the structure or schema of the Options.mdb database. In this diagram, the relationships are represented by arrows.

All the relationships in the Options.mdb database are one to many. As you may be able to gather from the diagram, a one-to-many relationship exists between the Stock and OptionContracts tables. Clearly, a single stock can have many options contracts on it. But in the opposite direction, it is not the same. A single option contract can have only one underlying stock associated with it.

Earlier in the chapter, we briefly described a many-to-many relationship between two tables. Although not represented in the Options.mdb diagram, let's consider a quick example. A single option contract may be involved in many trades, but an individual trade could have more than one option contract associated with it if we assume spreads are included in a SpreadTrades table. In this way, a single option contract could be related to several spread trades, and a single spread trade could be related to several option contracts.

F I G U R E 11.1

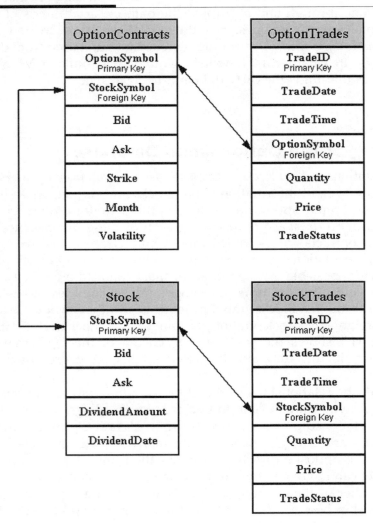

SUMMARY

When doing financial modeling and certainly when building production trading and risk management systems, relational databases are superior to Excel as a way to store and manage data.

The database field has its own language that we must learn before we can begin creating databases and interacting with them. In this chapter, we looked at and defined several database terms. Furthermore, creating new relational databases necessitates the use of a design methodology. We very briefly reviewed the seven steps of a well-known methodology.

There are three Access databases included on the CD with this book—Finance.mdb, DirtyFinance.mdb, and Options.mdb. We will be building VB.NET Windows applications in later chapters that access them.

PROBLEMS

1. What are operational and analytical databases?
2. What is SQL?
3. Describe tables, rows, and columns.
4. What are relationships and how are they created? Describe the three types of relationships.
5. What is the process to go through to design a relational database?

PROJECT 11.1

Assuming you have MS Access, create a simple relational database called Futures.mdb in MS Access. This database should consist of two tables named Futures and FuturesTrades. The Futures table should have columns named FuturesSymbol, Expiration, Bid, and Ask. The FuturesTrades table should have columns named TradeID, TradeDate, TradeTime, FuturesSymbol, Quantity, and Price.

In Access, open a blank Access database. Next, under Objects click on Tables and then on New. In Design View, enter the column names for the Futures table. On the FuturesSymbol field, right-click and select Primary Key. Close the Design View window and name this table Futures.

F I G U R E 11.2

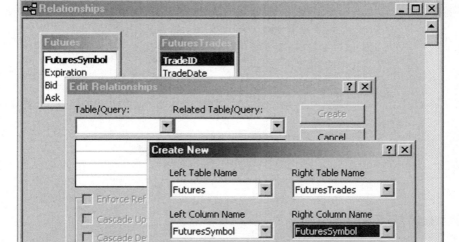

Next click on New again. In Design View, enter the column names for the FuturesTrades table. Set TradeID as the primary key. Close the Design View window and name this table FuturesTrades.

Under the Tools menu bar item, select Relationships. Add both the Futures and FuturesTrades tables.

On the menu bar, select Relationships and Edit Relationships. In the Edit Relationships window, click on Create New. Add a relationship between the FuturesSymbol field in the Futures table and the FuturesSymbol field in the FuturesTrades table as shown in Figure 11.2.

Back in the Edit Relationships window, click on Enforce Referential Integrity and Create. You should now see the one-to-many relationship shown graphically in the Relationships window—see Figure 11.3.

Now try adding some hypothetical data to the tables by opening the table.

F I G U R E   11.3

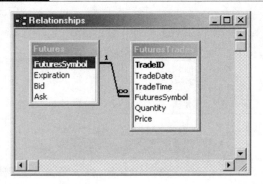

PROJECT 11.2

Design a relational database to hold bond trading data and create it in MS Access. Your database should contain at least two tables related to each other in a one-to-many way.

CHAPTER 12

ADO.NET

ADO.NET is an application programming interface used to interact with databases in VB.NET programming code using ActiveX Data Objects (ADO). ADO is a proprietary set of Microsoft objects that allows developers to access relational and nonrelational databases, including MS Access, Sybase, MS SQL Server, Informix, and Oracle among others. So if we need to write a program that provides a connection to a database, we can use ADO objects in our application to perform database transactions. These objects are found in the data and XML namespaces, as for example:

Namespace	Description
System.Data	ADO.NET classes, including the DataSet class
System.Data.Common	Classes for database access
System.Data.OleDb	Classes for connection to OleDb-compatible databases
System.Data.SqlClient	Classes for connection to SQL Server 7.0 databases
System.Data.SqlTypes	Classes for SQL Server 7.0 data types
System.XML	Classes for XML message creation and parsing

ADO.NET is part of Microsoft's overall data access strategy for universal data access, which attempts to permit connectivity to the vast array of existing and future data sources. In order for universal data access to work, Microsoft and several database companies provide interfaces between their databases and Microsoft's OleDb objects. OleDb (Object Linking and Embedding Databases) objects enable connection to just about any data source, whereas SqlClient objects enable optimized interaction with MS SQL Server databases. Furthermore, ADO supports the use of data-aware components, such as DataGrids in Visual Basic.NET, which allow us to see the data from the database. So we can, if need be, look at the data in a running Windows application.

ADO is a complex technology, and mastering it can take a tremendous amount of effort. In fact, several good books have been written about this subject alone. The remainder of this chapter will focus on a discussion of the ADO.NET classes and their uses, which enable us to open a connection to a data source, get data from it, and put the data into an in-memory cache of records called a DataSet. Then we can close the connection to the database. In a nutshell, ADO allows us to connect to and disconnect from a database, get data from a database, and view and manipulate data, including making changes to the data itself.

The model just mentioned is the one we will use in all examples in this chapter. But there is another model. The alternative is to perform operations or calculations on the database directly using a data command object, OleDbCommand, with an SQL statement. Direct database interaction in this manner uses less overhead since it bypasses storage of data in a data set, which of course requires memory. We will examine briefly this alternative model in the following chapter.

The main advantage of the DataSet model, though, is that DataSet allows us to work with multiple tables, from multiple data sources such as databases, Excel spreadsheets, or XML files, and use them in multiple applications. The long and the short of it is that the advantages of the DataSet methodology outweigh the disadvantage of increased memory usage.

The following sections will introduce you to some ADO objects that have evolved since previous versions of Visual Basic and some that are new.

CONNECTIONS

To interact with a database, we first need to establish a persistent connection to it. A persistent connection is one that will stay open until it is explicitly closed. VB.NET supports many different types of connection classes in the OleDb and SqlClient namespaces. We will use the OleDbConnection class.

DATAADAPTER

A DataAdapter is the object that communicates with the database via an SQL statement to get data and put it in something called a DataSet. Then, if need be, the DataAdapter can send updated data back to the database to make changes in the data, based on operations performed while the DataSet held the data. In an effort to make multitiered applications more efficient, data processing is turning to a message-based approach that revolves around chunks of information. At the center of this approach is the DataAdapter, which acts as a conduit to get and send data between a DataSet and a database. It accomplishes this by means of SQL queries and commands made against the database. In Chapter 13 we will discuss SQL in depth. Here are the important properties and methods of the OleDbDataAdapter class, which we will use:

Public Constructor	Description
New()	Initializes a new instance of the class

Public Properties	Description
DeleteCommand	Gets or sets an SQL statement for deleting records from the database
InsertCommand	Gets or sets an SQL statement used to insert new records into the database
SelectCommand	Gets or sets an SQL statement used to select records in the database
UpdateCommand	Gets or sets an SQL statement used to update records in the database

Public Methods	Description
Fill	Adds rows from a data source to a specified DataSet
FillSchema	Adds a DataTable to a DataSet so that the schema matches schema of the data source
Update	Calls the INSERT, UPDATE, or DELETE statements for each row in the DataSet

DATASET

A DataSet can be thought of as in-memory representation of a relational database, complete with tables, columns, rows, and relations. DataSets can be used then for storing, remoting, and programming against flat, XML, and relational data. The important distinction between this evolved stage of ADO.NET and previous Microsoft data architectures is that a DataSet is separate and distinct from any data sources. For this reason, DataSet functions are stand-alone entities that know nothing about the source or destination of the data within it. The DataSet does not interact directly with the database and is only a cache of data, with database-like structures such as tables, columns, and relationships within it. This allows us to work with a programming model that is always consistent, regardless of where the source data resides. Data coming from a database, an XML file, code, or user input can all be placed into a DataSet object. Then as changes are made to the DataSet, they can be tracked and verified before updating the source data. This DataSet is then used by a DataAdapter to update the original data source.

The DataSet class, the related Columns collection of DataColumns, the Rows collection of DataRows, and Constraints classes are all defined in the System.Data namespace.

Here are the important public properties and methods of the DataSet class:

Public Constructor	Description
New	Initializes an instance of the class

Public Properties	Description
HasErrors	Indicates whether there are errors in any of the records, or rows, of the DataSet
Tables	Gets the collection of tables within the DataSet

Public Methods	Description
Clear	Clears all data from the DataSet
Clone	Copies the structure of the DataSet, but not the data
Copy	Copies the structure and the data of the DataSet
GetChanges	Creates a second DataSet that contains the changes
GetXML	Gets an XML representation of the DataSet
Merge	Merges the DataSet with another DataSet
ReadXML	Reads data and schema from XML into the DataSet
ReadXMLSchema	Reads an XML schema in the DataSet
Reset	Resets the DataSet to its original state
WriteXML	Writes XML data from the DataSet
WriteXMLschema	Writes the XML schema from the DataSet

DataSets are made up primarily of a collection of DataTables and DataRelations. DataTables are in turn made up of collections of columns, rows, and constraints. Actual data is then contained in the Rows collection of DataRow objects. As in a relational database, constraints maintain the data, entity, and relational integrity of the data through the ForeignKeyConstraints, the UniqueConstraints, and the PrimaryKey. The DataRelation collection acts as an interface between related rows in different tables, as shown here:

Data Set Object

```
DataTable collection
    Columns (DataColumnCollection)
        DataColumns
    Rows (DataRowCollection)              DataRelation collection
        DataRows
    Constraints
        Constraint
```

As we describe the pieces of the DataSet puzzle, we will also show you the code snippets to build a DataSet with a DataTable. In more situations than not, the DataAdapter will do these things automatically, but an understanding of how a DataSet is constructed is absolutely necessary to higher-level programming.

Step 1 Create a new Windows application named DataSetExample. On the form, place a label. All the code we add to the program will be in the Form1_Load event. Add the code shown here to create a DataSet:

```
Private Sub Form1_Load(ByVal sender As ...)Handles MyBase.Load
        Dim myDataSet As New DataSet()
        ' Add new code in here later.
End Sub
```

DATATABLE

Because DataTables actually hold the data in a DataSet, DataTables are the main topic in any discussion of ADO.NET. A DataTable holds a Columns collection, which defines the table's schema; a Rows collection, which contains the records in DataRow objects;

and Constraints, which ensure the integrity of the data along with the PrimaryKey of the DataTable. We can add a DataTable to a DataSet's collection of tables using the overloaded Add method:

Public Methods	Description
Tables.Add	Creates a DataTable in the DataSet
Tables. Add(myName)	Creates a DataTable in the DataSet with a name
Tables.Add(myDataTable)	Adds a DataTable to the DataSet

Here are the important properties, methods, and events of a DataTable:

Public Constructor	Description
New	Creates a DataTable
New(TableName)	Creates a DataTable with the name

Public Properties	Description
Columns	Returns a reference to the DataColumnCollection, a collection of DataColumn objects
Constraints	The Constraints collection
DataSet	The DataSet to which the DataTable belongs
HasErrors	Indicates whether there are errors in any of the DataTable's DataRows
PrimaryKey	The primary key of the DataTable
Rows	Returns a reference to the DataRowCollection, a collection of DataRow objects
TableName	The name of the DataTable within the DataSet

Public Methods	Description
AcceptChanges	Changes all the DataRows
Clear	Deletes all DataRow objects from the DataTable
Clone	Copies the schema of the DataTable, but not the data
Compute	Performs an operation on the DataTable
Copy	Copies the schema and the data of the DataTable
ImportRow	Copies a DataRow into a DataTable
NewRow	Creates a row with the schema of the DataTable as defined by the DataColumnCollection
Select	Returns an array of DataRow objects that match a specified criterion

Public Events	Description
ColumnChanged	Fires after a DataColumn has been changed
RowChanged	Fires after a DataRow has been changed
RowDeleted	Fires after a DataRow has been deleted

Step 2 Let's create a DataTable and add it to the DataSet.

```
Dim dtIBMdata As New DataTable("IBMdata")
myDataSet.Tables.Add(dtIBMdata)
```

COLUMNS, DATACOLUMNCOLLECTIONS, AND DATACOLUMNS

The DataTable's Columns property returns a reference to a DataColumnCollection, an object that holds a collection of DataColumn objects and defines the schema of the table. Usually the DataColumnCollection is defined automatically by a DataAdapter's Fill method, and we can then access the DataColumnCollection through the DataTable's Columns property. Because the DataColumnCollection inherits from the CollectionBase class, it uses the Add, Remove, Item, and Count methods to (respectively) insert, delete, get a specified DataColumn from, and count the number of DataColumn objects within it. As we will see, in some cases we may want to define the schema ourselves using the DataTable's Columns properties and methods. We will discuss Collection objects in greater detail in Chapter 14.

We can add DataColumns to the DataColumnCollection using the Columns.Add method as follows:

Public Method	Description
Columns.Add(DataColumn)	Adds a DataColumn to a DataTable

Here are the important properties of DataColumns:

Public Properties	Description
New	Creates a DataColumn
New(ColumnName)	Creates a DataColumn with a name
New(ColumnName, DataType)	Creates a DataColumn with a name and a data type

Public Properties	Description
AllowDbNull	Specifies whether a column can be empty
AutoIncrement	Specifies whether the system will increment the value of the column automatically

Public Properties	Description
Caption	The name of the column if different from ColumnName
ColumnName	The name of the column
DataType	The type of data the DataColumn can hold
DefaultValue	The default value of elements in the DataColumn
ReadOnly	Specifies whether elements in the DataColumn can be changed
Unique	Specifies whether each element in the DataColumn must be unique

Step 3 Let's create a DataColumn and add it to the DataTable.

```
Dim colClose = New DataColumn("ClosePrice")
dtIBMdata.Columns.Add(colClose)
```

ROWS, DATAROWCOLLECTIONS, AND DATAROWS

The Rows property of a DataTable returns a reference to a DataRowCollection, a collection that contains the data in DataRow objects. Because the DataRowCollection inherits from the Collection class, it uses the Add, Remove, Item, and Count methods to (respectively) insert, delete, get a specified DataRow from, and count the number of DataColumn objects within it. So we can add DataRows to the DataTable through the Rows property using the Rows.Add methods as follows:

Public Methods	Description
Rows.Add(DataRow)	Adds a DataRow to a DataTable
Rows.Add(datavalues())	Adds a DataRow to a DataTable and sets the respective DataColumn values according to the datavalues array

Here are the important properties and methods of a DataRow object:

Public Properties	Description
HasErrors	Indicates whether there are errors in the DataRow
Item	Specifies a DataColumn within the DataRow
ItemArray	An array of all the values of the DataColumns in the DataRow
Table	The DataTable to which the DataRow belongs

Public Methods	Description
AcceptChanges	Makes all changes to a DataRow
BeginEdit	Starts an editing operation
CancelEdit	Stops an editing operation
Delete	Deletes a DataRow
EndEdit	Finishes an editing operation
IsNull	Specifies whether a DataColumn within the DataRow has a null value

Step 4 Now let's create a DataRow and add it to the DataTable.

```
Dim rowData As DataRow = dtIBMdata.NewRow()
dtIBMdata.Rows.Add(rowData)
```

We can define the value of this "cell" or any other "cell" in the table this way:

```
dtIBMdata.Rows(0).Item("ClosePrice") = 65.34
```

In the case where the DataTable is created by the DataAdapter, we can reference a specific cell this way:

```
Label1.Text = myDataSet.Tables("IBMdata").Rows(0).Item("ClosePrice")
```

See Figure 12.1.

F I G U R E 12.1

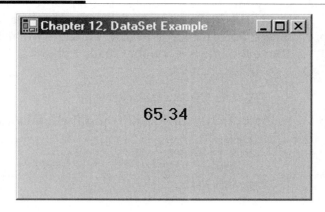

CONNECTING TO A DATABASE

As mentioned earlier, for the purposes of this book, we will use an OleDbConnection to interface with databases. The System.Data. OleDb namespace contains several classes we can use to access OleDb-compatible data sources, such as MS Access databases.

To connect to a database, we will use an OleDbConnection object, which represents a unique connection to a data source. An instance of this class specifies the connection provider and the name and path of the database to which our application will connect.

We will use the OleDbDataAdapter class to hold an SQL statement and the connection upon which it will be executed. After we have declared an OleDbDataAdapter object, we can create a DataSet object in which to place the data the DataAdapter returns to us. Unlike the DataSet example shown previously, we will not have to construct the DataSet's DataTable ourselves. Rather, the DataAdapter will create the DataSet's schema for us.

Step 1 The database to which we will connect will be the Finance.mdb MS Access database, which can be found on the CD. Create a copy of the Finance.mdb database in the ModelingFM folder on your C:\ drive so that the absolute path to the database is C:\ModelingFM\Finance.mdb.

Step 2 In VB.NET, open a new Windows application called ADOExample.

Step 3 On your Form1, add a Button, a Label, and a DataGrid. You can leave the names to their defaults.

Step 4 In the Form1 code window, all the way at the top, above the line of code that reads Public Class Form1, type the statement:

```
Imports System.Data.OleDb
```

Step 5 In the Button1_Click event, add the following code:

```
Private Sub Button1_Click(ByVal sender As ...)    Handles Button1.Click
    Dim myConnect As New OleDbConnection("Provider=Microsoft.Jet _
                     .OLEDB.4.0;Data Source=C:\ModelingFM\Finance.mdb")
    Dim myAdapter As New OleDbDataAdapter("select * from AXP", myConnect)
    Dim myDataSet As New DataSet()
    myConnect.Open()
```

```
      myAdapter.Fill(myDataSet, "AXPdata")
      myConnect.Close()
      DataGrid1.DataSource = myDataSet
      DataGrid1.DataMember = "AXPdata"
      Label1.Text = myDataSet.Tables("AXPdata").Rows(0).Item("ClosePrice")
   End Sub
```

Step 6   Run your program (see Figure 12.2).

In the above code example, the first line creates an OleDbConnection object called myConnect and supplies the connection string. In this case the Microsoft JET driver is specified as well as the local path for the MS Access database known as Finance.mdb. With the connection string specified, a new instance of the OleDbConnection is created. Notice that the connection string is passed in the constructor, the New() method, of the OleDbConnection object. A few lines down, the myConnect.Open() method is called. At that point, assuming no errors and that the database actually exists, the database connection is made.

The second line of code creates an OleDbDataAdapter object. Two arguments are passed to its constructor: a string containing an

F I G U R E   12.2

Date	Open	High	Low	Close	Volume
8/15/1991	6.4116	6.4412	6.3525	6.3821	1039400
8/16/1991	6.3525	6.4116	6.1457	6.1752	1727000
8/19/1991	5.9093	5.998	5.673	5.9093	2031400
8/20/1991	6.0275	6.0571	5.9684	6.0275	1293200
8/21/1991	6.1457	6.2343	6.0866	6.2048	1640900
8/22/1991	6.2048	6.2048	6.0866	6.1457	982700
8/23/1991	6.0866	6.2048	6.0866	6.1161	1384500
8/26/1991	6.1161	6.2934	6.0866	6.2639	939700
8/27/1991	6.2639	6.2934	6.1752	6.2343	797000
8/28/1991	6.2639	6.4707	6.2639	6.4412	1328400

Connect

Here is the first Close price: 6.3821

SQL statement that indicates that we are selecting *, which means all the columns, from the table named AXP, and the database connection against which the SQL statement will be executed, namely myConnect.

The third line of code in the example creates a DataSet object called myDataSet.

Once our three objects are created and the connection is open, we can execute the SQL statement by calling the myAdapter.Fill() method of our OleDbDataAdapter object. This method takes two arguments. The first argument is the DataSet that will hold all the data returned by the SQL query. The second is a string value that represents the name of the resulting DataTable. This name is an arbitrary string that we supply. Once the data is in the DataSet, we close the connection to the database using myConnect.Close().

At this point in the program, all the data from the table named AXP in the database now exists in memory in myDataSet. We display the data by telling DataGrid1 which DataSet, myDataSet, and which DataMember, which is the DataTable that we arbitrarily named AXPdata.

As in the DataSet example we looked at earlier in the chapter, we can retrieve any specific element in the DataTable by referencing its DataSet, its DataTable, its row, and its column. As you can see, the DataAdapter constructed the DataSet with the same schema that we manually created in the previous program.

Now that the data is in memory, we can perform mathematical operations on it. In its current form, the data set consists of a date column and open, high, low, close, and volume columns. Primarily when doing quantitative research, we are interested in log returns as opposed to actual prices. So the log returns must be calculated. We can choose to pass a reference to the DataRowCollection directly to a new function, or we may wish to create a one-dimensional array of log returns first, which then can be used with the functions discussed in Chapter 8. Let's look at both methods.

Step 7 First let's pass a reference to the DataRowCollection to a new function called ColumnAverage(). Change the last line of code to the following:

```
Label1.Text = ColumnAverage(myDataSet.Tables("AXPdata").Rows, 5)
```

Step 8 Now add the definition of the ColumnAverage() function:

```
Function ColumnAverage(ByRef myDataPoints As DataRowCollection, _
                        ByVal intCol As Integer) As Double
        Dim dblTotRet As Double
        Dim x As Integer
        For x = 0 To myDataPoints.Count-1
            dblTotRet += myDataPoints(x).Item(intCol)
        Next x
        Return dblTotRet / (x + 1)
End Function
```

Notice that the ColumnAverage() function accepts a reference to a DataRowCollection and an integer specifying the column to be averaged. In this case, we are averaging column 5, the volume column, and so our program will print into the label the average volume. The calling statement uses the Rows property, which returns a reference to a DataRowCollection, as mentioned earlier.

Step 9 Run the program (see Figure 12.3).

F I G U R E 12.3

Date	Open	High	Low	Close	Volume
8/15/1991	6.4116	6.4412	6.3525	6.3821	1039400
8/16/1991	6.3525	6.4116	6.1457	6.1752	1727000
8/19/1991	5.9093	5.998	5.673	5.9093	2031400
8/20/1991	6.0275	6.0571	5.9684	6.0275	1293200
8/21/1991	6.1457	6.2343	6.0866	6.2048	1640900
8/22/1991	6.2048	6.2048	6.0866	6.1457	982700
8/23/1991	6.0866	6.2048	6.0866	6.1161	1384500
8/26/1991	6.1161	6.2934	6.0866	6.2639	939700
8/27/1991	6.2639	6.2934	6.1752	6.2343	797000
8/28/1991	6.2639	6.4707	6.2639	6.4412	1328400

Connect

Here is the average Volume: 2060785.09076864

The alternative method is to create an array of log returns, which can then be used with the statistical functions we looked at previously.

Step 10 Add the following code to your Button1_Click event:

```
Dim intLength As Integer = myDataSet.Tables("AXPdata").Rows.Count
Dim x%
Dim dblAXPreturns As Double() = New Double(intLength - 2) {}
For x = 1 To intLength - 1
  dblAXPreturns(x - 1) = _
  Math.Log(myDataSet.Tables("AXPdata").Rows(x).Item("ClosePrice") / _
  myDataSet.Tables("AXPdata").Rows(x - 1).Item("ClosePrice"))
Next x
Label1.Text = Average(dblAXPreturns)
```

Step 11 Now add the code for the Average() function that we looked at in Chapter 8. You can either type it or paste it in from the file on the CD.

```
Public Function Average(ByRef Returns As Double()) As Double
        Dim dblTotRet As Double
        Dim x As Integer
```

F I G U R E 12.4

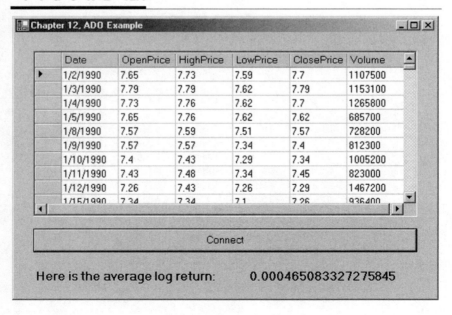

Date	OpenPrice	HighPrice	LowPrice	ClosePrice	Volume
1/2/1990	7.65	7.73	7.59	7.7	1107500
1/3/1990	7.79	7.79	7.62	7.79	1153100
1/4/1990	7.73	7.76	7.62	7.7	1265800
1/5/1990	7.65	7.76	7.62	7.62	685700
1/8/1990	7.57	7.59	7.51	7.57	728200
1/9/1990	7.57	7.57	7.34	7.4	812300
1/10/1990	7.4	7.43	7.29	7.34	1005200
1/11/1990	7.43	7.48	7.34	7.45	823000
1/12/1990	7.26	7.43	7.26	7.29	1467200
1/15/1990	7.34	7.34	7.1	7.26	936400

Chapter 12, ADO Example

Connect

Here is the average log return: 0.000465083327275845

```
    Dim dblLength# = UBound(Returns, 1)
    For x = 0 To dblLength
        dblTotRet += Returns(x)
    Next x
    Return dblTotRet / (dblLength + 1)
End Function
```

Step 12   Run the program (see Figure 12.4).

In the following chapter, we will learn how to add columns to tables to allow us to add this calculated data back to a database itself.

SUMMARY

In this chapter we briefly discussed the ADO.NET architecture and some of the OleDb objects for connecting to databases. Specifically, we looked at a model for database interaction that includes the use of OleDbConnection objects, OleDbDataAdapters, and DataSets. DataSets contain DataTables, which in turn contain collections of DataColumns and DataRows. Understanding the structure of a DataSet allows us to access the data within the DataSet.

PROBLEMS

1. What is an OleDbConnection object? What is an OleDb-DataAdapter?
2. Describe the model we use to interact with a database.
3. Describe the structure of a DataSet object.
4. What code can we use to access a specific item of data within a DataSet?
5. Write the lines of code necessary to add a DataRow to a DataTable named myDataTable.

PROJECT 12.1

The Finance.mdb database contains several tables. Create a Windows application that gets all the columns from the IBM table and displays them in a DataGrid.

Further, your program should allow the user to enter an index number corresponding to a specific row in the DataTable. In labels, print out the date, open, high, low, and closing prices and the volume associated with this index.

PROJECT 12.2

Create a Windows application that connects to the SPY table in the Finance.mdb database and downloads all the columns into a DataSet. Create a one-dimensional array and populate it with the daily log returns from the DataSet. Add the function definitions for the four moments of a distribution: Average(), Variance(), Skew(), and Kurtosis(). Print out these values in two labels.

What can we say about the distribution of returns on the SPY over the DataSet from the values you have calculated?

Structured Query Language

Structured Query Language is a computer language for communication and interaction with databases. SQL was created to be a single syntax to extract and manipulate data from disparate database systems. So in theory the same SQL queries written for an Oracle database will work on a Sybase database or an Access database and so on. However, database vendors have also developed their own versions of SQL such as Transact-SQL and Oracle's PL/SQL. This chapter will focus on writing standard SQL and will not use any vendor-specific SQL code.

SQL is the engine for communicating with the databases from programming code. The communicating parties are typically a "front-end" application or program, in our case a VB.NET application that sends an SQL statement across a connection via an OleDbDataAdapter, and a "back-end" data source that holds the data. That statement, the SQL code, contains instructions to read or change the data within the database or to manipulate the database itself in some other way. The universal rules of SQL have been established by ANSI, the American National Standards Institute, and therefore are open, meaning that SQL is not owned or controlled by any single company.

The strength of SQL is its universal acceptance by database vendors, and while there has been a lot of talk and marketing about "write once, run anywhere" languages, for database programmers it is really true. Understanding SQL is the ticket to "learn once, profit anywhere."

SQL is not a programming language in the way that VB.NET is. It is a pure language. There is no development environment built into SQL. It does not have user forms like Windows applications. SQL is a nonprocedural programming language consisting of only about 100 specialized words that we can combine into statements. We can embed these statements into VB.NET programs to perform everything from simple data retrieval to high-level operations on databases.

The SQL statements that we may most often be concerned with when developing quantitative trading or risk management systems are those that retrieve data, called queries. However, we will at times also need to write data to a database or delete data from a database. For example, since historical data is almost never perfectly clean, we may need to remove or change bad quotes, which requires changing data in the database. Also we may need to calculate values, such as log returns, that are not included in the raw data and that then must be saved back to a database. So although SQL has many capabilities, we will need to at least learn how to read data, create new fields and records to hold new calculated values, and change or delete existing data.

By the end of this chapter, you should have a good understanding of the syntax of SQL. In addition, you should be able to write SQL code to perform basic queries. Our experience is that understanding the basics of SQL is much easier than mastering all the intricacies of it. In other words, it is relatively easy to get good at SQL, but very difficult to get great at it.

We are confident that SQL is a language in which you can become fairly proficient in a relatively short amount of time. As we mentioned, SQL consists of only about 100 or so words, and SQL statements are simply groups of those words logically arranged to pull specific data from the data source or manipulate the data in the data source. These types of SQL statements are referred to as data manipulation language (DML). Also, however, SQL can be used to actually manipulate the database itself. These SQL statements are called data definition language (DDL). In this chapter, we will get a chance to look at both DML and DDL.

DATA MANIPULATION LANGUAGE

We use DML to work with the actual data held within databases.

The SELECT Statement

Reading data is the most common task we want to perform against a database. A SELECT statement queries the database and retrieves selected data that matches the criteria that we specify. The SELECT statement has five main clauses, although a FROM clause is the only required one. Each of the clauses has a wide array of options and parameters. Here we will show the general structure of a SELECT statement with clauses. However, each of them will be covered in more detail later in the chapter.

```
SELECT [ALL | DISTINCT] column1,column2
      FROM table1,table2
      [WHERE "conditions"]
      [GROUP BY "column-list"]
      [HAVING "conditions"]
      [ORDER BY "column-list" [ASC | DESC] ]
```

Again, in the SELECT syntax, only SELECT and the FROM clause are required. In English, a SELECT statement means that we want to *select* columns *from* a table. When selecting multiple columns, a comma must delimit each of them except for the last column. Also be aware that as with VB.NET, SQL is not case-sensitive. Uppercase or lowercase letters will do just fine. Be aware too that most, but not all, databases require the SQL statement to be terminated by a semicolon.

Before we get too in-depth, let's create a VB.NET program to test out the SQL statements we look at as we go along.

Step 1   Create a new Windows application named SQLexample.

Step 2   To Form1 add a text box, a button, and a data grid.

Step 3   In the Form1 code window add the following code. Most of this code should look very familiar. It follows closely the example presented in the previous chapter. This time, however, we will use the Options.mdb database.

```
Imports System.Data.OleDb
Public Class Form1
    Inherits System.Windows.Forms.Form
Windows Form Designer generated code
Dim myConnect As New OleDbConnection("Provider=Microsoft.Jet.OLEDB. _
                        4.0;DataSource=C:\ModelingFM\Options.mdb")
Dim myAdapter As OleDbDataAdapter
Dim myDataSet As DataSet
Private Sub Button1_Click(ByVal sender As ...) Handles Button1.Click
    Try
        myAdapter = New OleDbDataAdapter(TextBox1.Text, myConnect)
        myConnect.Open()
        myDataSet = New DataSet()
        myAdapter.Fill(myDataSet, "myData")
        DataGrid1.DataSource = myDataSet
        DataGrid1.DataMember = "myData"
    Catch
        MsgBox("Please enter a valid SQL statement.")
    Finally
        myConnect.Close()
    End Try
End Sub
End Class
```

This program will allow the user to provide an SQL statement during run time. Furthermore, we will be able to test out several SQL statements without having to rerun the program. Also we have included a Try...Catch block so the program won't crash if you make a mistake in the SQL statement.

Step 4   Run the program and enter into the text box the simple SQL statement shown below. See also Figure 13.1.

```
SELECT OptionSymbol,StockSymbol,Year,Month,Strike,Bid,Ask,OpenInt
    FROM OptionContracts;
```

This SQL statement will work in any programming language or development environment, including, as you can see, VB.NET. Note in Figure 13.1 that the columns are displayed in the order that they appear in the SELECT statement. If all columns from a table are needed to be part of the result set, we do not need to explicitly specify them. Rather, in the case where all columns are to be selected, we can use the * symbol. As we saw in the previous chapter's example, the resulting SQL statement would look like this:

```
SELECT * FROM OptionContracts;
```

F I G U R E   13.1

```
Chapter 13, SQL Example                                                    _ □ ×
```

SELECT OptionSymbol,StockSymbol,Year,Month,Strike,Bid,Ask,OpenInt FROM OptionContracts;

OptionSym	StockSymb	Year	Month	Strike	Bid	Ask	OpenInt
AXPCX	AXP	3	Mar	22.5	13	13.2	70
AXPCE	AXP	3	Mar	25	10.5	10.8	220
AXPCY	AXP	3	Mar	27.5	8	8.3	180
AXPCF	AXP	3	Mar	30	5.5	5.8	1071
AXPCZ	AXP	3	Mar	32.5	3	3.3	1844
AXPCG	AXP	3	Mar	35	0.95	1.15	7530
AXPCU	AXP	3	Mar	37.5	0.05	0.2	2155
AXPCH	AXP	3	Mar	40	0	0.05	913
AXPCV	AXP	3	Mar	42.5	0	0.05	302
AXPCI	AXP	3	Mar	45	0	0.05	0

Execute Query

For now, leave your SQLexample Windows application running. You can test out the SQL statements as you read through the rest of the chapter.

The WHERE Clause

The previous example retrieved a result set that included all the rows in the table from the specified columns. Usually, however, some rows need to be filtered out. Most queries we will write will not retrieve all the rows from a table, but only a subset of them. This is where the WHERE clause comes in. The WHERE clause filters out rows from a table according to some condition. For example, as in the Finance.mdb database example, if we want to look at the price data for only the year 1994, we could achieve this by using a comparison operator in the WHERE statement. Here is a list of SQL comparison operators:

Comparison Operator	Description
<	Contents of the field are less than the value
<=	Contents of the field are less than or equal to the value
>	Contents of the field are greater than the value
>=	Contents of the field are greater than or equal to the value
=	Contents of the field are equal to the value
<>	Contents of the field are not equal to the value
BETWEEN	Contents of the field fall between a range of values
LIKE	Contents of the field match a certain pattern
IN	Contents of the field match one of a number of criteria

If we are interested in only the option contracts with open interest greater than 1000, our SQL would look like this:

```
SELECT * FROM OptionContracts WHERE OpenInt > 1000;
```

Try this out in your SQLexample application. The WHERE clause can also have multiple conditions using AND or OR. If we want to see all contracts where open interest is over 1000 and the bid is greater than 0, it would look like this:

```
SELECT * FROM OptionContracts WHERE OpenInt > 1000 AND Bid > 0;
```

The Options.mdb database does not have any string-type fields. If we need to build a WHERE clause for such a field, MS Access requires that we use single quotes for string comparison like this:

```
SELECT * FROM OptionContracts WHERE StockSymbol = 'IBM';
```

Date comparison requires the use of the pound sign, #. For example, if we want to see all the options trades done in February 2003, we would use this SQL statement:

```
SELECT * FROM OptionTrades
      WHERE TradeDateTime >= #2/01/2003# AND TradeDateTime <= #2/28/2003#;
```

The ORDER BY Clause

We can sort our result set with the ORDER BY clause. ORDER BY is an optional clause that allows us to display the results of our query in a sorted order, either ascending or descending, based on the columns we specify to order by. Here is an example:

```
SELECT * FROM OptionContracts
      WHERE StockSymbol = 'MSFT' ORDER BY OpenInt;
```

This statement selects all the MSFT option contracts and orders the data from the lowest open interest to the highest.

To view the data in descending order, we simply add DESC to the end, as shown here:

```
SELECT * FROM OptionContracts
      WHERE StockSymbol = 'MSFT' ORDER BY OpenInt DESC;
```

If we need to order based on multiple columns, we must separate the columns with commas:

```
SELECT * FROM OptionContracts
     WHERE StockSymbol = 'MSFT' ORDER BY OpenInt DESC, Strike;
```

Notice that the contracts that have the same open interest are now listed in order of strike price. Also the DESC applies only to the OpenInt. Strike is sorted with the default ASC order.

The LIKE Clause

We have looked at the comparison operators that can be used in a WHERE clause, and most of them are self-explanatory and do not warrant further discussion. The exception to this is the LIKE operator.

So far we have learned how to find exact matches with SQL. However, there may be times you need to search for partial strings. SQL provides a LIKE operator for just this type of query.

The LIKE operator can only be used on fields that have one of the string types set as their data type. LIKE cannot be used on dates or numbers.

String comparison employs a wildcard sign, %, which can be used to match any possible character that might appear before or after the characters specified. For the sake of examples, we will use the standard SQL % wildcard symbol. If you want to view all the IBM option contracts with an 80 strike, you would write this statement:

```
SELECT * FROM OptionContracts
     WHERE StockSymbol = 'IBM' AND OptionSymbol LIKE '%P';
```

The LIKE operator proves to be very useful as we write more complex SQL statements since it enables us to find partial matches without performing any complicated string manipulation. Keep in mind, however, that the LIKE operator is not the most efficient SQL command, and it will degrade overall performance. If we know the exact string we are looking for in a field, then we should use the = operator instead of LIKE. Adding an index on a field that is often searched using the LIKE operator may increase system performance.

In addition to the % wildcard, there are two other important wildcards used with the LIKE operator: the underscore (_) and the square brackets ([]). Whereas the % wildcard is used to find a string with any number of characters before and/or after the specified characters, the underscore is used to limit the search to a single leading or trailing character. A search of '%D%' would return MCDRE and IBMDP. Say, for example, we want to find all the April calls for all the stocks. Omitting the IBM WHERE class and changing the LIKE expression to '%D_' would limit the return values to just those calls with April expiration since we are now looking for any option contract with a D as the second-to-last letter in its symbol.

```
SELECT * FROM OptionContracts WHERE OptionSymbol LIKE '%D_';
```

Additionally, we can use the brackets ([]) to further limit ranges of characters. With the brackets, we can specify particular characters that must appear in a particular position. For instance, if we were looking for April and May calls, then we need to modify our criteria. We limit our search to option contracts that have either D or E in the second-to-last position, and so we specify this by putting these characters within brackets, in the appropriate place:

```
SELECT * FROM OptionContracts WHERE OptionSymbol LIKE '%[DE]_';
```

Keep in mind that the brackets may only contain single characters, and so we cannot use them for lists of strings. This is the biggest limitation to the bracket wildcard, but there are still a large number of possibilities for expression searching in strings.

AGGREGATE SQL FUNCTIONS

So far the SQL that we have been using retrieves rows of data from the database. But SQL can do a lot more. Among other things, SQL has a few built-in functions that can tell us things about the data as a whole. For example, what if we wanted to know what contract has the largest open interest? How about the total number of trades for a given month? As you can see, these numbers are not contained within the columns of a table. Rather, they must be computed.

ANSI SQL contains aggregate functions that can compute simple information from the data in a database. The aggregate functions in the table below are the official ones that are supported by SQL-compliant databases. Specific RDBMSs may support additional aggregate functions that are proprietary and also very useful. We refer you to the documentation of your RDBMS for a list of nonstandard aggregate methods.

Aggregate Function	Description
AVG	Returns the average of the values in a column
COUNT	Returns the total number of values in a column
COUNT(*)	Returns the number of rows in a table
MAX	Returns the largest value in a column
MIN	Returns the smallest value in a column
SUM	Returns the sum of the numeric values in a column

The SUM Function

Let's begin by taking a look at the SUM function. It is used within a SELECT statement and, predictably, returns the summation of a series of values. In this example we will compute the total number of shares traded in the month of January 2003.

```
SELECT SUM(Quantity) FROM StockTrades
    WHERE TradeDateTime >= #1/1/2003# AND TradeDateTime <= #1/31/2003#;
```

Notice in Figure 13.2 that the result set only contains one row of data. This is to be expected when using any of the SQL aggregate functions. Also notice the name of the column. Since we asked SQL to return an aggregate value, SQL named the column for us. When this occurs, we say that an SQL-computed column is being used.

Of course, the column name Expr1000 is not descriptive of the data it contains. Fortunately SQL column naming is simple. To rename computed columns, use the AS modifier. The AS modifier allows us to give meaningful names to any computed columns. If we wanted to give a meaningful name—say, TotalShares—to the computed column shown in Figure 13.2, we could write it as:

```
SELECT SUM(Quantity) AS TotalShares FROM StockTrades
    WHERE TradeDateTime = #1/1/2003# AND TradeDateTime <= #1/31/2003#;
```

FIGURE 13.2

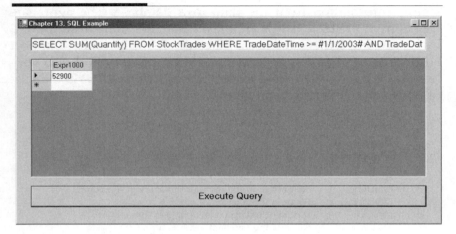

The AVG/COUNT/MIN/MAX Functions

Predictably, these aggregate functions will return the average of the data in a column, the lowest and highest values in a column, and the count or number of elements in a column. If we want to obtain the respective values for the month of January 2003, our SQL statements would look as follows:

```
SELECT MIN(Quantity) FROM StockTrades
    WHERE TradeDateTime >= #01/01/2003# AND TradeDateTime <= #1/31/2003#;

SELECT MAX(Quantity) FROM StockTrades
    WHERE TradeDateTime >= #01/01/2003# AND TradeDateTime <= #1/31/2003#;

SELECT AVG(Quantity) FROM StockTrades
    WHERE TradeDateTime >= #01/01/2003# AND TradeDateTime <= #1/31/2003#;

SELECT COUNT(*) FROM StockTrades
    WHERE TradeDateTime >= #01/01/2003# AND TradeDateTime <= #1/31/2003#;
```

The DISTINCT Function

The SQL DISTINCT function is useful when only the first occurrence of a desired series of data is needed. For example, if we are interested in seeing a list of all the stocks that have been traded, we would not care to see duplicates. That is, we may have traded MSFT several times, and we don't care to see it listed more than once. We can filter out duplicates with the DISTINCT function.

```
SELECT DISTINCT(StockSymbol) FROM StockTrades
       ORDER BY StockSymbol;
```

The GROUP BY Clause

As we have just seen, using aggregate functions such as SUM and MIN will get us the appropriate value for all records or a group of records. What if, however, we want to write an SQL statement that would show the SUMs of the quantities traded of each individual option symbol? The GROUP BY will return the results of aggregate functions for a group of values.

```
SELECT OptionSymbol,SUM(Quantity) FROM OptionTrades GROUP BY OptionSymbol;
```

Notice in Figure 13.3 that option symbols are only displayed when they have a value greater than zero. If, for example, the summation of the quantity for AXPDZ were zero, it would not be included in the result set. The GROUP BY clause can only be used when selecting multiple columns from a table or tables and at least one aggregate function appears in the SELECT statement.

When there are multiple columns beyond the one being aggregated, we can GROUP BY all the other selected columns. For example, if we want the total quantity for all option symbols by BuySell, the SQL would look like the following:

F I G U R E 13.3

	OptionSymbol	Expr1001
►	AXPDZ	10
	AXPPZ	10
	GEIE	40
	GMFF	40
	GMFU	60
	IBMDP	100
	IBMGP	10
	IBMSP	40
	JNJGJ	10
	MCDIW	20
	MCDDC	20

SELECT OptionSymbol,SUM(Quantity) FROM OptionTrades GROUP BY OptionSymbol;

Execute Query

```
SELECT OptionSymbol,BuySell,SUM(Quantity) FROM OptionTrades
    GROUP BY OptionSymbol,BuySell;
```

Note that the above SQL has two columns in the GROUP BY clause. Remember, if the column appears in the SELECT and the SELECT has aggregate functions, the column must appear in a GROUP BY clause.

The HAVING Clause

The HAVING clause is like a WHERE clause for groups. By definition an SQL statement that uses a GROUP BY clause cannot use a WHERE clause. We must use a HAVING clause instead. For example, if we want to see only those option contracts that have total quantities traded that are greater than or equal to 50, the SQL statement would look like this:

```
SELECT OptionSymbol,SUM(Quantity) FROM OptionTrades
    GROUP BY OptionSymbol HAVING SUM(Quantity) >= 50;
```

Figure 13.4 shows how the results would look on your screen.

The HAVING clause is reserved for aggregate functions and is usually placed at the end of an SQL statement. Also, an SQL statement with a HAVING clause may or may not necessarily

F I G U R E   13.4

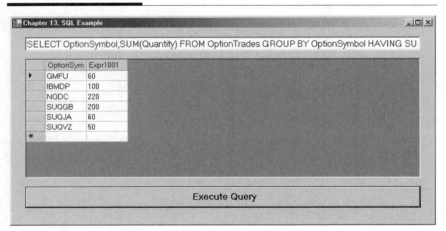

include the GROUP BY clause. The following SQL statement is valid:

```
SELECT COUNT(OptionSymbol) FROM OptionTrades
      HAVING SUM(Quantity) >= 50;
```

Aliasing

Anytime an aggregate function or computed column appears in an SQL statement, SQL will rename it. As we ran the previous examples, we noticed that the column headings looked something like Expr1000. And we saw that with the AS modifier, the column can be aliased with a name we supply. Using a column alias greatly makes the output much more readable. We can also make mathematical calculations in our SQL statements. The following SQL uses a column alias to describe the (quantity * price) of a trade:

```
SELECT OptionSymbol,Price,Quantity,(Price * Quantity * 100) AS TradeCost
      FROM OptionTrades;
```

If you run the above SQL, you will notice that the column title is changed. The column holding the cost of each trade has been aliased. Tables can also be aliased in a FROM clause. The following example creates an alias named OT for the OptionTrades table:

```
SELECT * FROM OptionTrades OT;
```

This is convenient when you want to retrieve information from two or more separate tables, an operation known as joining. The advantage of using a table alias when joining will become apparent over the course of the rest of the chapter.

Joining Tables

So far in our examples, we have retrieved data from only one table. In many instances, however, we may need to retrieve data from two or more tables. Anytime more than one table is being queried, they must be joined. The Stock table and the OptionContracts table above contain information about individual stocks and options contracts on those stocks. In a real-world application, we may be interested in returning data from both tables in a single SQL statement. To join these two tables we must first identify a column in each table that contains the same data. In this example the OptionContracts table contains a StockSymbol column that matches the StockSymbol column in the Stock table.

The two tables can be joined on these StockSymbol columns, although it is just a coincidence that both these tables are named the same. In order to join tables, the data must match, but not necessarily the column names. When creating an SQL SELECT statement containing more than one column, we first specify the join. Here is an example using table aliasing for readability:

```
SELECT * FROM Stock S, OptionContracts OC
      WHERE S.StockSymbol = OC.StockSymbol;
```

In this example the join is performed within the WHERE clause. The above SQL will return all columns for each table joined by the stock symbol.

With the two tables joined, the SELECT and the WHERE clause can now be modified. For example:

```
SELECT OC.OptionSymbol,OC.StockSymbol,OC.Bid,OC.Ask,S.DividendAmount
      FROM Stock S, OptionContracts OC
      WHERE S.StockSymbol = OC.StockSymbol AND S.StockSymbol = 'IBM';
```

Figure 13.5 shows a screen shot of the results.

F I G U R E 13.5

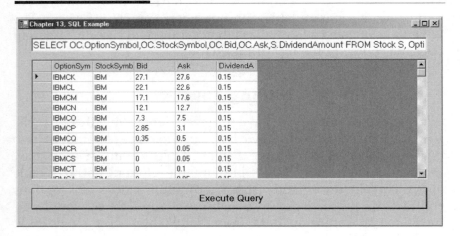

The UNION Keyword

A UNION is useful if you want to get data from two tables within the same result set. For example, if we want to see the bid and ask for INTC as well as the bids and asks for all the INTC options in one result set, the SQL statement would read as follows:

```
Select StockSymbol,Bid,Ask FROM Stock
    WHERE StockSymbol = 'IBM'
UNION
Select OptionSymbol,Bid,Ask FROM OptionContracts
    WHERE StockSymbol = 'IBM';
```

See Figure 13.6.

The data type for the columns in each SELECT statement must match for a UNION to work. This is not an issue in the above example because each of the tables has identical column sets.

The INSERT Statement

Up to this point we have only queried the Options.mdb database and looked at the results. We may, however, also be interested in changing the data. In order to add, delete, or modify the data in the

F I G U R E 13.6

Options.mdb database, we will first need to add some elements to our SQLexample program.

Step 5   Add another button to your form.

Step 6   Add the following code to the Button2_Click event:

```
Private Sub Button2_Click(ByVal sender As ...) Handles Button2.Click
        Try
            myConnect.Open()
            Dim command As New OleDbCommand(TextBox1.Text, myConnect)
            command.ExecuteNonQuery()
        Catch
            MsgBox("Please enter a valid SQL statement.")
        Finally
            myConnect.Close()
        End Try
    End Sub
```

An OleDbCommand object is an SQL statement that we can use to perform transactions against a database. We use the ExecuteNonQuery() member method to execute UPDATE, INSERT, and DELETE statements.

For the remainder of the chapter, SELECT statements should be executed using the first button, and all other transactions should be executed using this new, second button.

The SQL INSERT statement enables us to add data to a table in a database. Here is an example showing the syntax for adding a record to the OptionTrades table:

```
INSERT INTO OptionTrades
       (TradeDateTime, OptionSymbol, BuySell, Price, Quantity, TradeStatus)
       VALUES (#02/27/2003#,'IBMDP','B',2.60,10,'F');
```

You can verify that this data has been added to the table by writing a simple SELECT statement.

Notice that all values for all columns have been supplied save for the TradeID column, which is generated automatically. If a value for a column is to be left blank, the keyword NULL could be used to represent a blank column value. In regard to data types, notice that strings are delimited by single quotes, numerical data does not need single quotes, and dates are defined with pound signs. As we have mentioned previously, each RDBMS is different, and so you should look into the documentation of your system to see how to define the data types. Whatever your RDBMS, the comma-delimited list of values must match the table structure exactly in the number of attributes and the data type of each attribute.

The UPDATE Statement

The SQL UPDATE clause is used to modify data in a database table existing in one or several rows. The following SQL updates one row in the stock table, the dividend amount for IBM:

```
UPDATE Stock SET DividendAmount = .55
    WHERE StockSymbol = 'IBM';
```

SQL does not limit us to updating only one column. The following SQL statement updates both the dividend amount and the dividend date columns in the stock table:

```
UPDATE Stock SET DividendAmount = .50,DividendDate = #03/18/2003#
    WHERE StockSymbol = 'IBM';
```

The update expression can be a constant, any computed value, or even the result of a SELECT statement that returns a single row and a single column. If the WHERE clause is omitted, then the specified attribute is set to the same value in every row of the table. We can also set multiple attribute values at the same time with a comma-delimited list of attribute-equals-expression pairs.

The DELETE Statement

As its name implies, we use an SQL DELETE statement to remove data from a table in a database. Like the UPDATE statement, either single rows or multiple rows can be deleted. The following SQL statement deletes one row of data from the StockTrades table:

```
DELETE FROM StockTrades
    WHERE TradeID = 40;
```

The following SQL statement will delete all records from the StockTrades table that represent trades before January 4, 2003:

```
DELETE FROM StockTrades
    WHERE TradeDateTime < #01/04/2003#;
```

If the WHERE clause is omitted, then every row of the table is deleted, which of course should be done with great caution.

BEGIN, COMMIT, and ROLLBACK

Transaction commands such as INSERT, UPDATE, and DELETE may also contain keywords such as BEGIN, COMMIT, and ROLLBACK, depending upon the RDBMS you are using. For example, to make your DML changes visible to the rest of the users of the database, you may need to include a COMMIT. If you have made an error in updating data and wish to restore your private copy of the database to the way it was before you started, you may be able to use the ROLLBACK keyword.

In particular, the COMMIT and ROLLBACK statements are part of a very important and versatile Oracle capability to control sequences of changes to a database. You should consult the documentation of your particular RDMBS with regard to the use of these keywords.

DATA DEFINITION LANGUAGE

We use DDL to create or modify the structure of tables in a database. When we execute a DDL statement, it takes effect immediately. Again, for all transactions, you should click Button2 to execute these nonqueries. You will be able to verify the results of the SQL statements by creating simple SELECT statements and executing a query with Button1 in your program.

Creating Views

A view is a saved, read-only SQL statement. Views are very useful when you find yourself writing the same SQL statement over and over again. Here is a sample SELECT statement to find all the IBM option contracts with an 80 strike:

```
SELECT * FROM OptionContracts
     WHERE StockSymbol = 'IBM' AND OptionSymbol LIKE '%P';
```

Although not overly complicated, the above SQL statement is not overly simplistic either. Rather than typing it again and again, we can create a VIEW. The syntax for creating a VIEW is as follows:

```
CREATE VIEW IBM80s as SELECT * FROM OptionContracts
    WHERE StockSymbol = 'IBM' AND OptionSymbol LIKE '%P';
```

The above code creates a VIEW named IBM80s. Now to run it, simply type in the following SQL statement:

```
SELECT * FROM IBM80s;
```

Views can be deleted as well using the DROP keyword.

```
DROP VIEW IBM80s;
```

Creating Tables

As you know by now, database tables are the basic structure in which data is stored. In the examples we have used so far, the tables have been preexisting. Oftentimes, however, we need to build a table ourselves. While we are certainly able to build tables ourselves with an RDBMS such as MS Access, we will cover the SQL code to create tables in VB.NET.

As a review, tables contain rows and columns. Each row represents one piece of data, called a record, and each column, called a field, represents a component of that data. When we create a table, we need to specify the column names as well as their data types. Data types are usually database-specific but often can be broken into integers, numerical values, strings, and Date/Time. The following SQL statement builds a simple table named Trades:

```
CREATE TABLE Trades
    (myInstr Char(4) NOT NULL,myPrice Numeric(8,2) NOT NULL,myTime Date _
    NOT NULL);
```

The general syntax for the CREATE TABLE statement is as follows:

```
CREATE TABLE TableName (Column1 DataType1 Null/Not Null, ...);
```

The data types that you will use most frequently are the VARCHAR2(n), a variable-length character field where n is its maximum width; CHAR(n), a fixed-length character field of width n; NUMERIC(w.d), where w is the total width of the field and d is the number of places after the decimal point (omitting it produces an integer); and DATE, which stores both date and time in a unique internal format. NULL and NOT NULL indicate whether a specific field may be left blank.

Tables can be dropped as well. When a table is dropped, all the data it contains is lost.

```
DROP TABLE myTrades;
```

Altering Tables

We have already seen that the INSERT statement can be used to add rows. Columns as well can be added to or removed from a table. For example, if we want to add a column named Exchange to the StockTrades table, we can use the ALTER TABLE statement. The syntax is:

```
ALTER TABLE StockTrades ADD Exchange char(4);
```

As we have seen in the previous chapter, all tables must have a primary key. We can use the ALTER TABLE statement to specify TradeID in the Trades table we created previously.

```
ALTER TABLE Trades ADD PRIMARY KEY(TradeID);
```

Columns can be removed as well using the ALTER TABLE statement.

```
ALTER TABLE StockTrades DROP Exchange;
```

SUMMARY

Over the course of this chapter, we have looked at SQL data manipulation language and data definition language. While we have certainly not covered all of SQL, you should now be fairly proficient at extracting and modifying data in a database as well as changing the structure of tables within a database.

SQL consists of a limited number of SQL statements and keywords, which can be arranged logically to perform transactions against a database. While it is easy to get good at SQL, it is very difficult to become an expert.

PROBLEMS

1. What is SQL? What are DDL and DML?
2. What document should you consult to find out the specifics of SQL transactions against your RDBMS?
3. What is an OleDbCommand object, and what is the ExecuteNonQuery() method?
4. If we found corrupt data in a database, what statements might we use to either correct it or get rid of it?
5. What is the syntax of CREATE TABLE?

PROJECT 13.1

The Finance.mdb database contains price data. However, we very often will be interested in a time series of log returns. Create a VB.NET application that will modify the AXP table to include a Returns column. Then make the calculations for the log returns and populate the column.

PROJECT 13.2

Create a VB.NET application that will connect to the Finance.mdb database and return the average volume for a user-defined stock between any two user-defined dates.

Introduction to Data Structures

In Chapter 8 we looked at arrays, which are the simplest data structures and have fixed sizes, although they can be redimensioned. Visual Basic.NET offers several other more dynamic data structures known as collection objects, which are convenient for holding groups of objects such as, for example, a portfolio of options. These data structures include the Collection object itself and the objects found in the System.Collections namespace, the most notable of which for right now are array lists, queues, stacks, hash tables, and sorted lists. Oddly enough, the Collection class itself is not located in the System.Collections namespace.

COLLECTION OBJECT

The Collection class allows us to store groups of objects of different data types and to easily count, look up, and add or remove objects within the collection using the Count and Item properties and the Add and Remove methods of the Collection class. Furthermore we can iterate through the elements in a collection using a For Each...Next loop. Collections do not have fixed sizes, and memory allocation is completely dynamic, and so in many cases they will be a superior way of handling data compared with arrays.

As with arrays, it will be important to note the index of the first element. Most often, the Collection objects we will use will be 1-based. That is, the index of the first element will be by default 1 and not zero as with arrays. Also Collection objects allow us to access elements of the collection by either index or an optional string key. As we will see later, other collection types allow only numeric index references and may not have a key. Here are the properties and methods associated with Collection objects:

Collection Properties	Description	Example
Count	Returns the number of objects in the collection	dblNum = myColl.Count
Item	Returns a specific element of the collection	dblObj = myColl.Item(1) or dblObj = myColl.Item(strKey)

Collection Methods	Description	Example
Add	Adds an object to the collection	myColl.Add(myObj)
Remove	Removes an object from the collection	myColl.Remove(2) or myColl.Remove(strKey)

We have in fact already had some experience with Collection objects. As you may recall, several of the ADO.NET objects we looked at in Chapter 12, like DataRowCollections and DataColumnCollections, are Collection objects and as such inherit from the CollectionBase class.

Here is an example using a Collection object.

Step 1 Create a new Windows application named Portfolio.

Step 2 In the Project menu item, select Add Class twice and add two new classes. Into these class code modules, paste in the code for the StockOption and CallOption classes.

Step 3 Go back to the Form1 code window, and in the Form1_Load event, add the code to create a Collection object named MyPortfolio.

```
Dim MyPortfolio As New Collection()
```

Step 4 Next add the code to create a CallOption object called myOption.

```
Dim myOption As New CallOption("IBMDP")
```

Step 5   Add myOption to MyPortfolio.

```
MyPortfolio.Add(myOption)
```

Step 6   Now we can actually destroy myOption using the Nothing keyword.

When we assign Nothing to an object, the object reference no longer refers to that object instance.

```
myOption = Nothing
```

Step 7   Still within the Form1_Load event, let's create another option and add it to MyPortfolio.

```
myOption = New CallOption("SUQEX")
MyPortfolio.Add(myOption)
myOption = Nothing
```

MyPortfolio now consists of two CallOption objects, neither known by the name myOption, but rather by their respective indexes within the MyPortfolio collection.

Step 8   We could find the Strike price of the Sun MicroSystems option (SUQEX) in the following way:

```
Label1.Text = MyPortfolio.Item(2).Strike
```

Or simply:

```
Label1.Text = MyPortfolio(2).Strike
```

as shown in Figure 14.1.

F I G U R E   14.1

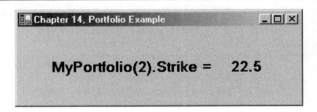

CREATING A CUSTOMIZED COLLECTION CLASS

In this simple example, we will create our own collection class that will hold a portfolio of options. This new Collection class will allow us only to add option objects. As in the previous example, any object type, not just CallOptions, can be added to an instance of the generic Collection class since it is not strongly typed. There is an inherent advantage and a disadvantage with using this approach. The advantage is that any object representing a tradable instrument can be added to our MyPortfolio object. However, the disadvantage is that if we try to use a For Each CallOption In MyPortfolio. . .Next loop to process a portfolio of options, an error will occur since one element in MyPortfolio may be, for example, a GovtBond object.

In cases where we require a more robust collection, we can, through inheritance from the CollectionBase class, create our own Collection class and add our own functionality. The CollectionBase class, found in the System.Collections.namespace, includes the public Clear method, the Count property, and a protected property called List that implements the IList interface. The methods and properties—Add, Remove, and Item—require that we codify the implementation, as you will see. Here are the important properties and methods of the MustInherit CollectionBase class:

IList Implementations	Description
Count	Returns the number of elements in the CollectionBase object

Public Methods	Description
Clear	Deletes all elements from the CollectionBase object
Equals	Determines whether two objects in the CollectionBase are equal
GetEnumerator	Returns an enumerator that can iterate through the elements of a CollectionBase
RemoveAt	Deletes an element from the CollectionBase object at a specified index

IList Implementations	Description
CopyTo	Copies the elements of a CollectionBase to a one-dimensional array
Add	Adds an element at the end of the CollectionBase
Contains	Determines whether a specified element is contained in a CollectionBase

IList Implementations	Description
IndexOf	Returns the index of the first occurrence of a specified element in a CollectionBase
Insert	Inserts an element into the CollectionBase at the specified index
Remove	Removes the first occurrence of a specified element from the CollectionBase

In this example, we will create an OptionCollection that only accepts CallOptions as opposed to any object. Then we will add methods to buy, implementing IList.Add(), and sell, IList.RemoveAt(), CallOptions. Also we will need to implement the Item property that returns the CallOption at a specified index. This customized OptionCollection class will be zero-based.

Step 1 Start a new Windows application and name it OptionCollection.

Step 2 In the same way as in the previous example, add the code for the StockOption and CallOption classes.

Step 3 Now add a code module for a third class called OptionCollection with the following code:

```
Public Class OptionCollection
     Inherits System.Collections.CollectionBase
Public Sub Buy(ByVal myOption As CallOption)
     List.Add(myOption)
End Sub
Public Sub Sell(ByVal myIndex As Integer)
     List.RemoveAt(myIndex)
End Sub
Public ReadOnly Property Item(ByVal myIndex As Integer) As CallOption
     Get
             Return List.Item(myIndex)
     End Get
End Property
End Class
```

Notice that the public Buy and Sell methods implement the Add() and RemoveAt() methods and the Item property implements the Item property of the List property of the parent CollectionBase class.

Step 4 In the Form1_Load event, create an instance of the OptionCollection class called MyOptionPortfolio. Also create two CallOption objects

```
Dim myOptionPortfolio As NewOptionCollection()
Dim myFirstOption As New CallOption("IBMDP")
Dim mySecondOption As New CallOption("SUQEX")
```

F I G U R E   14.2

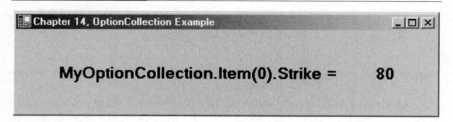

Step 5   Add the two CallOptions to MyOptionPortfolio by "buying" them.

```
myOptionPortfolio.Buy(myFirstOption)
myOptionPortfolio.Buy(mySecondOption)
```

Step 6   Sell the IBMDP option.

```
myOptionPortfolio.Sell(0)
```

Step 7   The SUQEX option is left in the portfolio as you can see in Figure 14.2.

```
Label1.Text = myOptionPortfolio.Item(0).Strike
```

CLEANING DATA

Financial modeling and forecasting requires clean data for testing and simulation. But almost no data is perfectly clean. In fact, we should assume that all data is dirty. As a result, financial engineers often spend large amounts of time cleaning data. It is very easy and very common to underestimate the amount of time it will take to clean data. Literally half the time required for high-quality analysis can typically be spent cleaning data, and every analyst can recall wasting countless hours of time testing and coding only to draw bad conclusions due to dirty data. Failing to adequately consider the impact of bad data can lead to the creation of bad models and, worse, losses. Clean data can be profitable, but bad data will be ruinous. As you might imagine, the quality of data purchased from different data vendors can range from very clean to terribly dirty.

Using high-quality data almost always pays off even though it's more expensive. In any case, though, time spent finding good data and giving it a good once-over is worth the effort and expense.

All data should be cleaned before use. But serious data cleaning involves more than just visually scanning data in Excel and updating bad records with good data. Rather, it requires that we decompose and reassemble data. This takes time.

Data cleaning is a process that consists of first detection and then correction of data errors and of updating the dirty data source with clean data or preferably creating a new data source to hold the entire cleaned data set. Maintaining the original dirty data source in its original form allows us to go back if we make a mistake in our cleaning algorithms and consequently further corrupt the data.

Another problem requiring data cleaning occurs when, depending on the time interval we're looking at, the data we have is not in the individual ticks or bars we desire (bars being fixed units of time with a date/time, an open, a high, a low, a close, and maybe even a volume and/or open interest). We may, for example, possess tick data and want to analyze bars of several different durations—a minute in length, 5 minutes, a day, a week, or a month. It is, of course, possible to convert raw tick data into a series of bars by writing a simple VB.NET program to generate the bar data and save it to a new database.

Let's look at some of the common types of bad data we often encounter in financial markets:

Type of Bad Data	Example
Bad quotes	Tick of 23.54 should be 83.54
Missing data	Blank field or data coded as "9999," "NA," or "0"
Bad dates	2/14/12997
Column-shifted data	Value printed in an adjacent column
File corruption	CD or floppy disk errors
Different data formats	Data from different vendors may come in different formats or table schemas

As we know, the use of a large amount of in-sample data will produce more stable models and have less curve-fitting danger, thereby increasing the probability of success out-of-sample and consequently during implementation. Sophisticated models, such as GARCH(1,1), are often more affected by bad data as compared with simpler models.

Since many forecasting models, like GARCH, are extremely sensitive to even a few bad data points, we should be sure to look at means, medians, standard deviations, histograms, and minimum and maximum values of our data. A good way to do this is to sort through the data set to examine values outside an expected range. Or we can run scans to highlight suspicious, missing, extraneous, or illogical data points. Here are a few, but certainly not all, methods often used to scan data:

Scanning for Bad Data

Intraperiod high tick less than closing price
Intraperiod low tick greater than opening price
Volume less than zero
Bars with wide high-low ranges relative to some previous time period
Closing deviance. Divide the absolute value of the difference between each closing price and the previous closing price by the average of the preceding 20 absolute values
Data falling on weekends or holidays
Data with out-of-order dates or with duplicate bars

As mentioned, data cleaning has three components: auditing data to find bad data or to highlight suspicious data, fixing bad data, and applying the fix to the data set or preferably saving the data to a new data source. The methods we choose to accomplish these three tasks constitute a data transformation management system (DTMS). The hope is that our DTMS will improve the quality of the data as well as the success of our models. To review, a DTMS should capture data from your data source, clean it, and then save it back or create a new data source with the clean data.

As with any process, it pays to plan ahead when building a DTMS. Before you begin, identify and categorize all the types of errors you expect to encounter in your data, survey the available techniques to address those different types of errors, and develop a system to identify and resolve the errors.

Of course, as we mentioned, you should purchase data only from reputable vendors who take data integrity seriously. Even so, you should always scan and clean your data. It's just that dealing with quality vendors will nonetheless save time and improve results.

CREATING A DATA TRANSFORMATION MANAGEMENT SYSTEM

Let's look at an example of how to use a collection to build a simple DTMS.

Step 1 Create a new Windows application called DTMS.

Step 2 In the Form1_Load event make an OleDbConnection to the DirtyFinance.mdb database, retrieve all the columns in the AXP table with an OleDbDataAdapter and an SQL statement, and place the data into myDataSet with the name "AXPdata." Be sure to declare myDataSet in the declarations section of the Form1 class code window.

```
Imports System.Data.OleDb

Public Class Form1
    Inherits System.Windows.Forms.Form

Dim myDataSet As New DataSet()

Private Sub Form1_Load(ByVal sender As ...) Handles MyBase.Load
 Dim myConnect As New OleDbConnection("Provider=... ...\DirtyFinance.mdb")
 Dim myAdapter As New OleDbDataAdapter("select * from AXP", myConnect)
 myConnect.Open()
 myAdapter.Fill(myDataSet, "AXPdata")
 myConnect.Close()
End Sub
```

At this point, you may notice a particularly advantageous situation. The AXP price data is now already held in a collection, namely a DataRowCollection. So we can, without any additional machinations, loop through the collection's elements, which are DataRow objects, and search for bad data. We prefer, of course, to contain individual data-cleaning algorithms in separate procedures or objects. Then we can simply pass a reference to the collection as an input argument to the procedure and commence cleaning. In the AXPdata DataTable, let's search for intraday high prices that are less than the closing price.

Step 3 Create a subroutine called CleanHighLessThanLow() that accepts as an input argument a reference to a

DataRowCollection object. This subroutine should loop through the element of a collection and find instances where the intraday high is less than the close.

As we discussed in Chapter 11, the DirtyFinance.mdb Access database contains dirty data. For simplicity, your subroutine should, upon finding a dirty data point, show a message box alerting the user to the bad data as well as its index.

```
Private Sub CleanHighLessThanClose(ByRef myDataPoints As _
                          DataRowCollection)
Dim x As Integer
For x = 0 To myDataPoints.Count - 1
   If myDataPoints(x).Item("HighPrice") < myDataPoints(x).Item("ClosePrice")
          Then
          MsgBox("Bad Data Point: High of " & _
             myDataPoints(x).Item("HighPrice") & _
             " and Close of " & myDataPoints(x).Item("Close") & _
             " at " & Str(x))
   End If
Next x
End Sub
```

Step 4   Add a button to Form1, and in the Button1_Click event, call the subroutine to clean the table passing a reference to the DataRowCollection. The Rows property of the DataTable returns a reference to the DataRowCollection.

```
Private Sub Button1_Click(ByVal sender As ...) Handles Button1.Click
       CleanHighLessThanClose(myDataSet.Tables("AXPdata").Rows)
End Sub
```

Step 5   Run the program. Figure 14.3 shows the result.

F I G U R E 14.3

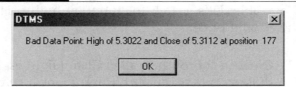

In the AXP table, there are three instance of a high that is greater than the low. Your program should find them at indexes of 177, 1200, and 2342.

SUMMARY

In this chapter we learned how to use the Collection object as well as how to create our own Collection class by inheriting from the CollectionBase class for adding Option objects to a strongly typed Portfolio object. Further we looked at the importance of using clean data when making financial calculations and forecasts. Since data stored in a DataSet is already in a DataRowCollection, we can immediately scan data for errors by passing a reference to the DataRowCollection to procedures containing data-cleaning algorithms.

PROBLEMS

1. What is a collection?
2. How does a collection differ from an array?
3. What are common types of data corruption?
4. What are some techniques for scanning for dirty data?
5. What is the CollectionBase class?

PROJECT 14.1

In the DirtyFinance.mdb database, the IBM table contains missing data. Create a VB.NET Windows application that finds the three bad entries and deletes them from the database.

To complete this project you will need to use the IsDBNull() function. The IsDBNull() function returns True or False indicating whether a given object is of type System.DBNull. A System.DBNull object represents missing data in a data set. As may be intuitively deduced, missing data is not held as a Nothing value, nor is it held as a string with no value such as "".

PROJECT 14.2

The MRK table in the DirtyFinance.mdb database is rife with bad data, including bad and missing data points, bad dates, and column-shifted data. Create a DTMS to find the bad data. Also, allow the user to view the bad data and either update it or delete it.

CHAPTER 15

Advanced Data Structures

The System.Collections namespace contains several classes for collections of objects. These Collection classes differ from the Collection class we discussed in Chapter 14. Notice, however, the inclusion in this namespace of the CollectionBase, which we looked at briefly in the previous chapter. Here is a list of the Collection classes in the System.Collections namespace:

System.Collections Namespace Classes	Description
ArrayList	An array whose size is dynamic
BitArray	A compact array of bit values represented as Booleans
CaseInsensitiveComparer	Compares two nonstring objects for equivalence
CaseInsensitiveHashCodeProvider	Supplies a hash code for a nonstring object
CollectionBase	The abstract base class for a collection
Comparer	Compares two objects for case-sensitive equivalence
DictionaryBase	The base class for a collection of key-and-value pairs
Hashtable	A collection of key-and-value pairs organized by hash code
Queue	A first-in, first-out collection of objects
ReadOnlyCollectionBase	The abstract base class for a read-only collection
SortedList	A collection of key-and-value pairs that are sorted by key and are accessible by both key and index
Stack	A last-in, first-out collection of objects

Structure	Description
DictionaryEntry	Defines a dictionary key-and-value pair

We will not discuss fully each of these classes. However, we will illustrate a hash table and leave it to the reader to investigate the various members of each of the classes should the need for them arise. For now, be aware that they exist, and understand their differing descriptions.

HASH TABLES

A hash table is a collection of key-and-value pairs based upon the hash code of the element's key. Each element is then stored in a DictionaryEntry object. Because of the way they are constructed, hash tables allow for speedy retrieval of elements in the hash table. When an application needs to store elements, it creates a scheme to convert the element's key value to a subscript, which then becomes the location of that object in the collection. To retrieve the object then, the program converts the key value using the same scheme to find and return the object from its location. This process is called hashing.

When we convert a key to an index value, we are scrambling the bits. Problems can arise, however, when two different keys hash into the same element in an array. Since we certainly cannot store two different records in the same location, we need to find an alternative location via some method. The VB.NET Hashtable class solves this problem by having each cell of the hash table be a bucket, which is a collection of all the key-value pairs that hash to that cell. This entire process is invisible to us since the hash table's hashing function calculates where to put the value in the hash table. This function is applied to the key of the key-value pair of objects. By using this process, any object can be added to a hash table.

The VB.NET Hashtable class implements the IDictionary, ICollection, IEnumerable, ISerialization, IDeserializationCallback, and ICloneable interfaces. As a result, there are several member variables, properties, and methods associated with Hashtable objects. Some of the more important members to be aware of are:

Public Constructor	Description
Constructor	Initializes a hash table

Public Properties	Description
Count	Returns the number of elements in the hash table
Item	Returns or sets the value of an element in the hash table

Public Properties	Description
Keys	Returns a collection containing the keys in the hash table
Values	Returns a collection containing the values in the hash table

Public Methods	Description
Add	Adds an element to the hash table
Clear	Deletes all elements from the hash table
ContainsKey	Determines whether the hash table contains a specific key
ContainsValue	Determines whether the hash table contains a specific value
CopyTo	Copies the elements of the hash tables to a one-dimensional array
Equals	Determines whether two objects are equal
GetEnumerator	Returns an IDictionaryEnumerator that can iterate through the hash table
Remove	Deletes a single element from the hash table

Protected Methods	Description
GetHash	Returns the hash code for a specified key
KeyEquals	Compares an object with a specific key in the hash table

Since the elements of a hash table may be of different types, we can loop through the elements in a hash table using an IDictionaryEnumerator. Here is an example from the program presented later in the chapter:

```
Dim enumerator As IDictionaryEnumerator = myPortfolio.GetEnumerator()
txtPortfolio.Text = "PORTFOLIO ELEMENTS:" & vbCrLf
While enumerator.MoveNext()
    txtPortfolio.Text += enumerator.Value.ToString & vbCrLf
End While
```

An IDictionaryEnumerator itemizes the elements of a DictionaryEntry object. When an enumerator is created, its position is before the first element in the dictionary. As a result, we must call the MoveNext() method in order to advance to the first element. We can then use the Current() property or the Value() property to retrieve the element at which the enumerator is positioned. And then we can call MoveNext() and iterate through all the elements in the hash table. If the enumerator runs off the end of the hash table, the MoveNext() method will simply return a false value. So we can loop while MoveNext() is True, as in the example shown above. An enumerator will be invalidated if changes are made to the hash table while it is being used. Here are the key properties and methods of an IDictionaryEnumerator:

Public Properties	Description
Current	Retrieves the current element in the dictionary
Entry	Returns both the key and the value of the current dictionary entry
Key	Returns the key of the current dictionary entry
Value	Retrieves the current element in the dictionary

Public Methods	Description
MoveNext	Moves the enumerator to the next element in the dictionary
Reset	Moves the enumerator to the position before the first element

Now let's use a hash table to create a robust portfolio object with a great deal more functionality than the one using the Collection class that we looked at in the previous chapter.

Step 1 Open a new Windows application named Portfolio.

Step 2 Create the GUI shown in Figure 15.1.

Step 3 On your GUI, there should be seven text boxes. In the Properties windows, rename these controls txtSymbol, txtQuantity, txtStockPrice, txtVolatility, txtDelta, txtPortfolio, and txtPortStatus. The large text box in the middle, txtPortfolio, should have the multiline property set to True and the scroll bar property set to Vertical. Also on your GUI, there should be a combo box. Rename this combo box cboCallPut. There should be eight buttons on your form. Rename these controls cmdBuy, cmdSell, cmdGetMeOut, cmdContains, cmdIsEmpty, cmdRetrieve, cmdCompute Delta, and cmdListKeys, respectively.

Step 4 Now to add some code. Add a reference to Options.dll and Import Options as well as System.Collections at the top of your Form1 code window.

```
Imports System.Collections
Imports Options
```

F I G U R E 15.1

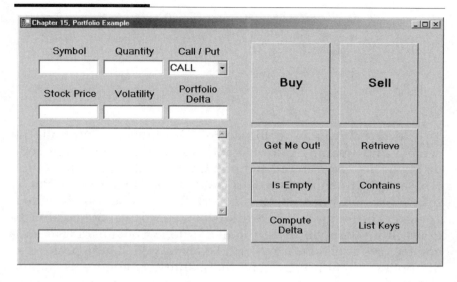

Step 5 In the general declarations section of the Form1 code window, create a new Hashtable object named myPortfolio.

```
Dim myPortfolio As New Hashtable()
```

Step 6 Add the following code to the cmdBuy_Click event subroutine:

```
Private Sub cmdBuy_Click(ByVal sender As ...) Handles cmdBuy.Click
    Dim intOptionQuantity As Integer = txtQuantity.Text
    Dim strSymbol As String = txtSymbol.Text
    If cboCallPut.Text = "CALL" Then
        If myPortfolio.ContainsKey(strSymbol) = False Then
            Dim myOption As New CallOption(txtSymbol.Text, _
                             intOptionQuantity)
            myPortfolio.Add(strSymbol, myOption)
        Else
            myPortfolio(strSymbol).Quantity += intOptionQuantity
            If myPortfolio(strSymbol).Quantity = 0 Then _
                          myPortfolio.Remove(strSymbol)
        End If
    Else
        If myPortfolio.ContainsKey(strSymbol) = False Then
            Dim myOption As New PutOption(txtSymbol.Text, _
                             intOptionQuantity)
```

```
                    myPortfolio.Add(strSymbol, myOption)
            Else
                myPortfolio(strSymbol).Quantity() += intOptionQuantity
                If myPortfolio(strSymbol).Quantity = 0 Then _
                                myPortfolio.Remove(strSymbol)
            End If
        End If
        ListPortfolioElements()
    End Sub
```

Several things are going on in this routine. First of all, the symbol and quantity are read into variables. Second, the code distinguishes between call and put. If Call is selected in the combo box, a CallOption is added to myPortfolio. Likewise, if Put is selected, a PutOption object is added. Before either one is added, however, the program checks to see if that particular option already exists in myPortfolio using the myPortfolio.ContainsKey(strSymbol) member function. If myPortfolio already contains a position in that option, it simply increments the quantity of the current position. If there is no current position in that option in myPortfolio, then it creates the new CallOption or PutOption object and adds it to myPortfolio. Third and last, the procedure calls the ListPortfolio-Elements() subroutine, which we will look at shortly.

Step 7   Add the following code for the cmdSell_Click event subroutine. The cmdSell_Click event routine is the same as the cmdBuy routine except that it subtracts the quantity rather than adds it.

```
Private Sub cmdSell_Click(ByVal sender As ...) Handles cmdSell.Click
    Dim intOptionQuantity As Integer = txtQuantity.Text
    Dim strSymbol As String = txtSymbol.Text
    If cboCallPut.Text = "CALL" Then
            If myPortfolio.ContainsKey(strSymbol) = False Then
                Dim myOption As New CallOption(txtSymbol.Text, _
                                        -intOptionQuantity)
                myPortfolio.Add(strSymbol, myOption)
            Else
                myPortfolio(strSymbol).Quantity -= intOptionQuantity
                If myPortfolio(strSymbol).Quantity = 0 Then _
                                myPortfolio.Remove(strSymbol)
            End If
    Else
            If myPortfolio.ContainsKey(strSymbol) = False Then
                Dim myOption As New PutOption(txtSymbol.Text, _
                                        -intOptionQuantity)
                myPortfolio.Add(strSymbol, myOption)
```

```
                Else
                       myPortfolio(strSymbol).Quantity() -= intOptionQuantity
                       If myPortfolio(strSymbol).Quantity = 0 Then _
                                                myPortfolio.Remove(strSymbol)
                   End If
           End If
           ListPortfolioElements()
End Sub
```

Step 8   Add the following code to the cmdRetrieve_Click event:

```
Private Sub cmdRetrieve_Click(ByVal sender As ...) Handles cmdRetrieve.Click
        Dim strSymbol As String = txtSymbol.Text
        Dim resultOption As Object = myPortfolio(strSymbol)
        If Not resultOption Is Nothing Then
            txtPortStatus.Text = "Retrieved: " & resultOption.ToString()
        Else
            txtPortStatus.Text = txtSymbol.Text & " not in the Portfolio."
        End If
        ListPortfolioElements()
End Sub
```

The cmdRetrieve_Click event finds the specific element within myPortfolio, if it exists. In this example, we are just printing out in a text box the fact that it was found. In more sophisticated production programs and systems, we would probably want to do something more important.

Step 9   Add the following code to the cmdIsEmpty_Click event:

```
Private Sub cmdIsEmpty_Click(ByVal sender As ...) Handles cmdIsEmpty.Click
        If myPortfolio.Count = 0 Then
            txtPortStatus.Text = "Portfolio is empty."
        Else
            txtPortStatus.Text = "Portfolio is not empty."
        End If
        ListPortfolioElements()
End Sub
```

This event simply uses the myPortfolio.Count method, as you can see. The simplicity of using System.Collections classes is what makes them so powerful.

Step 10   Add the following code to the cmdContains_Click event:

```
Private Sub cmdContains_Click(ByVal sender As ...) Handles cmdContains.Click
        Dim strSymbol = txtSymbol.Text
        txtPortStatus.Text = "Contains: " & myPortfolio.ContainsKey(strSymbol)
End Sub
```

This subroutine simply calls the ContainsKey() method of myPortfolio to check and see whether a specific element is present in the library. The ContainsKey() method returns a Boolean.

Step 11   Add the following code to the cmdGetMeOut_Click event:

```
Private Sub cmdGetMeOut_Click(ByVal sender As ...) Handles cmdGetMeOut.Click
    myPortfolio.Clear()
    txtPortStatus.Text = "You are out. Portfolio is now empty."
    ListPortfolioElements()
End Sub
```

The cmdGetMeOut_Click event calls the Clear() method of the Hashtable object myPortfolio, which removes all the elements from the library.

Step 12   Add the following code to the cmdListKeys_Click event:

```
Private Sub cmdListKeys_Click(ByVal sender As ...) Handles cmdListKeys.Click
    Dim enumerator As IDictionaryEnumerator = myPortfolio.GetEnumerator()
    txtPortfolio.Text = "PORTFOLIO KEYS:" & vbCrLf
    While enumerator.MoveNext()
        txtPortfolio.Text += enumerator.Key & vbCrLf
    End While
End Sub
```

Here we see the IDictionaryEnumerator at work, as we discussed in the example.

Step 13   Add the following code for the ListPortfolio-Elements() subroutine:

```
Private Sub ListPortfolioElements()
    Dim enumerator As IDictionaryEnumerator = myPortfolio.GetEnumerator()
    txtPortfolio.Text = "PORTFOLIO ELEMENTS:" & vbCrLf
    While enumerator.MoveNext()
        txtPortfolio.Text += enumerator.Value.ToString & vbCrLf
    End While
End Sub
```

Here again we see the IDictionaryEnumerator at work calling the ToString() method of each successive enumerator.Value.

Step 14   Add the following code for the ComputeDelta_Click event:

```
Private Sub ComputeDelta_Click(ByVal sender As ...) Handles _
                                              ComputeDelta.Click
    Dim enumerator As IDictionaryEnumerator = myPortfolio.GetEnumerator()
```

```
        Dim myDelta As Double = 0
        While enumerator.MoveNext()
            enumerator.Value.StockPrice() = Val(txtStockPrice.Text)
            enumerator.Value.Volatility() = Val(txtVolatility.Text)
            myDelta += (enumerator.Value.Quantity * enumerator.Value.Delta)
        End While
        txtDelta.Text = Format(myDelta * 100, "#.00")
End Sub
```

The portfolio delta calculation takes the individual option deltas times the number of contracts times 100 shares per contract to arrive at a portfolio delta.

Step 15   Run the program (see Figure 15.2).

F I G U R E 15.2

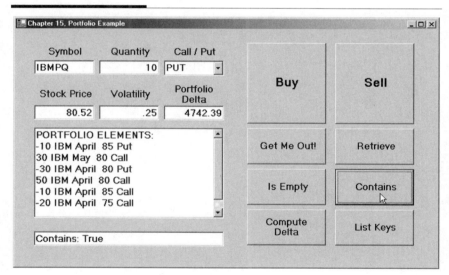

SUMMARY

In this brief chapter we have illustrated the use of a Hashtable object. Several classes, including hash tables, are defined in the System.Collections namespace. As you have seen, implementing collection objects greatly reduces the complexity of dealing with multiple objects of similar or even different types. In a later chapter we will create VB.NET applications that simulate placing buy and sell orders on real derivatives markets. As trades are "executed," you should think about how you can manage your portfolio of positions as a collection of objects. This will make the jump to calculating portfolio hedge ratios rather simple.

PROBLEMS

1. What is a hash table?
2. What are Queues and Stacks?
3. What is an IDictionaryEnumerator?
4. The properties of a CallOption differ from the fields in the OptionTrades and OptionContracts tables in the Options.mdb database. The process of converting the information in an object to another data structure is called mapping. How could we map an OptionTrades record in the database into a CallOption or PutOption object?
5. If our portfolio consisted of options on several different stocks, how could we keep track of the respective deltas?

PROJECT 15.1

The Windows application presented in the chapter example uses user inputs for stock price and volatility. Create a new VB.NET program that provides the same functionality, but connects to the Options.mdb database to retrieve the current bid as the stockprice and connects to the Finance.mdb database to calculate the historical volatility. You may use whatever time period you like to calculate volatility.

PROJECT 15.2

The Options.mdb databased contains information about several OptionTrades. Use this table to populate a portfolio object as in the chapter example.

Advanced VB.NET

Implementation

The world hates change, yet it is the only thing that has brought progress.

Charles F. Kettering

CHAPTER 16

Software Connectivity and Interoperability

As recently as 1990, the idea of automated trade execution was for the most part inconceivable. But today automated systems and electronic exchanges have completely redefined the industry. Without sophisticated technology, modern financial markets would cease to exist. Today global markets and global trading never stop. Opportunities come and go quickly, and trades must be sent in milliseconds. Securities and derivatives transactions have become instantaneous and inexpensive. As technology has evolved and will continue to evolve, it will completely redefine the tasks of traders. The only way for traders and firms to survive trading in the financial markets is through ever-better understanding of market processes and the use of ever-faster technology. Yesterday's trading ideas and technologies fade quickly. In the twenty-first century, real-time data is simply a raw material. Successful traders and trading firms will be the ones that develop the technological and analytic infrastructure to transform data into knowledge and then into action and then into continuously improving processes.

The rapid increase in the use of technology has made the trading of securities and derivatives more pervasive. It has freed markets and exchanges from their geographic boundaries and stimulated globalization. As more companies and instruments are listed for trading on electronic markets around the world, traders and trading firms will increasingly be seeking to get connected using legacy software and hardware ill-suited for the job, given the number and complexity of connections that will be needed.

Whatever the future holds, one thing is for sure: The ability of exchanges and trading firms to survive depends on the quality of their technology. The proliferation of live market feeds and the resulting tidal wave of data are increasing the complexity of the trading selection process and the architecture of trading technology. The new paradigm will necessitate open systems and application programming interfaces for connectivity and inter-operation. In other words, the future lies in middleware.

Middleware is a computing model that offers institutions a means to embrace the future of trading technology without destroying the foundation of systems created in the past. Large trading institutions often incorporate several disparate legacy systems for their front, middle, and back office, and as we will be able to see, the goals of straight-through processing (STP) and firmwide risk management are and will be severely hindered by the use of multiple systems. Middleware provides a solution.

Through the use of middleware, our trading systems can have the ability to back-test trading systems against historical data, assimilate real-time market information from a multiplicity of sources, perform complex quantitative calculations, scan the markets for profitable opportunities, place buy and sell orders automatically, and manage a portfolio of position and monitor risk. Through network connectivity and interoperation of software applications, automated trading systems can trade any instrument at anytime anywhere in the world.

Whether we realize it or not, virtually all software applications make requests to other programs to perform some tasks on their behalf. To accomplish the goals of market connectivity, of data transmission between disparate technologies, and of other higher-level quantitative processes, such as optimization, it will be necessary for our VB.NET applications to make requests to other software systems as well. This will largely be done through the use of application programming interfaces and, in the case of data transmission, XML. Some software applications, including some electronic exchanges, allow for connectivity and interoperation via both methods, APIs and XML. We will look at both over the next four chapters. Even within the Microsoft family of visual languages and even within Visual Basic itself, we will often confront issues relating to interoperability of systems, particularly in legacy systems using Component Object Model (COM) objects.

APPLICATION PROGRAMMING INTERFACES

In short, a software application's API defines the proper way for other applications to interact with and request services from it. In the trading industry, APIs facilitate the exchange of data between different software applications and will provide for interoperability between financial industry software packages and our own software built in VB.NET. Through APIs we are able to integrate multiple commercial off-the-shelf (COTS) software products with our own proprietary software to create customized trading and risk management systems—and at a fraction of the cost of developing a complete system from the ground up. APIs allow us to create a kind of middleware that shares data across different trading platforms and networks. Most, if not all, software packages that you will encounter as a financial engineer will have APIs that either are a free bundled part of their software package itself or are separately licensed packages available for a fee.

An API is a set of rules for writing function calls or instantiating objects that access function definitions or classes in a library, usually in the form of a .dll file. Programs we create that use these functions or classes can communicate with the COTS software to, for example, run an optimization routine, exchange information such as market data feeds, process buy and sell transactions, and post trade fill information to a database. Once we have created objects based upon the classes in the library, the API classes do all the work for us, totally transparent to our application. In addition to performing data-sharing tasks, APIs usually check network parameters and error conditions for us so as to deliver robust interoperation between the programs.

As opposed to fully open source code, which exposes the software maker's proprietary methods, APIs represent a stream-lined way to grant access to an application without giving away intellectual property. APIs grant less access than open source code but certainly more than entirely closed software.

Among financial markets COTS software, APIs exist in many different forms. You should fully understand the implementation of the API, contained in the software vendor's API documentation, before you proceed.

EXCHANGE APPLICATION PROGRAMMING INTERFACES

The major exchanges all have APIs to which developers can write to create market data feed and order routing applications. Writing to an exchange API, or alternatively to the FIX interface, and building proprietary software from the ground up requires a healthy amount of research, time, and money. As was discussed in Chapter 1, for most small firms this is not a feasible option for building automated trading systems. However, we can gain a somewhat greater understanding of market connectively and electronic exchange order routing if we briefly look at three exchange APIs.

The Chicago Board Options Exchange offers an API through which developers can access the CBOE's Electronic Trading System. The CBOE also supports the FIX messages for the purposes of order routing. This FIX interface is available as an alternative to connection through the API.

The all-electronic International Securities Exchange (ISE) offers an API to which member firms can program to access market data, send trades, and receive trade fill confirmations and information. Through this API, the ISE's electronic access members and market makers can develop applications for automated trading purposes or for back-office systems.

The Chicago Mercantile Exchange has the Globex system, which contains open APIs for market data and order routing so that trading firms can write applications to receive real-time market data from and place automated orders on the CME's electronic markets.

As we have seen previously, firms involved in trading on multiple markets will need to connect to multiple APIs for market data and order entry. And every exchange API is different. Furthermore, to add to the complexity, in most cases applications developed to interact with an exchange's API must be approved by the exchange itself. Fortunately several third-party developers have written customized applications to the respective exchange APIs for market data and execution of securities, futures, and options trades. We will look at how to connect to two of these COTS software applications in Chapter 17.

COM INTEROPERATION

As we have seen in Chapter 10, in order to create VB.NET code that requests services from an external component, we must first add a reference to it. The components can be of the following types:

- .NET class libraries
- COM components
- XML web services

We have, up till now, looked only at .NET class libraries. Although the new .NET libraries and assemblies are now a much-improved model for development, at times we need to make use of COM objects. .NET applications may someday replace COM ones, but until then, if we need to use a COM object in a VB.NET application, we will need to understand something about COM itself and how it differs from the .NET Framework.

COM is a Microsoft specification used prior to .NET that controls library usage and compatibility and communication. Through COM, objects are exposed and their functionality is available to other applications. Via COM, libraries are ensured to be highly organized and reusable. Microsoft defined COM so that developers could create compatible libraries of classes and components. Virtually all Windows libraries that were constructed prior to the advent of the .NET Framework adhere to the COM specification, and most software today includes COM objects. But COM is difficult to program and deploy because developers must guarantee that new COM components are compatible. If a COM library is placed on a system without being properly registered, applications will be unable to find or use the library.

An understanding of COM involves an understanding of how COM objects exist in memory. Whereas .NET objects are held in managed memory, which is controlled by CLR (the common language run time), COM objects are held in unmanaged memory. The CLR in .NET manages certain tasks such as dynamic memory allocation and type checking. VB.NET uses managed code, but we can access the unmanaged COM code using interoperability assemblies. Many companies have invested significant amounts of time and effort into creating COM components but now find themselves eager for a migration to .NET. Fortunately Microsoft created tools for integrating legacy systems and COM components into .NET Framework implementations.

The .NET Framework provides for direct interaction between objects in managed and unmanaged memory. These tools enable interoperability with COM so that we can use existing COM objects in our VB.NET programs. This process is known within the .NET Framework as COM interop.

VB.NET uses an interoperability assembly to find COM methods and translate data between the .NET and COM types. This translation is performed by the run-time callable wrapper (RCW), which is created by .NET based upon the information in an object's interop assembly. As we discussed in Chapter 10, assemblies are collections of functionality usually in the form of classes contained in one or several files with their assembly manifest. Assembly manifests perform the same function in .NET as type libraries do in COM components. They include information about version numbering, constituent files, types and resources, compile-time dependencies, and permissions.

The RCW controls the COM object and carries out communication between .NET and COM code. When we create an instance of a COM object in VB.NET, we are really creating a new instance of the RCW of the object. Fortunately for VB.NET developers, the communication between an RCW and its COM object is completely transparent to us. So we can create and interact with COM objects as if they were .NET objects. Adding references to COM objects is the same as in previous incarnations of Visual Basic except that .NET adds the creation of this interop assembly to the process. References to the COM object properties and methods in VB.NET are routed to the interop assembly prior to proceeding to the actual COM object code. On the way back, responses are routed first to the interop assembly and before being forwarded back to calling code in .NET.

Should the need arise, we can create new COM objects in VB.NET by using the .NET Framework's COM class template, which can create a new class and configures the project so as to generate the COM class and register it with the operating system. COM objects referenced via interop assemblies must be registered, which we accomplish by using the Regsvr32 utility included with all Windows operating systems. If you are familiar with VB 6.0, you are aware that ActiveX controls are commonly used COM components. Through the interop assembly, we can import ActiveX controls into our .NET IDE toolbox using the Customize Toolbox option, which will list all the COM components that are registered with the operating system. We are then free to use the ActiveX control in our VB.NET application. .NET Framework components do not need to be registered since .NET components maintain all of their type identification information internally.

In Visual Basic .NET, adding references to COM objects that have type libraries is similar to doing so in previous versions of Visual Basic. However, Visual Basic .NET adds the creation of an interop assembly to the procedure. References to the members of the COM object are routed to the interop assembly and then forwarded to the actual COM object. Responses from the COM object are routed to the interop assembly and forwarded to your .NET application. If, for example, the input argument and return values of a COM object's properties and methods use different data types than .NET does, a process called interop marshaling converts equivalent data types as they flow back and forth between COM objects. In fact all .NET programs share a set of common types that permit interoperability of objects, regardless of the programming language.

While COM objects have been the foundation of Visual Basic applications for many years, .NET applications designed for CLR offer many advantages. In the .NET framework, COM components are no longer necessary. Through the use of assembly manifests, .NET components hold on to the benefits of COM while solving many of its inherent problems.

SUMMARY

The financial markets of the twenty-first century require connectivity and interoperability of disparate hardware and software systems. The use of APIs and XML will enable software we create in VB.NET to connect and exchange information with other systems. Furthermore, even within Visual Basic itself there are interoperability issues to confront, particularly those pertaining to legacy systems making use of COM components.

PROBLEMS

1. What is middleware?
2. What is an API?
3. Rather than connecting to exchange APIs ourselves, what is our alternative for creating automated trading systems?
4. What is COM?
5. What is an RCW?

Connecting to Trading Software

An important problem to solve when developing automated trading or risk management systems is market connectivity. Connecting to live electronic markets is no small task. Millions of dollars and literally years of time can be spent building such a system from the ground up. However, we can substantially reduce the amount of up-front time and expense needed to establish a connection to a market by licensing third-party software that already provides the required functionality. What's more, most of these software packages already connect to more than one market, sometimes dozens of them, around the world enabling traders, or financial engineers, to be active in multiple markets simultaneously. More often than not, this kind of third-party software will include an API that we can write to in VB.NET.

These APIs usually exist in a single .dll library file or a set of .dll files. These libraries contain classes that enable us to connect to the licensed COTS software. When we create objects based upon the classes in such a library, we can use the functionality provided by these objects to interact with the software and subsequently pass data back and forth. Such functionality might include getting live, real-time market quotes, placing buy and sell orders, or receiving trade fill confirmations.

Rather than require that you license some of this commercial software yourself, we have provided two libraries on the CD, called Trader API.dll and OptionsAPI.dll.

CONNECTING TO A FUTURES MARKET

The classes in the TraderAPI.dll library allow us to simulate a connection to a popular industry software package from Trading Technologies, Inc., called X_Trader. Trading Technologies, Inc. (TT) develops high-performance derivatives trading software including the X_TRADER product, which provides professional traders with connectivity to electronic derivatives markets around the world. Furthermore, the X_TRADER application contains an API consisting of 10 classes that financial engineers can instantiate for the purposes of developing, among other things, automated analytics, order entry, and trade fill information processing systems. However, you do not need to license X_Trader to use the TraderAPI.dll library included on the CD.

As we said, by creating objects from the classes in TraderAPI.dll, we achieve the goal of market connectivity, albeit simulated. As a result, a VB.NET program that adds a reference to TraderAPI.dll and instantiates the objects in it can see the "real-time" market price movements of the S&P 500 eMini futures market, can place market buy and sell orders, and can receive trade fill confirmations.

TraderAPI.dll can be used to create applications to customize order entry screens, monitor live fill feeds, perform live profit and loss calculations, and automatically execute trades based upon outside conditions and customized algorithms. While providing only a subset of all the possible functionalities, TraderAPI.dll will give our programs the look and feel of connecting to real markets through TT's X_Trader API. While APIs are always changing and being upgraded, we have, in every way possible, tried to make the architecture of TraderAPI.dll mimic the API that comes with X_TRADER.

The TraderAPI.dll file included with this book uses the same classes, method calls, and methodology, albeit somewhat abbreviated in functionality, as if you were in a real-life environment using the X_TRADER API. TraderAPI.dll contains five classes that simulate a portion of the X_TRADER API's functionality. The five classes are:

TraderAPI Classes	Description
InstrObj	A tradable object
InstrNotify	Must be attached to an InstrObj so when the instrument changes, messages can be sent
OrderProfile	Contains all order information for submission
OrderSet	Represents a subset of orders on this machine
FillObj	Stores all information about each fill

InstrObj Class

An InstrObj object represents a tradable object, that is, an instrument. If we want to receive prices or submit orders, we must create an InstrObj object. Attaching an InstrNotify object to an InstrObj object will allow us to receive price updates as they occur. To create an active InstrObj object, we must supply values for the Exchange, ProdType, Product, and Contract properties. Here are the public properties and methods associated with the InstrObj class.

Public Properties	Description
Contract	Contract identifier
Exchange	Gateway used by the instrument
ProdType	Product type of the instrument
Product	Product name of the instrument

Public Methods	Description
CreateNotifyObject()	Creates a notification object for the instrument
GetData()	Returns the current values of properties identified by parameter string
Open()	Establishes a connection to the instrument

InstrNotify Class

An InstrNotify object, which is attached to an InstrObj object, alerts our application when some aspect, namely the price, of an InstrObj changes. If we want to monitor a price feed for an instrument, we must create an InstrNotify object. To create an InstrNotify object, we must use the InstrObj object's CreateNotifyObject() method.

```
Dim myInstrument as New InstrObj()
Dim myInstrNotifyObj = New myInstrument.CreateNotifyObject()
```

Public Event	Description
OnNotifyFound()	Fires when a connection to the instrument is established

OrderProfile Class

An OrderProfile object contains the information needed for order submission. An OrderProfile uses an OrderSet object to actually send an order. The public properties and methods are listed here:

Public Properties	Description
BuySell	Buys or sells
GetPrice	Returns the price of an instrument
GetProduct	Returns the product name of an instrument
Instrument	Instrument to be traded
Price	Order price
Quantity	Order quantity

Public Methods	Description
SetTradeParams()	Market orders only; TraderAPI.dll does not support limit orders
SetTradeType()	Sets the trade type

OrderSet Class

An OrderSet object is used to submit orders. An OrderSet receives the order information from an OrderProfile object and then sends the order. Characteristics include the following:

Public Properties	Description
EnableOrderAutoDelete	Deletes all orders in the OrderSet
EnableOrderFillData	Returns all the fill information
EnableOrderSend	Orders send status

Public Methods	Description
Open()	Opens the order set. Default is not open
SendOrder()	Submits an order to the exchange
SetLimits()	Sets OrderSet limits

Public Event	Description
OnOrderFillData()	Fires when a fill has been received

FillObj Class

TraderAPI creates a new FillObj when it is notified of a new fill. The OrderSet's OnOrderFillData event will receive a fill object as an input argument. It's characterized by this public method:

Public Method	Description
GetFillInfo()	Returns the current values of the fill object

In our VB.NET applications, we can add a reference to the TraderAPI.dll file, import it, and instantiate objects based upon the classes in the library. In this way, we can "connect to the market" to get a simulated data feed, place buy and sell orders, and receive trade fill information. Again, TraderAPI.dll is a stripped-down version of TT's X_Trader API and provides only basic functionality, but it will give you the look and feel of creating real automated trading software.

Let's create a program that connects to the market in the eMini S&P 500 futures contracts traded on the Chicago Mercantile Exchange.

Step 1 Start a new Windows application named PriceFeed.

Step 2 To your Form1, add five labels in a row.

Step 3 In the Projects menu tab, select Add Reference. Select Browse and find the TraderAPI.dll file. In the code window, above the class definition for Form1, add:

```
Imports TraderAPI
```

Step 4 To get a price feed, we need to set up an InstrObj object and an InstNotify object. In the general declarations section of the Form1 code window, add the following code:

```
Private WithEvents InstNoti As InstrNotify
Dim Inst1 As InstrObj
```

Step 5 Also we will need an array of strings to receive the quote information. Add the code to declare and instantiate an array of strings in the general declarations section:

```
Dim MyData As String() = New String() {}
```

Step 6 In the form load event, add the code to create the objects and open the connection with the Chicago Mercantile Exchange for the eMini S&P 500 contract for December 2003. This will require setting the four properties of the InstrObj object.

```
Private Sub Form1_Load(ByVal sender As ...) Handles MyBase.Load
        Inst1 = New InstrObj()
        InstNoti = Inst1.CreateNotifyObj()
        Inst1.Exchange = "CME-S"      ' Setup gateway name
        Inst1.Product = "ES"          ' Setup Product name
        Inst1.ProdType = "FUTURE"     ' Setup Product type
        Inst1.Contract = "Dec03"      ' Setup Expiry information
        Inst1.Open()                  ' Open/access the instrument
End Sub
```

Step 7 The InstrNotify object has an event, OnNotify-Found(), that fires when the price of the instrument object changes. When this happens, we want to retrieve the new bid and ask prices, the bid and ask quantities, and the last price. Add the following event handler for the OnNotifyFound() event in the Form1 code window:

```
Private Sub InstNoti_OnNotifyFound(ByRef pInstr As InstrObj) _
                Handles InstNoti.OnNotifyFound
    MyData = pInstr.GetData("BidQty,Bid,Ask,AskQty,Last")
    Label1.Text = MyData(0)
    Label2.Text = MyData(1)
    Label3.Text = MyData(2)
    Label4.Text = MyData(3)
    Label5.Text = MyData(4)
End Sub
```

Step 8 Run the program. You should see the form window populated with a simulated moving market—with a moving bid and offer, moving quantities, and last prices hitting the bid and offer. See Figure 17.1.

Now let's add the ability to place some orders and get back trade fill confirmations.

Step 9 To place orders, we will need an OrderSet object and an OrderProfile object. In the general declarations section of the Form1 code window, add:

```
Dim WithEvents LiveOrderSet As OrderSet
Dim CurOrdProf As OrderProfile
```

F I G U R E 17.1

Bid Qty	Bid Price	Ask Price	Ask Qty	Last
430	999.87	999.89	50	999.87

Step 10 To the Form1_Load event, add the following code to create the OrderSet object and enable orders to be sent:

```
LiveOrderSet = New OrderSet()
LiveOrderSet.EnableOrderFillData = True
LiveOrderSet.EnableOrderAutoDelete = False
LiveOrderSet.SetLimits("NetLimits", False)
LiveOrderSet.EnableOrderSend = True
LiveOrderSet.Open()
```

Step 11 Add two buttons to your form. Change the text properties to say "Buy" and "Sell," respectively. In the Button Click events, add the following code:

```
Private Sub Button1_Click(ByVal sender As ...) Handles Button1.Click
    SendOrder("Buy")
End Sub
Private Sub Button2_Click(ByVal sender As ...) Handles Button2.Click
    SendOrder("Sell")
End Sub
```

Step 12 In the form code window, add the following subroutine called SendOrder():

```
Private Sub SendOrder(ByVal BuySell As String)
    CurOrdProf = New OrderProfile()
    Dim intSent As Integer
    CurOrdProf.Instrument = Inst1
    CurOrdProf.SetTradeType("M2", "L")
    CurOrdProf.SetTradeParams(BuySell, 1, "Market")
    intSent = LiveOrderSet.SendOrder(CurOrdProf)
    CurOrdProf = Nothing
End Sub
```

The SendOrder() subroutine creates an order profile, sets the Instrument property, and calls the SetTradeType() and SetTradeParams() methods. In the code above, we are sending a quantity of one contract. Later, when you become a more accomplished trader, we will allow you to trade larger amounts. Finally, we send the order by calling the SendOrder() method of the OrderSet object.

Our method of handling the trade fill confirmations that come back to us from the market will be to simply print them out in a message box.

Step 13 Add the following subroutine to handle the OnOrderFillData() event associated with the OrderSet object:

```
Private Sub LiveOrderSet_OnOrderFillData(ByRef my FillObj As FillObj) _
                              Handles LiveOrderSet.OnOrderFillData

    Dim strFillData As String()
    strFillData = myFillObj.GetFillInfo("Contract,BuySell,NetQty,Price")
    MsgBox(strFillData(0) & " " & strFillData(1) & " " & _
        strFillData(2) & " @ " & strFillData(3), , "TradeFilled")

End Sub
```

Step 14 Run the program. The results are shown in Figure 17.2.

On the CD you will find a program named TotalAPI, which shows the full functionality of the TraderAPI.dll together with a DataSet and a DataGrid to list trade fill confirmations. In addition to taking a look at the code, you can feel free to test your trading acumen using this program.

F I G U R E 17.2

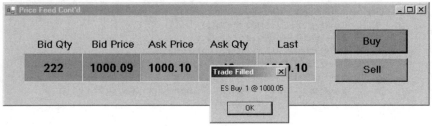

CONNECTING TO AN OPTIONS MARKET

The classes in the OptionsAPI.dll library allow us to simulate a connection to a popular options industry software package from MicroHedge, Inc. (MH). MH develops high-end equity options trading and analytics software that provides professional market makers and traders with a wealth of high-level option portfolio analytics and risk management tools. MH's flexible design, which includes a robust COM wrapper, enables efficient interoperation with third-party software systems like the one we will build in this chapter. As a result, trading institutions often use MicroHedge as a foundation on which they create proprietary systems.

With MH's Screen Based Trading (SBT) software suite, automated market analysis and order selection are greatly simplified through the use of its API, which consists of dozens of classes. Furthermore, SBT users can send orders to any of the major U.S. options exchanges, the NYSE, and AMEX, as well as several ECNs. Through the MH software developer's kit (SDK) and SBT, market makers create a single software application to autoquote markets, manage risk, and employ custom models. As another example of SBT flexibility, options traders can set implied volatility curves with one of twenty different calculations, analyze their portfolio risk under a multiplicity of "what-if" scenarios, and monitor the national best bids and offers.

As we discussed in Chapter 1, it is extremely important to realize that most, if not all, of the options exchanges prohibit automated order entry in their bylaws. There must be human intervention and trade approval at some point along the way to entering an order. We will demonstrate this functionality in the example program. As with the futures example, you do not need to license MicroHedge software in order to use the OptionsAPI.dll library included on the CD.

By creating objects from the classes in Options API.dll, we can achieve the goal of options market connectivity, albeit simulated and very stripped down. Options analytics requires a huge piece of software, which MicroHedge is, and we will be able to only demonstrate the simplest functionality. In any case, a VB.NET program that adds a reference to OptionsAPI.dll and instantiates the objects in it can monitor "real-time" price movements of the

S&P 500 options market, can place market buy and sell orders, and can receive trade fill confirmations.

OptionsAPI.dll can be used to gain practice creating applications to customize order entry screens, monitor live fill feeds, perform live profit and loss calculations, and execute trades based upon outside conditions and customized algorithms. While providing only a very small subset of all the possible functionalities, OptionsAPI.dll will give our programs the look and feel of connecting to real options markets through MicroHedge's API. The architecture of OptionsAPI.dll attempts to mimic the SBT API that you can license from MicroHedge.

The OptionsAPI.dll file included with this book uses the same classes, method calls, and methodology (although again they are abbreviated in functionality) as if you were in a real-life environment using the MH SBT API. As we said, OptionsAPI.dll contains classes that simulate a portion of the SBT API's functionality. Here are the classes included in the OptionsAPI.dll file:

OptionsAPI Classes	Description
MicroHedge	An instance of MicroHedge
MHSBT	An instance of Screen-Based Trading
CBOEorder	A CBOE option order
IndexOp	An index option instrument
MHposition	A position in MicroHedge

In our VB.NET applications, we can add a reference to the OptionsAPI.dll file, import it, and instantiate objects based upon the classes in the library. In this way we can "connect to the market" to monitor market quotes, place buy and sell orders, and receive trade fill information. Again, OptionsAPI.dll is a stripped-down version of MH's SBT API and provides only basic functionality, but it will give you the look and feel of creating real trading software.

Let's create a program that connects to the market in the S&P 500 options contracts traded on the Chicago Board Options Exchange.

Step 1   Start a new VB.NET Windows application named OptionOrders.

Step 2   To your Form1, add a single text box and a button. Change the Multiline property of the text box to True.

Step 3   In the Projects menu tab, select Add Reference. Select browse and find the OptionsAPI.dll file. In the code window, above the class definition for Form1, add:

```
Imports OptionsAPI
```

Step 4   To get market prices, we need to set up objects for the MicroHedge, MHSBT, and MHPosition classes. In the general declarations section of the Form1 code window, add the following code:

```
Public WithEvents mhApp As MicroHedge
Public WithEvents myMHSBT As MHSBT
Dim Pos As MHPosition
```

Step 5   In the form load event, add the code to create instances of the objects

```
Private Sub Form1_Load(ByVal sender As ...) Handles MyBase.Load
    myMHSBT = New MHSBT()
    mhApp = New MicroHedge()
    Pos = mhApp.GetSymbol("SPY.TEST", True, False)
End Sub
```

Because MicroHedge is actually a COM object, we would in the real world use the CreateObject() function to create an instance of "MicroHedge.Application" in the following way:

```
mhApp = CreateObject("MicroHedge.Application")
```

However, in our simulated environment where we may not have MicroHedge licensed software, we will use the method for instantiation as shown. COM objects use something called unmanaged code, which lacks the benefits of VB.NET's common language run time. But it should not prevent you from creating efficient applications in VB.NET. Since a certain amount of complexity is involved in mixing the VB.NET code with COM objects, we suggest you contact MicroHedge if you intend to use a .NET platform for development.

Step 6   To the Button1_Click event, add the following code:

```
Private Sub Button1_Click(ByVal sender As ...) Handles Button1.Click
    GetQuotes()
End Sub
```

The method for accessing options data is significantly different from what we looked at for futures data. In the previous example using TT and futures, we connected to the market for a single instrument and were able to see the market in real time. In this options example, however, we want to monitor several or maybe hundreds of option contracts at the same time. This will necessitate looping through the contracts and refreshing the data at specified intervals. In this case the data will refresh, GetQuotes(), when the user clicks the button.

> **Step 7**   Add the following code for the GetQuotes() function. For simplicity's sake, the OptionsAPI program will only show data for 20 call options on the SPY. The price of the underlying index is approximately 841.00 and will not move.

```
Private Sub GetQuotes()
    Dim i As Integer
    Dim cBid, cAsk, cThv, cSym, Days, Strike As Object
    cBid = Pos.OptionPairs.FieldArray("cBid")
    cAsk = Pos.OptionPairs.FieldArray("cAsk")
    cThv = Pos.OptionPairs.FieldArray("cThv")
    cSym = Pos.OptionPairs.FieldArray("cSym")
    Days = Pos.OptionPairs.FieldArray("Days")
    Strike = Pos.OptionPairs.FieldArray("Strike")
    TextBox1.Text = "SYMBOL" & vbTab & " BID" & vbTab & _
                    " ASK" & vbTab & "THEO" & vbCrLf & vbCrLf
    For i = 0 To 19
        TextBox1.Text &= cSym(i) & vbTab & Format(cBid(i), "##.00") & _
                        vbTab & Format(cAsk(i), "##.00") & vbTab & _
                        Format(cThv(i), "##.00") & vbCrLf
    Next i
End Sub
```

Here the GetQuotes() function retrieves the bid, ask, theoretical value, symbol, days till expiration, and strike every time it is called. Furthermore it prints the information into TextBox1.

> **Step 8**   Run the program. You should see the form window, similar to Figure 17.3, populated with simulated market data when you click the button. The data is not live, however, and will not change. Click the button again and you will see that the markets do change slightly with each refresh.

F I G U R E   17.3

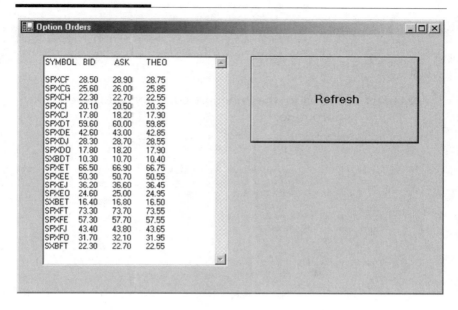

Now let's add the ability to place some orders and get back trade fill confirmations.

Step 9   To place orders, we will need to specify a quantity. In the general declarations section of the Form1 code window, add:

```
Const QUANT As Integer = 10
```

Step 10   In the GetQuotes() functions, add the following code. This code will loop through the market bids and offers and place orders, using the EnterOrder() subroutine, to buy orders when the ask price is 10 cents below the theoretical value and to sell orders when the bid is 10 cents above the theoretical value:

```
For i = 0 To 19
    TextBox1.Text &= cSym(i) & vbTab & Format(cBid(i), "##.00") & _
                vbTab & Format(cAsk(i), "##.00") & vbTab & _
                Format(cThv(i), "##.00") & vbCrLf
    If cAsk(i) + 0.1 < cThv(i) Then
        EnterOrder(Month(DateAdd("d", Days(i), #3/1/2003#)), _
```

```
                    Year(DateAdd("d", Days(i), #3/1/2003#)), cSym(i), _
                    Strike(i), cAsk(i), QUANT)
        ElseIf cBid(i) - 0.1 > cThv(i) Then
            EnterOrder(Month(DateAdd("d", Days(i), #3/1/2003#)), _
                    Year(DateAdd("d", Days(i), #3/1/2003#)), cSym(i), _
                    Strike(i), cBid(i), -QUANT)
        End If
    Next i
```

Step 11 Now add the function code for the EnterOrder() subroutine:

```
Private Sub EnterOrder( ByVal ExMonth As Integer, _
                        ByVal ExYear As Integer, _
                        ByVal OPRA As String, _
                        ByVal Strike As Double, _
                        ByVal Price As Double, _
                        ByVal Quant As Long)
    Dim Inst As New IndexOp()
    Dim CBOEOrd As New CBOEorder()
    Inst.ExpyMonth = ExMonth
    Inst.ExpyYear = ExYear
    Inst.OpenClose = 1                              'Open
    Inst.CoverNaked = 2                             'Naked
    Inst.Root = Microsoft.VisualBasic.Left(OPRA, 3)
    Inst.Strike = Strike
    Inst.Underlier = Pos.SYMBOL
    Inst.CallPut = 1                                'Call
    CBOEOrd.OrdPrice = Price
    CBOEOrd.OrdQty = Math.Abs(Quant)
    CBOEOrd.Account = Pos.Account
    CBOEOrd.Duration = 1                            'Day
    CBOEOrd.Instrument = Inst
    CBOEOrd.PriceType = 2                           'Limit
    If Quant > 0 Then
        CBOEOrd.Side = 1
    Else
        CBOEOrd.Side = 2
    End If
    myMHSBT.PlaceOrder(CBOEOrd)
End Sub
```

The EnterOrder() subroutine creates an index option object, IndexOp, and a CBOEorder object and sets the values necessary to send an order. In this example, we are sending a quantity of 10 contracts. As you will be able to see, though, an order of 10 contracts can grow into a position of 50 or 100 contracts quickly if the market price does not come back into line with the theoretical value. Applications that you build will need to devise a way to handle these situations from a portfolio perspective.

Step 12 In order to receive trade fill confirmations, add the following event handler:

```
Private Sub myMHSBT_OrderEvent(ByVal Order As CBOEorder) _
                                         Handles myMHSBT.OrderEvent
        MsgBox('Filled: " & Order.ToString)
End Sub
```

Our method of handling the trade fill confirmations that come back to us from the market will be to simply print them out in a message box.

Step 13 Run the program. Figure 17.4 shows the results.

Now let's add a timer, so that the data refreshes automatically without a button click.

Step 14 Remove Button1 and the Button1_Click event routine. In the toolbox you will find a Timer control. Add a timer control to your Form1. In the

F I G U R E 17.4

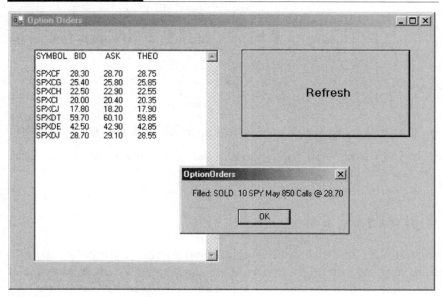

F I G U R E   17.5

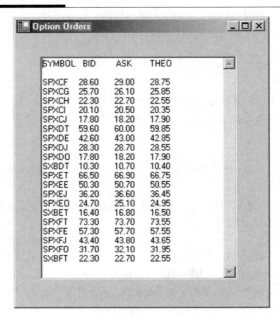

Properties window for Timer1, set the Enabled property to True and the Interval property to 5000. Add the following code to the Timer1_Tick event routine:

```
Private Sub Timer1_Tick(ByVal sender As ...) Handles Timer1.Tick
    GetQuotes()
End Sub
```

Step 15   Run the program. Figure 17.5 shows the results.

The timer will tick every 5 seconds and refresh the data. Trades will execute as before.

SUMMARY

In this chapter we have looked at two methods for connecting to real markets through connections to the APIs of two popular financial industry software packages. Building software for

monitoring real-time prices, performing analytics, and monitoring trade fills and portfolio risk are absolutely necessary for implementation of an automated trading system. Several of these key components may already be present in COTS software. APIs allow for proprietary analytics to be built on top of these systems.

You should contact the software provider for full documentation of its API before attempting to build a trading system. The documentation will have all the information on the classes and their functionalities in the API along with sample programs.

PROBLEMS

1. What is the rule regarding automated order entry of options orders?
2. What is the problem situation with options order entry that we need to resolve?
3. If the COTS application is a COM object, what would you do?
4. What is the process for creating objects out of the classes in an API?
5. Where can you find out more about the objects in an API?

PROJECT 17.1

Create a single VB.NET application that connects to both the S&P 500 eMini market on the CME and the S&P 500 cash options market on the CBOE using the TraderAPI and the OptionsAPI libraries.

PROJECT 17.2

To the program in Project 17.1, add a Portfolio object that keeps track of the instruments bought and sold and the net positions. This will require the use of the StockOption class, the CallOption class, and a Futures class, which you will need to create yourself.

XML

Over the last 5 or so years, the ever-increasing demand for flexibility in application messaging has spawned the Extensible Markup Language (XML). XML is a fully portable and open markup syntax for data description and messaging. Further, beyond being just a markup language, XML is a metalanguage—a language used to define new markup languages. Whereas Hypertext Markup Language (HTML) is used for formatting and displaying data, XML allows users to represent the contextual meaning of the data they wish to model using human readable tags.

In this chapter we will cover the basics of XML notation as well as ways to describe and encapsulate data in an XML document, also called an XML message. In addition, we will go over how to write VB.NET programs that encapsulate data in XML messages and how to send them over the Internet. While only skimming the surface of XML, this chapter will give you the knowledge and the context you need to use XML in your VB.NET programs.

XML AND FINANCIAL MARKETS

The ultimate goal of developing firmwide, real-time global positioning systems that exploit profitable trading opportunities and manage risk will require a much higher degree of interconnectivity between departments within a firm, trading counterparties, and exchanges than exists today. As a result, institutions involved in the financial markets have caught on to

XML as a way to move large quantities of data in real time between different technology systems. Financial markets, firms, and professionals who utilize XML find it to be a powerful tool for financial data representation and messaging and see it as the key technology in meeting the challenges of global interconnectivity (Bradley, 2002).

Because XML is a metalanguage, segments of the financial markets industry have already been able to create their own markup languages specifically for their own domains. In addition to learning the technology of XML in this chapter, we will be able to see some of the business reasons why financial institutions are so keen on developing XML-based technologies, even to the point of inventing their own customized markup languages using XML. In the following chapter, we will look at some specific XML technologies used in the financial markets and create programs in a new industry XML protocol called FIXML.

CREATING A MARKUP LANGUAGE

As we mentioned, XML allows us to represent the contextual meaning of the data we wish to describe and transmit. This is done through the definition of customized tags. As long as the application that sends an XML message and the application that receives it agree on what these tags mean, they can communicate and exchange data. If you are not familiar with markup languages, this idea of inventing or defining our own tags may seem somewhat vague. So let's take a quick look at an example.

Imagine for a minute that we could invent our own markup language for describing a trade. What kind of tags might we want to invent, and how would an XML document written with these tags look? Intuitively, we would first probably describe the information structure of a trade:

Trade Information

Exchange
Ticker symbol
Buy/sell
Quantity
Price

Trade Information

Clearing firm
Trader
Time
Etc.

Now that we have listed the information about a trade, let's define a markup language using XML tags to describe it and then rewrite our trade in that language. We will call our new markup language FMML—the Financial Markets Markup Language, pronounced "fimmel." In the same way that a variable in VB.NET should be named using a naming convention, which describes the data held in the variable, our FMML tags should represent the contextual meaning of the data being held.

So the tag for a trade should probably be named < Trade > . The tag for the exchange name should probably be < Exchange > . And so on. Simple, right? It is exactly this simplicity that makes XML so popular. It is a completely intuitive way to describe data. Before we go ahead and write our trade using these tags, we must consider one more thing. It may be possible that a FMML document representing a trade may at times consist of more than one trade. For example, we may want to describe a spread trade, which would have two legs. So we will need a root tag, or a root element, within which we can place a trade or trades. Let's call our root element <Tradedoc> for trade document.

Now we are ready to describe our trade in XML using our FMML tags.

```xml
<?xml version='1.0' ?>
<Tradedoc>
<Trade>
   <Exchange Acronym='FMEX'/>
   <Ticker>IBMDP</Ticker>
   <BuySell Type='Buy'/>
   <Quantity>10</Quantity>
   <Price Type='Market'/>
   <ClearingFirm>001</ClearingFirm>
   <Trader>Ben</Trader>
   <Time>3/6/2003 1:45:06 PM</Time>
</Trade>
</Tradedoc>
```

Again, so far we have simply invented our own markup tags that represent the contextual meaning of the data in a trade. Let's take a closer look at the rules of XML using this particular document or message, which is written in FMML, because the rules of XML are very strict.

On the CD a file named sampleXML.xml contains the XML message shown above. Double-clicking on this file will cause it to open in MS Internet Explorer (see Figure 18.1. Well-formed XML documents such as this one will successfully open in Internet Explorer. XML documents that are not well formed will generate an error statement in the Internet Explorer window. Fortunately the XML document we created is both well formed and valid.

F I G U R E 18.1

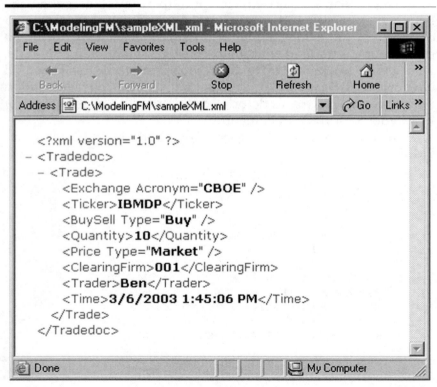

Well-Formed XML Documents

Every XML document must be well formed. A well-formed XML document follows all the structural rules for XML, and make no mistake, XML definitely does not allow ambiguous structure. This is because part of the information contained in an XML message has to do with how different elements relate to one another. If the structure is ambiguous, so is the information. A clean and consistent structure is what allows XML documents to be processed as data structures or trees, as we will briefly describe later. Programs that intend to process XML, called parsers, will reject any message that does not follow the structural rules for being well formed. Among the most important rules are that XML is case-sensitive and that unclosed tags and overlapping tags are not permitted.

Every start tag must have a corresponding end tag. The start tag begins an enclosed area of text, known as an item, according to the tag name. <Ticker> is a start tag. </Ticker> is an end tag. The element, defined by a tag, ends with the end tag. As we will point out later, XML tags may also include one of a list of attributes consisting of an attribute name and an attribute value.

A tag that opens inside another tag must close before the containing tag closes. For example, take a look at this sequence:

```
<ClearingFirm>001<Trader>Ben</ClearingFirm>
</Trader>
```

Obviously this XML message is not well formed because <Trader> opens inside <ClearingFirm> but does not close prior to the closing tag </ClearingFirm>. Put differently, the structure of an XML document must be strictly hierarchical.

Assuming a particular XML message is, in fact, well formed, we can turn our attention to whether or not it is valid. Just because an XML document is well formed does not mean it is valid. Making sure our XML document is well formed is only half the battle. The other half is validation.

Valid XML Documents

When the XML tags in a well-formed document are queried for their meanings, we say the document is being validated. A well-formed XML message simply means that it has met all the syntax requirements, whereas a valid XML message means that both the sending and receiving parties are able to correctly identify the document's content according to an agreed-upon set of tag definitions.

Earlier in the chapter, we defined XML as a syntax, because it is not truly a programming language. It is a plain markup language; we developers make up the tags and the definitions associated with those tags. The set of tag names that we came up with to describe a trade we gave the name FMML. In this way FMML can be thought of as a dialect of the XML language. FMML is a specific set of XML tags with their respective meanings.

Eventually, if we intend to transmit our FMML trade document to another application over a network or over the Internet, we will need to make sure that the tag names are used correctly with respect to our FMML definition. That is, we must speak the dialect correctly. We could not, for example, use a tag names <ExpMonth>, because it is not part of FMML as we defined it. Furthermore the application that receives our FMML message must be able to understand the FMML dialect as well. As long as the receiver of our message understands FMML, we can communicate using this dialect. If we sent our FMML message to a widget factory for example or some other non-FMML speakers, they would not be able to read it.

When sending or receiving an XML document, both parties must agree on the meaning of the XML tags; that is, they must agree on the dialect. Just because we are placing the number of contracts in a trade within a <Quantity> tag does not mean that the server receiving our document will understand the contents of the <Quantity> element. What we need then is a system that both the sender and receiver can use to validate the meaning of the tags. Of course, these types of systems have already been developed.

There are two different methods used to validate XML documents—document type definition (DTD) and XML schema. The system we will look at is DTD.

The purpose of a DTD is to define the legal building blocks of an XML document. It defines the document structure along with a list of acceptable elements and tags. In addition to defining names for tags, a DTD defines the business rules or valid values that may be contained within the tags. As we will see, a DTD can be an external reference.

If several financial institutions and exchanges get together and agree on a dialect, or DTD, they can communicate between themselves using that dialect of XML. As you can imagine then, DTDs are very powerful. They define industry standards for the meanings and business rules of an XML document. Earlier in this chapter we mentioned that XML tags mean nothing to the computer. But to people, they mean a lot. Technology professionals of entire segments within the financial markets industry meet and define DTDs that become the standard within their particular domain. Any XML message creator who sends an XML document based on the agreed-upon DTD can be assured that the recipient of the document will be able to read it. This is one of the main advantages of using XML to transfer data. It allows individual firms or even entire industries to create their own customized markup language.

Again, in the following chapter, we will look at a few examples of DTDs for financial markets. But for right now, let's take a look at how a DTD validates an XML document.

DOCUMENT TYPE DEFINITION

Seen from a DTD point of view, all XML documents are made up of simple building blocks—elements, tags, attributes, entities, PCDATA, and CDATA.

Elements

Elements are the main building blocks of XML documents. Examples of XML elements that we have looked at are <Trade> and <Ticker>. Elements can contain text, can contain other elements, or can be empty.

Tags

Tags are used to mark up elements. A starting tag like <Ticker> marks up the beginning of an element, and an ending tag like

</Ticker> marks up the end of an element. Furthermore XML permits empty tags, denoted by a slash before the final right-angle bracket in the tag like this <Ticker/>. This tag opens and closes in one statement. Empty tags of this sort may have within them attributes and attribute values.

Attributes

Attributes provide extra information about elements and are always placed inside the starting tag of an element. Attributes always come in name-value pairs and are allowed to be empty if not supplied at all. However, XML does not allow naked attribute values. Attribute values must be in quotes. For example, we allow the <BuySell> tag to take on an attribute of either Buy or Sell:

```
<BuySell Value='Buy'/>.
```

Entities

Entities are variables used to define common text or characters. Entities are then expanded when an XML parser parses a document. For example, because they are special characters for XML, <, >, &, ", and ' must be represented by special-character entities. An XML message using, say, the double-quote character in text enclosed in a tag would not be well formed. Correctly designed XML parsers will produce an error for such input. The following entities are predefined in XML:

Entity References	Character
&lt;	<
&gt;	>
&amp;	&
&quot;	"
&apos;	'

PCDATA

PCDATA means parsed character data. Character data is the text found between the start tag and the end tag of an XML element. PCDATA is text that will be parsed by a parser. Tags inside the text will be treated as markup, and entities will be expanded.

CDATA

CDATA means character data. CDATA is text that will not be parsed by a parser. Tags placed inside the text will not be treated as markup, and entities will not be expanded.

Parsers

As we discussed previously, an XML message's structure should be validated against a DTD. This is done through the use of a parser, a program that actually conducts the validation and reads the data. A parser that has access to a DTD guarantees that all the required elements and attributes are present in an XML document according to the DTD. As with XML itself, the rules for validation are very strict.

XML validation is order-sensitive, and elements must appear in the same order as they are specified in the DTD. Additional fields may not be added without first defining them in the DTD or in the XML message itself. There are two methods for parsing and processing XML documents: the document object model (DOM) and the simple API for XML (SAX) model. We will employ a SAX parser in an example program later.

A parser using DOM reads the entire XML document into a hierarchical tree structure. A tree is a nonlinear, two-dimensional data structure capable of holding the elements of an XML message in nodes. The root node is the first node of the tree and corresponds to the root element in an XML document. Every other element is a child of the parent root node. Unlike the tree-based structure in DOM, SAX is event-based. SAX parsers notify our application of a stream of parsing events. Since both DOM and SAX are widely standardized and supported, developers have a choice of free, high-quality, third-party parsing software.

As we will see, classes for creating and reading XML messages are found in the System.XML namespace. For now let's take a look at the DTD for FMML and gain an understanding of how a parser validates a FMML message.

```
<?xml version='1.0' encoding='us-ascii'?>
<!ELEMENT Tradedoc (Trade+)>
```

```
<!ELEMENT Trade (Exchange,Ticker,BuySell,Quantity,Price,ClearingFirm,Trader,
               Time)>
<!ELEMENT Exchange (#PCDATA)>
<!ELEMENT Ticker (#PCDATA)>
<!ELEMENT BuySell (#PCDATA)>
<!ELEMENT Quantity (#PCDATA)>
<!ELEMENT Price (#PCDATA)>
<!ELEMENT ClearingFirm (#PCDATA)>
<!ELEMENT Trader (#PCDATA)>
<!ELEMENT Time (#PCDATA)>
<!ATTLIST Exchange Acronym (CBOE|ISE|BOX|AMEX|FMEX) #REQUIRED>
<!ATTLIST BuySell Type (Buy|Sell) #REQUIRED>
<!ATTLIST Price Type CDATA #FIXED "Market">
```

Let's go through line by line and describe what is going on.

```
<!ELEMENT Tradedoc (Trade+)>
```

This line specifies that this DTD is meant to validate an XML
message called a Tradedoc and that a Tradedoc is made up of at
least one element named Trade.

```
<!ELEMENT Trade (Exchange,Ticker,BuySell,Quantity,Price,ClearingFirm,Trader,
               Time)>
```

Here we can see that a <Trade> element contains eight child
elements. No other elements are allowed.

```
<!ELEMENT Exchange (#PCDATA)>
<!ELEMENT Ticker (#PCDATA)>
<!ELEMENT BuySell (#PCDATA)>
<!ELEMENT Quantity (#PCDATA)>
<!ELEMENT Price (#PCDATA)>
<!ELEMENT ClearingFirm (#PCDATA)>
<!ELEMENT Trader (#PCDATA)>
<!ELEMENT Time (#PCDATA)>
```

These lines in the DTD specify the children within a Trade tag in the
order in which they must be supplied. The #PCData notation
specifies that the contents of each tag are to be parsed character
data. This is a bit misleading because it suggests that the contents of
XML tags are data-type-specific like numbers, strings, and dates.
XML is not data-type-specific. Rather, think of character data as the
text found between the start tag and the end tag of an XML element
and nothing more. The DTD has no way to define an element's data
type. In the FMML DTD above, the <Ticker> element is defined to

be an empty element with an attribute named type of PCDATA. Parsed character data means that the parser reads the data extracted from the tag.

The DTD up to this point has only specified which elements along with their children and tag names must be found in the XML document, written in our made-up language called FMML. The DTD has done nothing yet to help us determine whether good information is contained in the tags. When simple business rules need to be applied, attributes and attribute value lists may be included. XML attributes can be added to elements if more detailed information needs to be known about them. For example, the <Exchange> tag can include an attribute to give us more information on which exchange we are dealing with, such as CBOE, ISE, or AMEX.

An XML element can contain as many attributes as needed. The <Exchange> element has a single attribute as described in the DTD and is known as Acronym.

```
<!ATTLIST Exchange Acronym (CBOE|ISE|BOX|AMEX|FMEX)
          #REQUIRED>
```

The Acronym attribute will be validated against a set of legal values: CBOE, ISE, BOX, AMEX, and FMEX. (As we will later see, FMEX is the Financial Markets Exchange, a simulated, hypothetical exchange we can communicate with over the Internet using FMML to place orders and receive fills.) Notice that enumerated values are contained in an open-close set of parentheses and are separated by the pipe character, |. Also notice that this list of enumerated values does not need to be in single or double quotes; in XML everything is a string.

The <BuySell> and <Price> tags have attributes as well:

```
<!ATTLIST BuySell Type (Buy|Sell) #REQUIRED>
<!ATTLIST Price Type CDATA #FIXED "Market">
```

The <BuySell> tag has a required Type attribute, which can take on the value of either Buy or Sell. The <Price> tag's fixed Type attribute can only take on the value "Market". That is, according to the definition of FMML, only market orders are permissible. So limit or stop orders are not allowed.

The attribute type can have the following values:

Value	Description
CDATA	The value is character data
(X|Y| ...)	The value must be one from an enumerated list
ID	The value is a unique ID
IDREF	The value is the ID of another element
IDREFS	The value is a list of other IDs
NMTOKEN	The value is a valid XML name
NMTOKENS	The value is a list of valid XML names
ENTITY	The value is an entity
ENTITIES	The value is a list of entities
NOTATION	The value is a name of a notation
xml:	The value is a predefined XML value

The default value of an attribute can be:

Value	Description
Value	The default name of the attribute
#REQUIRED	The attribute value must be included in the element and is not optional
#IMPLIED	The attribute is optional
#FIXED value	The attribute value is fixed

For the sake of simplicity, our FMML DTD only deals with PCDATA. Although there is a lot more to XML than we can fit into this chapter, the FMML DTD will be sufficient to validate messages, in the form of trades, that we will send over the Internet, as long as we include the name and location of the .dtd file in our FMML message.

The FMML.dtd file we will use to validate our FMML messages will actually be external to the XML documents we create and send. External DTDs can exist as flat files both on the local machine and on the local network or as a uniform resource locator (URL) on the Internet. Whatever the case, DTDs usually exist as publicly available, human readable ASCII files.

In our XML messages we will need to specify the name and location of the DTD against which it should be validated by the receiving parser. If the DTD is located in the current folder, the following syntax should be included in the XML document:

```
<!DOCTYPE Tradedoc SYSTEM 'fmml.dtd'>
```

If needed, the entire path to the .dtd file can be specified—for example, C:\ModelingFM\xml\fmml.dtd. If the DTD is public as in the FMML case, meaning that it is available on the Internet, the syntax will be:

```
<!DOCTYPE Tradedoc SYSTEM 'http://yorkville.rice. _
                            iit.edu:8100/FMML.dtd'>
```

When a DTD exists as a URI, it becomes especially powerful. Assuming that all partners who exchange XML messages can access the DTD, they all can use it to create and validate their XML documents anywhere in the world. Let's take a look.

CREATING XML DOCUMENTS

Before we create an Internet application, let's first develop a simple VB.NET application that will write an XML document and save it to the C:\drive.

Step 1   In VB.NET create a new Windows application named XMLexample.

Step 2   On your Form1, add controls to build the GUI shown in Figure 18.2.

There should be two combo boxes on your form. Name them cboExchange and cboBuySell. In the Collection property of cboExchange, add the elements CBOE, ISE, BOX, AMEX, and FMEX. In the Collection property of cboBuySell, add the elements Buy and Sell. Give the text boxes the appropriate names: txtTicker, txtQuantity, txtPrice, txtClearingFirm, and txtTrader.

Step 3   To the Button1_Click event, add the following code:

```
Imports System.IO
Public Class Form1
    Inherits System.Windows.Forms.Form
[Windows Form Designer Generated Code]
Private Sub Button1_Click(ByVal sender As ...) Handles Button1.Click
    Dim strTradeDoc As String
    strXMLtrade = "<?xml version = '1.0'?>"
    strXMLtrade &= "<Tradedoc>"
    strXMLtrade &="<Trade>"
    strXMLtrade &= "<Exchange Acronym = '" & cboExchange.Text & "'/>"
    strXMLtrade &= "<Ticker>" & txtTicker.Text & "</Ticker>"
```

F I G U R E 18.2

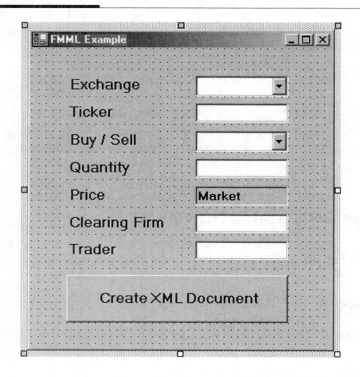

```
    strXMLtrade &= "<BuySell Type = '" & cboBuySell.Text & "'/>"
    strXMLtrade &= "<Quantity>" & txtQuantity.Text & "</Quantity>"
    strXMLtrade &= "<Price Type = '" & txtPrice.Text & "'/>"
    strXMLtrade &= "<ClearingFirm>" & txtClearingFirm.Text & "</ClearingFirm>"
    strXMLtrade &= "<Trader>" & txtTrader.Text & "</Trader>"
    strXMLtrade &= "<Time>" & Now & "</Time>"
    strXMLtrade &= "</Trade>"
    strXMLtrade &= "</Tradedoc>"
    Dim objWriter As New StreamWriter("C:\ModelingFM\myFirstXMLdoc.xml")
    objWriter.Write(strXMLtrade)
    objWriter.Close()
End Sub
End Class
```

Step 4 Run the program. Your results should look like the screen shown in Figure 18.3.

Step 5 Now find the file named myFirstXMLdoc.xml in your C:\ModelingFM folder and double-click on it, which will cause it to open in MS Internet Explorer.

F I G U R E 18.3

If your XML document is well formed, it will successfully open. If it is not well formed, Internet Explorer (IE) will generate an error statement.

SENDING XML MESSAGES

Creating an XML message and saving it to a file is not really all that exciting. After all, XML was designed for communication. Let's change our program so we can send our FMML trade over the Internet and receive a trade confirmation. We will be sending our pseudo trades to the Financial Markets Exchange, FMEX, which is a server that will receive FMML "trades," post them in a database, and send back FMML trade confirmations. Once you have placed your trade, you can see whether the FMEX has received it at *http:// yorkville.rice.iit.edu:8100/servlet/fmex.GetTrades*. This website shows the contents of the FMEX database. So if your FMML document was successfully received, it will be viewable on this site.

Step 6 To communicate with the FMEX over the Internet, we will need to create a few objects that are based upon classes found in the System.Net and System.XML namespaces. Add the Imports System.Net and Imports System.XML code at the very top of the Form1 code window. In the general declarations section of the Form1 code window, declare the following objects:

```
Dim myUrl As Uri
Dim myReq As WebRequest
Dim myRes As WebResponse
Dim myReader As XmlTextReader
```

A URI is an object representation of a URL. A WebRequest object, found in the System.Net namespace, makes a request to a URI over the Internet. A WebResponse objects receives a message from a URI.

An XmlTextReader object, found in the System.XML namespace, gives us fast, read-only access to an XML stream. So by using an XMLTextReader to read a stream, we will be implementing a form of SAX parser to make sure the XML message is well formed. However, an XmlTextReader object will not perform data validation against a DTD. To perform data validation, we could use an XmlValidatingReader object, but creating a full, validating parser is beyond the scope of this chapter.

Step 7 Change the Button1_Click event to include the following code:

```
Private Sub Button1_Click(ByVal sender As ...) Handles Button1.Click
    Dim strCurrentTag, strStatus, strBuySell, strQty, strTicker, _
        strPrice, strDate, strXMLtrade As String
    strXMLtrade = "<?xml version = '1.0'?>"
    strXMLtrade += "<!DOCTYPE Tradedoc SYSTEM _
        'http://yorkville.rice.iit.edu:8100/FMML.dtd' > "
    strXMLtrade += "<Tradedoc>"
' This code is the same as before.
    strXMLtrade += "</Tradedoc>"
    myUrl = New _
Uri("http://yorkville.rice.iit.edu:8100/servlet/fmex.XMLTrade?xmlfile=" _
        & strXMLtrade)
    myReq = WebRequest.Create(myUrl)
```

```
Try
        myRes = myReq.GetResponse
        myReader = New XmlTextReader(myRes.GetResponseStream())
        Do While (myReader.Read())
            If myReader.NodeType = XmlNodeType.Element Then
                strCurrentTag = myReader.Name
            End If
            If myReader.NodeType = XmlNodeType.Text Then
                Select Case strCurrentTag
                    Case "Status"
                        strStatus = myReader.Value
                    Case "BuySell"
                        strBuySell = myReader.Value
                    Case "Quantity"
                        strQty = myReader.Value
                    Case "Ticker"
                        strTicker = myReader.Value
                    Case "Price"
                        strPrice = myReader.Value
                    Case "Time"
                        strDate = myReader.Value
                End Select
            End If
        Loop
        myReader.Close()
    Catch exc As Exception
        MsgBox(exc.Message)
        Exit Sub
    End Try
    lblConfirm.Text = strStatus & " " & strBuySell & " " & strQty & " _
                    " & strTicker & " at " & strPrice & " at " & strDate
End Sub
```

Step 8 One last thing: Add a label named lblConfirm to the bottom of your Form1.

Step 9 Run the program (see Figure 18.4).

You can view the FMEX server at *http://yorkville.rice.ii-t.edu:8100/servlet/fmex.GetTrades*. When the server receives your "trade," it will be posted on this website.

XML DATA SOURCES

ADO.NET provides additional functionality that allows us to convert data in a database into XML. VB.NET DataSet objects provide methods that create XML documents from a data table and that also can convert XML data into a data source. This is accomplished through the use of the GetXML(), WriteXML, and ReadXML() member methods. Let's look at a quick example:

F I G U R E 18.4

Step 1 Open a new VB.NET Windows application named XMLdatasource.

Step 2 To your Form1 add a text box with the multilane property turned to True and with a vertical scroll bar. Also add a button and a data grid. Leave these controls with their default names.

Step 3 Add the following code to the Form1 code window:

```
Imports System.Data.OleDb
Public Class Form1
    Inherits System.Windows.Forms.Form
[Windows Form Designer generated code]
```

F I G U R E   18.5

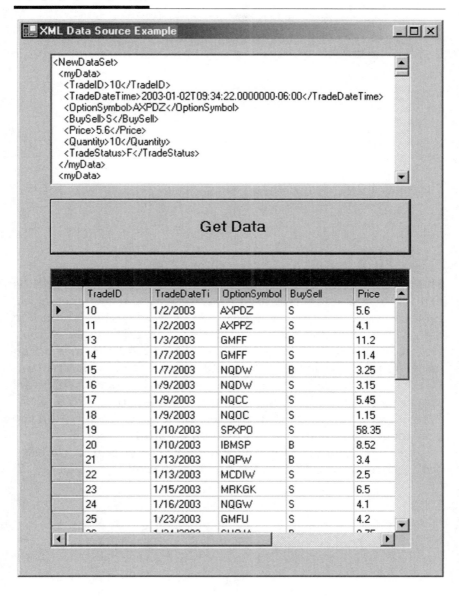

```
Private Sub Button1_Click(ByVal sender As ...) Handles Button1.Click
     Dim myConnect As New _
           OleDbConnection("Provider=Microsoft.Jet.OLEDB.4.0;Data _
           Source=C:\ModelingFM\Options.mdb")
     Dim myAdapter As New OleDbDataAdapter("Select * From OptionTrades, _
           myConnect)
     Dim myDataSet As New DataSet()
     myConnect.Open()
     myAdapter.Fill(myDataSet, "myData")
     DataGrid1.DataSource = myDataSet
     DataGrid1.DataMember = "myData"
     myDataSet.WriteXml("OptionTrades.XML")
     TextBox1.Text = myDataSet.GetXml()
     myConnect.Close()
End Sub
End Class
```

Step 4   Run the program. It should look like Figure 18.5.

SUMMARY

This chapter presented the basics of the XML language, which is really a metalanguage. We used XML to create our own messaging protocol, which we named FMML. All XML messages should be both well formed and valid according to some DTD. In the chapter we broke down the elements of the FMML.dtd file to gain an understanding of elements, tags, attributes, entities, CDATA, and PCDATA. Furthermore, we briefly discussed parsers, which are programs that read XML files. Finally, we used some of VB.NET's System.Net and System.XML namespace objects to communicate over the Internet with a server using the FMML protocol.

In the following chapter we will look at some real-world XML protocols used every day in the financial markets.

PROBLEMS

1. What is a metalanguage?
2. What is the difference between a well-formed XML message and a valid one?
3. What is FMML, and how is it different from XML?
4. What is a DTD?
5. What objects are contained in the System.Net and System.XML namespaces?

PROJECT 18.1

Trade confirmations received from FMEX should be posted in the
OptionTrades table of the Options.mdb database. Create a VB.NET
Windows application that inserts the necessary information into
the appropriate columns in the table.

PROJECT 18.2

As trades are made on FMEX, your portfolio will change. Create a
VB.NET application that will hold call and put objects in a portfolio.
Be sure to add the functionality necessary to keep track of your
portfolio statistics in real time.

CHAPTER 19

XML Protocols in Financial Markets

Although electronic trading has become widespread over the last decade, communication between institutional trading firms is still often done using such last-millennium technologies as the telephone. Over the coming years, the advantages of new technologies such as XML will change the way all companies do business, but especially those involved in the financial markets since the details of virtually all tradable instruments can be represented and communicated in digital format. Furthermore, as we have argued in this book, financial industry firms will increasingly use electronic trading systems (to select trades and manage portfolios) and electronic markets (to execute trades). The benefits of an entirely electronic platform will pave the way for straight-through processing (STP). STP will require the transmission of trade information across electronic networks using a common messaging protocol.

STP is a set of business processes that will one day achieve the goal of automating end-to-end trade processing for all financial instruments, thereby streamlining back-office activities and lowering trading costs. Thanks to the advent of web services technology and messaging protocols, the focus of attention with regard to STP is moving away from issues relating to connectivity between software applications and more toward the business content of the information being exchanged.

As we showed in the previous chapter, a messaging protocol such as FMML can be created and defined as a standardized way of

communicating trade information between two market participants without the necessity of human intervention. Processes such
as this, where the messaging protocol is not identical to a
proprietary data description methodology, are the very definition
of the issues around connectivity and system interoperability.
System interoperation permits individual market participants to
share the fixed costs of technological infrastructure development as
well as the benefits of subsequently lower transaction costs.

Within the financial markets industry, several XML protocols
have been developed for system interoperation within specific
industry segments. These XML standards provide a framework for
encoding information relating to different parts of the industry and
are being promoted by consortiums and organizations that set
document definitions in the form of XML DTDs or schemas. As we
learned in the previous chapter, a DTD describes the valid structure
and sequence of a message spoken in a particular dialect of XML.
The most interesting of these XML protocols or dialects used in the
financial markets are:

- FIX/FIXML. FIXML is the XML version of FIX.
- FpML. The Financial Products Markup Language.
- Swift/SwiftML. SwiftML is the XML version of Swift.
- RIXML. The Research Information Exchange Markup
  Language.
- MDDL. The Market Data Definition Language.
- FinXML.
- SFXL. The Securities Financing Extensible Markup
  Language.
- OFX. Open Financial Exchange.
- XBRL. The Extensible Business Reporting Language.
- IFX. Interactive Financial Exchange.
- IRML. The Investment Research Markup Language.
- XFRML. The Extensible Financial Research Markup
  Language.
- MDML. The Market Data Markup Language.
- WeatherML. The Weather Markup Language.
- STPML. The Straight-through Processing Markup
  Language.

As you can imagine, an institution of any size may need to support a multiplicity of standards within its trading, risk management, and back-office systems. The most widely used of the protocols mentioned above, however, are FIX, Swift, and FpML. Both Swift, promoted by the Society for Worldwide Interbank Financial Telecommunications, and FIX, promoted by FIX Protocol, Ltd. (FPL), are currently non-XML protocols, but they are being converted to XML formats known as SwiftML and FIXML, respectively.

Furthermore, since there is obviously a fair amount of overlap between the protocols listed, we will likely see convergence of the standards over the coming years. In fact, the FPL and Swift organizations have recently agreed to team up and merge their two messaging standards into a single, ISO 15022 XML-based protocol. [ISO 15022 is the current International Standards Organization (ISO) standard that defines electronic messages exchanged between institutions involved in the securities industry.] It is hoped that the new XML protocol will combine FIX's agility in trade execution and Swift's post-trade talents to further the goal of straight-through processing.

Rather than delve into each of the listed protocols in depth, we will briefly discuss FpML and then focus in more depth on FIXML, leaving it to the reader to further investigate the others should the need arise. Whatever the case, since all the other listed standards are XML-based protocols, messages written in any of these formats must be well-formed XML documents and valid according to their respective DTDs.

FpML

The Financial Products Markup Language (FpML) is a freely licensed XML protocol for trading complex over-the-counter financial derivative instruments, including equity, interest rate, and foreign exchange derivatives such as options, spots, forwards, swaps, and swaptions. Eventually it is hoped that FpML will automate the flow of information for electronic trading and confirmations in all the types of negotiated OTC derivatives.

Let's take a look at a sample FpML message taken from the FpML Version 2.0 documentation, which can be found at *www.FpML.org*. As you will see, this document contains the information about a forward rate agreement trade. In some areas we have abbreviated less interesting content.

On May 14, 1991, ABN AMRO Bank and Midland Bank entered into a forward rate agreement in which ABN AMRO was the seller of the contract and Midland was the buyer. The terms of the contract are as follows:

- Effective date: 01/07/1991
- Termination date: 01/17/1992
- Notional amount: CHF 25,000,000
- Fixed rate: 4.00%
- Day count fraction: Actual/360

Here is an XML representation of this OTC trade of a forward rate agreement using the FpML protocol:

```
<?xml version="1.0" ?>
<FpML version="2-0" BusinessCenterSchemeDefault=http://www.fpml.org/...>
<trade>
   <tradeHeader>
      <partyTradeIdentifier>
        <partyReference href="#MIDLAND" />
        <tradeId tradeIdScheme="http://www.hsbc.com/...>123</tradeId>
      </partyTradeIdentifier>
      <partyTradeIdentifier>
         <partyReference href="#ABNAMRO" />
         <tradeId tradeIdScheme="http://www.abnamro.com/...>456</tradeId>
      </partyTradeIdentifier>
      <tradeDate>1991-05-14</tradeDate>
   </tradeHeader>
   <fra>
      <buyerPartyReference href="#MIDLAND" />
      <sellerPartyReference href="#ABNAMRO" />
      <adjustedEffectiveDate id="resetDate">1991-07-17 _
                                        </adjustedEffectiveDate>
      <adjustedTerminationDate>1992-01-17</adjustedTerminationDate>
      <paymentDate>
         <unadjustedDate>1991-07-17</unadjustedDate>
         <dateAdjustments>
            <businessDayConvention>FOLLOWING</businessDayConvention>
            <businessCenters>
                  <businessCenter>CHZU</businessCenter>
            </businessCenters>
         </dateAdjustments>
      </paymentDate>
      <fixingDateOffset>
```

```
        <periodMultiplier>-2</periodMultiplier>
        <period>D</period>
        <dayType>Business</dayType>
        <businessDayConvention>NONE</businessDayConvention>
        <businessCenters>
            <businessCenter>GBLO</businessCenter>
        </businessCenters>
        <dateRelativeTo href="#resetDate">ResetDate</dateRelativeTo>
    </fixingDateOffset>
    <dayCountFraction>ACT/360</dayCountFraction>
    <calculationPeriodNumberOfDays>184</calculationPeriodNumberOfDays>
    <notional>
        <currency>CHF</currency>
        <amount>25000000.00</amount>
    </notional>
    <fixedRate>0.04</fixedRate>
    <floatingRateIndex>CHF-LIBOR-BBA</floatingRateIndex>
    <indexTenor>
        <periodMultiplier>6</periodMultiplier>
        <period>M</period>
    </indexTenor>
    <fraDiscounting>true</fraDiscounting>
</fra>
<party Id="MIDLAND">
    <partyId>MIDLGB22</partyId>
</party>
<party id="ABNAMRO">
    <partyId>ABNANL2A</partyId>
</party>
</trade>
</FpML>
```

Although this XML document is quite lengthy, you should be able to not only read it but, based upon what we learned in the previous chapter, also understand the underlying structure and determine how it may be created in VB.NET and how it could be sent to a URL over the Internet. Now let's look in more depth at FIXML.

FIX AND FIXML

The Financial Information Exchange (FIX) protocol is a public domain, non-XML messaging standard targeted toward institutional trading of exchange-traded securities and derivatives. FIX was originally designed by Salomon Brothers and Fidelity to automate messages between themselves, but over the years it has become widely used by most major market participants. Today FIX

Protocol, Ltd. (FPL), an industry consortium, oversees the ongoing development of FIX and FIXML, the XML version of the FIX protocol.

FPL has designed FIX for the express purpose of communicating trades electronically and exchanging transaction data in real time between exchanges, ECNs, FCMs, and broker-dealers. Every day, FIX-compliant trading institutions and exchanges use FIX to route and manage their flow of orders and confirmation information more quickly and efficiently than prior or alternative methods. The use of FIX messages greatly reduces the time and expense necessary to perform transactions and transaction processing in the financial markets. Due to its wide acceptance by securities and derivatives exchanges as well as their member firms, FIX is becoming a necessary and integral component of any real-time trading system.

FIXML, on the other hand, is an attempt by the FPL consortium to create an XML version of FIX. That is, the consortium is aiming to rewrite the FIX protocol in XML. As we have learned, since FIXML is an XML-based language, the definition of FIXML is encompassed in a DTD that is available on the Internet, as we will see shortly. Although FIXML is only now narrowly used in the industry, FPL is designing it in such a way as to minimize effort and expense for FIX-compliant firms to convert to it from their legacy FIX-based systems. In general, FIXML simply takes FIX tag values and represents them in XML format. The new FIXML messages then are actually put inside the established FIX headers and trailers. The result is that FIX firms can convert to FIXML by simply adding an XML parser on top of their existing FIX engine. Alternatively, FIXML messages can also stand on their own outside the FIX framework.

Although FIXML messages are bigger and therefore require more bandwidth than traditional FIX messages, the advantages of using an XML format, and the additional functionalities it enables, clearly outweigh the disadvantages. One of the biggest advantages of the XML format is that it allows for interoperation between FIXML systems and other similar standards such as OFX. Software applications can easily pass fields through to connected systems that use other DTDs to, for example, describe trades in terms of price, quantity, and security name.

As we have said, over the long run the use of XML formats, like FIXML, SwiftML, and OFX, will motivate a convergence of the various protocols. The ultimate prize will be a single dictionary for the entire financial industry, which will clearly ease the transition to straight-through processing.

As we mentioned before, just as with any XML standard, there is a corresponding DTD with FIXML. It is known as fixmlmain.dtd and is available on the FPL website, *www.FIXprotocol.org.*

Before we dive in to creating a FIXML document, let's take a quick look at some peculiarities of FIXML. FIXML messages, of course, require that the content of a message be ordered. That is, as with any XML protocol, elements must be in a specific order. Also, FIXML supports conditionally required content. So, for example, options trades must contain the <StrikePrice> element, whereas futures trades do not. And lastly, FIXML makes use of certain commonly used and well-known financial abbreviations. Here are some examples:

Abbreviation	Description
Amt	Amount
Comm	Commission
Comp	Company
Curr	Currency
DK	Don't know
Exch	Exchange
Forex	Foreign
Fut	Futures
ID	Identifier
IOI	Indication of interest
Mkt	Market
Opt	Option
Ord	Order
Px	Price
Qty	Quantity

In the following example, we will build a FIXML document step-by-step, element-by-element, from the ground up. Further, we will be able to modify this document for use with equity trades, options trades, and futures trades. As with all XML messages, FIXML documents start with headers, including the XML version and the FIXML document type, which defines the DTD against which a parser will validate the document.

```
<?xml version='1.1' encoding='UTF-8' ?>
<?DOCTYPE FIXML SYSTEM 'http://www.fixprotocol.org/specification/ _
                          fixml4.3v1.0.dtd'>
```

Next we add the root element <FIXML> with opening and closing tags.

```
<?xml version='1.1' encoding='UTF-8' ?>
<?DOCTYPE FIXML SYSTEM 'http:\... .dtd'>
<FIXML>
</FIXML>
```

According to the DTD, a <FIXML> element can contain one or more <FIXMLMessage> elements. A <FIXMLMessage> must contain one <Header> and one <ApplicationMessage>. The <Header> element will contain the information about the parties involved in a transaction. The <ApplicationMessage> element will contain information about the transaction itself.

```
<?xml version='1.1' encoding='UTF-8' ?>
<?DOCTYPE FIXML SYSTEM 'http:\... .dtd'>
<FIXML>
        <FIXMLMessage>
                <Header>
                </Header>
                <ApplicationMessage>
                </ApplicationMessage>
        </FIXMLMessage>
</FIXML>
```

The <Header> element must contain a <Sender> and a <Target> element. Optionally it can also contain an <onBehalfOf>, <DeliverTo>, <SendingTime>, <PossDupFlag>, or <PossResend> element.

```
<Header>
        <Sender>
        </Sender>
        <Target>
        </Target>
        <SendingTime/>
</Header>
```

The <Sender> and <Target> elements must each contain <CompID> and optionally a <SubID> and a <LocationID>.

```
<Header>
      <Sender>
              <CompID></CompID>
              <SubID></SubID>
      </Sender>
      <Target>
              <CompID></CompID>
              <SubID></SubID>
      </Target>
      <SendingTime/>
</Header>
```

We can complete the header by adding some data.

```
<Header>
      <Sender>
              <CompID>BVV</CompID>
              <SubID>BEN</SubID>
      </Sender>
      <Target>
              <CompID>BH</CompID>
              <SubID>Bob</SubID>
      </Target>
      <SendingTime>20030203-9:30:00</SendingTime>
</Header>
```

Now that the <Header> is complete, we can turn our attention to the <ApplicationMessage> content. The <ApplicationMessage> element can contain one of several elements, including but not limited to the following: <Advertisement>, <Indication>, <News>, <Email>, <QuoteReq>, <Quote>, <Order>, <ExecutionReport>, <DK_Trade>, <OrderModificationRequest>, <OrderCancelRequest>, <OrderCancelReject>, <OrderStatusRequest>, <SettlementInstructions>, <MarketData>, <MarketDataReq>, <QuoteCancel>, and <SecurityStatus>. For the purposes of this example, we are sending an order.

```
<ApplicationMessage>
      <Order>
      </Order>
</ApplicationMessage>
```

The <Order> element must include tags for <ClOrdID>, <HandInst>, <Instrument>, <Side>, <TransactTime>, <Order-

Quantity>, and <OrderType>. Optionally, <Order> can also include other tags such as <ClientID>, <ExecBroker>, <Account>, <PrevClosePx>, <Currency>, <OrderDuration>, <Commission>, <Rule80A>, <Text>, <ClearingFirm>, or <ClearingAcct>. For this example we will include the required elements as well as the optional <Currency> element.

Furthermore, the <Instrument> element will contain a required <Symbol> element and may include one of the optional elements such as <SymbolSfx>, <SecurityID>, <SecurityType>, <SecurityExch>, and <Issuer>.

```
<ApplicationMessage>
      <Order>
            <ClOrdID></ClOrdID>
            <HandInst />
            <Instrument>
                  <Symbol></Symbol>
                  <SecurityType></SecurityType>
            </Instrument>
            <Side />
            <TransactTime></TransactTime>
            <OrderQuantity></OrderQuantity>
            <OrderType></OrderType>
            <Currency />
      </Order>
</ApplicationMessage>
```

Now let's add some parsed character data as well as some attributes to our order elements.

```
<ApplicationMessage>
      <Order>
            <ClOrdID>12345</ClOrdID>
            <HandInst Value="1"/>
            <Instrument>
                  <Symbol></Symbol>
                  <SecurityType></SecurityType>
            </Instrument>
            <Side Value="1"/>
            <TransactTime>20030203-9:30:00</TransactTime>
            <OrderQuantity></OrderQuantity>
            <OrderType></OrderType>
            <Currency Value="USD"/>
      </Order>
</ApplicationMessage>
```

Let's take a more in-depth look at the <Instrument> element. The <SecurityType> element may contain elements corresponding to the different tradable instruments, including <Equity>, <FixedIncome>, <ForeignExchange>, <Future>, <MutualFund>, <Option>, and <Warrant>. The format for a common stock trade looks like this:

```
<Instrument>
        <Symbol>IBM</Symbol>
        <SecurityType>
                <Equity Value="CS">
        </SecurityType>
</Instrument>
```

The format for a call <Option> trade looks like the following example. In this example, a put is a code "0" and a call is a code "1".

```
<Instrument>
        <Symbol>IBM</Symbol>
        <SecurityType>
                <Option>
                        <PutCall Value="1"/>
                        <Maturity>
                                <MonthYear>200304</MonthYear>
                        </Maturity>
                        <StrikePx>80.00</StrikePx>
                </Option>
        </SecurityType>
</Instrument>
```

Now let's take a look at the finished FIXML document, which incorporates the <Header> and the <ApplicationMessage> along with some additional information for <OrderQuantity> and <OrderType>. In this final message we have included the <Instrument> element for the purchase of 10 IBM April 80 call options at a limit price of $5.00.

```
<?xml version='1.0' encoding='UTF-8' ?>
<!DOCTYPE FIXML SYSTEM 'http://www.fixprotocol.org/specification/ -
                                        fixml4.3v1.0.dtd'>
<FIXML>
<FIXMLMessage>
    <Header>
        <Sender>
            <CompID>BVV</CompID>
```

```
            <SubID>BEN</SubID>
        </Sender>
        <Target>
            <CompID>BH</CompID>
            <SubID>Bob</SubID>
        </Target>
        <SendingTime>20030203-9:30:00</SendingTime>
    </Header>
    <ApplicationMessage>
        <Order>
            <ClOrdID>12345</ClOrdID>
            <HandInst Value='1'/>
            <Instrument>
                <Symbol>IBM</Symbol>
                <SecurityType>
                    <Option>
                        <PutCall Value='1'/>
                        <Maturity>
                            <MonthYear>200304</MonthYear>
                        </Maturity>
                        <StrikePx>80.00</StrikePx>
                    </Option>
                </SecurityType>
            </Instrument>
            <Side Value='1'/>
            <TransactTime>20030203-9:30:00</TransactTime>
            <OrderQuantity>
                <OrderQty>10</OrderQty>
            </OrderQuantity>
            <OrderType>
                <LimitOrder>
                    <Price>5.00</Price>
                </LimitOrder>
            </OrderType>
            <Currency Value='USD'/>
        </Order>
    </ApplicationMessage>
</FIXMLMessage>
</FIXML>
```

On the CD, the file sampleFIXML.xml contains the completed code above. Try opening this file in Internet Explorer. Since this FIXML message is both well formed and valid, the only thing left to do is to build a VB.NET application that creates FIXML messages.

This program mimics the FMML program in the previous chapter and creates a FIXML document.

Step 1   In VB.NET create a new Windows application named FIXMLexample.

Step 2   On your Form1, add controls to build the GUI shown in Figure 19.1

F I G U R E 19.1

There should be two combo boxes on your form. Name them cboExchange and cboBuySell. In the Collection property of cboExchange, add the elements CBOE, ISE, BOX, AMEX, and FMEX. In the Collection property of cboBuySell, add the elements Buy and Sell. Give the text boxes the appropriate names: txtTicker, txtQuantity, txtPrice, txtClearingFirm, and txtTrader.

Step 3 To the Form1 code window, add the following code:

```
Imports System.IO
[Windows Form Designer generated code]
Public Class Form1
    Inherits System.Windows.Forms.Form
Private Sub Button1_Click(ByVal sender As ...) Handles Button1.Click
        Dim strXMLtrade As String
        strXMLtrade = "<?xml version='1.0' ?>"
```

```
strXMLtrade &= "<!DOCTYPE FIXML SYSTEM _
    'http://www.fixprotocol.org/specification/fixml4.3v1.0.dtd'>"
strXMLtrade &= "<FIXML>"
strXMLtrade &= "<FIXMLMessage>"
strXMLtrade &= "<Header>"
strXMLtrade &= "<Sender>"
strXMLtrade &= "<CompID>" & txtClearingFirm.Text & "</CompID>"
strXMLtrade &= "<SubID>" & txtTrader.Text & "</SubID>"
strXMLtrade &= "</Sender>"
strXMLtrade &= "<Target><CompID>" & cboExchange.Text & "</CompID>
    </Target>"
strXMLtrade &= "<SendingTime>" & Now & "</SendingTime>"
strxmlTRADE &= "</Header>"
strxmltrade &= "<ApplicationMessage>"
strXMLtrade &= "<Order>"
strXMLtrade &= "<ClOrdID>Test</ClOrdID>"
```

F I G U R E 19.2

```
        strXMLtrade &= "<HandInst Value='1' SDValue = '" & cboBuySell.Text & "'/>"
        strXMLtrade &= "<Instrument>"
        strXMLtrade &= "<Symbol>" & txtTicker.Text & "</Symbol>"
        strXMLtrade &= "<SecurityExchange Value = '" & cboExchange.Text & "'/>"
        strXMLtrade &= "</Instrument>"
        strXMLtrade &= "<Side Value='1'/>"
        strXMLtrade &= "<TransactTime>" & Now & "</TransactTime>"
        strXMLtrade &= "<OrderQtyData><OrderQty>" & txtQuantity.Text & _
                       "</OrderQty></OrderQtyData>"
        strXMLtrade &= "<OrdType Value = '1' SDValue = '" & txtPrice.Text & "'/>"
        strXMLtrade &= "</Order>"
        strXMLtrade &= "</ApplicationMessage>"
        strXMLtrade &= "</FIXMLMessage>"
        strXMLtrade &= "</FIXML>"
        Dim objWriter As New StreamWriter("C:\ModelingFM\myFirstFIXMLdoc.xml")
        objWriter.Write(strXMLtrade)
        objWriter.Close()
End Sub
```

Step 4   Run the program (see Figure 19.2).

Since this program produces a well-formed and valid FIXML document, you may view it in Internet Explorer.

SUMMARY

In this chapter we looked at some real-world XML protocols used everyday in the financial markets. Specifically, we presented the basics of the FpML and in more depth, FIXML. As with XML messages, those written in FpML and FIXML must be both well formed and valid according to their respective DTDs.

PROBLEMS

1. What is the relationship between FIX and FIXML?
2. What is FpML primarily used for?
3. What are Swift and SwiftML?
4. Why is convergence of XML protocols likely?
5. What two pieces must every FIXML message contain? What do these two elements represent?

PROJECT 19.1

Create a VB.NET Windows application that accepts user inputs regarding an OTC derivatives trade and builds a valid FpML document. Your program should save this document as myFirstFpMLdoc.xml.

PROJECT 19.2

The program in the chapter does not distinguish between stocks, futures, and options. Create a VB.NET application that accepts trade information from the user similar to the example program in the chapter. Add a combo box so the user can select the product type. Then build the correct FIXML message for the instrument type selected according to the instructions in the chapter.

Object-Oriented Programming

Risk Management

In theory, there is no difference between theory and practice.
But, in practice, there is.

Jan van de Snepscheut

Unified Modeling Language

As we hope you have been able to see over the last several chapters, object-oriented programming allows us to break down computer programs into separate objects in a very intuitive way. If you were new to programming when you first opened this book, you may very well have started with Chapter 3, fired up VB.NET, and started to code. While this approach might work for simple programs, it will certainly not work for larger ones. For example, what if you were asked to create a large value-at-risk system to monitor several automated trading systems. A project of this magnitude is too big to immediately start programming. Clearly, a good bit of planning would be required first.

In order to create larger applications, we should follow a detailed planning process for program design. This process must include a comprehensive analysis of the project requirements and result in a design, or blueprint, of the objects to be used in the program, as well as a plan for project completion. As you will no doubt learn over your career as a financial engineer, quality time spent on planning will save countless hours of coding and may even prevent failure of projects.

Large software projects have large probabilities of failure. Very rarely, if ever, do large software applications meet all the requirements as planned on time and within budget. Proper planning is the only way to ensure against failure before you start to program. Furthermore, it is not enough just to plan; be sure to have your designs and plans approved by management before you build anything.

As described in Chapter 2, the Kumiega–Van Vliet Trading System Development Methodology requires that we build an objects and program document as well as gain management buy-in prior to programming. This document should lay out all the objects along with all their functionalities that will be needed to construct the system. Again, the process should include requirements analysis, to define the specifications of the software; object-oriented analysis, to provide a framework within which all the objects can cooperate to satisfy the requirements; and object-oriented design, to lay out the class hierarchy. Fortunately, there is a graphical language created expressly for this purpose—the Unified Modeling Language.

UNIFIED MODELING LANGUAGE

Although it's also possible to describe a software system and its design in words, most developers prefer to use pictures to help visualize the system's pieces and the relationships between them. UML is a way to represent object-oriented applications using a standard set of graphical notations. With UML we can create blueprints in the form of diagrams before we start to program. Planning with UML makes the entire software development process much more structured and makes it easier to communicate ideas about system architecture. UML is not, however, a project management tool. Project management tools and software coordinate the various parts of a software project into a time line for completion. UML diagrams show, from an architectural perspective, the objects and the interrelationships between objects in a software application.

We can model just about any object-oriented application using UML. By creating models first, we can assure ourselves not only that trading algorithms are completely and correctly formulated, but also that the thorny issues of object-oriented implementation are worked out before construction begins and changes become expensive. Blueprints of classes and code modules, either drawn by hand or built in a UML software suite, are much easier to change than existing systems.

CHAPTER 20

In fact, dozens of products are available that facilitate the creation of UML diagrams. The most well-known UML design tool is Rational Rose (*www.rational.com*). Using these tools, we can build new applications or analyze existing code to reverse-engineer the UML diagrams. At the extreme end, some software will even go so far as to generate program code from UML diagrams, producing most of a production application.

Large automated trading systems must be structured in a way that facilitates error-free execution and a clear architecture so that financial engineers can find and fix bugs quickly. UML helps us visualize trading system design from a technology standpoint and document the results of the modeling process. This visualization is enabled through the use of UML's twelve diagram types, which are defined in three categories—model management, structural, and behavior diagrams.

High-level model management diagrams lay out the way we organize and manage the components of an application and consist of:

- Model diagrams
- Subsystem diagrams
- Package diagrams

Structural diagrams are used to model the static structure of a software application and consist of:

- Class diagrams
- Object diagrams
- Component diagrams
- Deployment diagrams

Behavior diagrams show the different behaviors of objects in an application and consist of:

- Use case diagrams
- Sequence diagrams
- Activity diagrams
- Collaboration diagrams
- State chart diagrams

MODEL MANAGEMENT DIAGRAMS

The process of modeling a software application is a process of breaking down a large system into smaller and smaller subsystems, because as systems get larger, it becomes more and more difficult to understand how the pieces fit together.

Model management diagrams are high-level designs to illustrate the organization and management of application components. Model management diagrams describe how the different pieces of a UML design will fit together. Subsequent diagrams will refine the details, but for now model management diagrams will incorporate all the other diagrams we will look at in order to show how the system is structured.

Model Diagrams

Our model diagram follows the Kumiega–Van Vliet paradigm presented in Chapter 2 of this book for developing automated trading systems. Thus the whole trading system software design process is defined by the models corresponding to each of the four steps along the waterfall.

For each of the four models, as an example, subsets of the twelve UML diagrams have been selected to show the relevant areas of communication. In each of the four models, instances of all the diagram types may be required, but nonetheless the focus will be on the diagrams listed in Figure 20.1.

So, as shown in Figure 20.1, modeling of the algorithms for trade selection will concentrate on structural diagrams and package diagrams. Data and implementation models will focus on package diagrams and behavior diagrams. Portfolio and risk management models will focus on structural class diagrams as well as behavior diagrams.

Subsystem Diagrams

Software systems are made up of subsystems. And subsystems are made of packages. A subsystem diagram breaks down a model diagram into the constituent subsystems of a software system and provides a hierarchical view of a system's overall structure.

F I G U R E 20.1

Automated Trading System Models			
Algorithm Documentation	**Data Documentation**	**Implementation Documentation**	**Portfolio and Risk Management Documentation**
Class Diagrams	Class Diagrams	Package Diagrams	Class Diagrams
Object Diagrams	Package Diagrams	Sequence Diagrams	Use Case Diagrams
Package Diagrams	Use Case Diagrams	Activity Diagrams	Activity Diagrams

As we saw in Chapter 2, the implementation of a trading system must manage three concurrent processes—trade selection, portfolio management, and risk management. So our subsystem diagram organizes the models into these logical components. Examples of the pieces of subsystems are shown in Figure 20.2.

Package Diagrams

Package diagrams break subsystems into packages of classes and subpackages. Packages simplify complex class diagrams and group together logically related program elements.

We draw packages as rectangles with small tabs on the top right-hand side (see Figure 20.3). As we will see, lines of different types show relationships between packages. We might say, for example, that one package has a relationship with another package if changes in one cause changes in the other.

F I G U R E 20.2

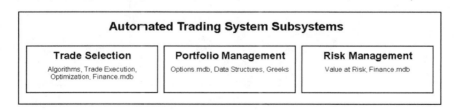

Automated Trading System Subsystems		
Trade Selection	**Portfolio Management**	**Risk Management**
Algorithms, Trade Execution, Optimization, Finance.mdb	Options.mdb, Data Structures, Greeks	Value at Risk, Finance.mdb

F I G U R E   20.3

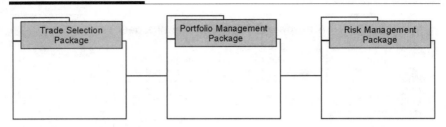

The three subsystems in our trading system are packages. We can break down these subsystems further, into other subsystems and classes.

The classes and subpackages in Figure 20.4 are connected by relationships to illustrate the fact that classes send messages to one another. We will look at these relationships in greater detail when we examine structural diagrams. One of the arts of UML design is to minimize the dependencies between classes, which will have the result of reducing the impact of changing a class or package definition.

Over the remainder of this chapter, we will not be able to diagram all the aspects of a trading system in detail. From the package diagram shown in Figure 20.4, however, and the knowledge gained over the past chapters, you should be able to

F I G U R E   20.4

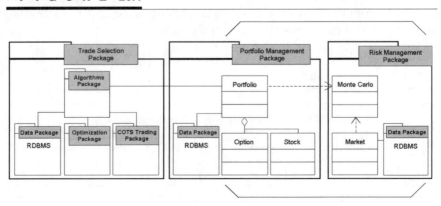

piece together the elements and subsystems of a full trading system. For this chapter, though, we will focus on a simplified project implementing portfolio and risk management using value at risk and UML. The project will encompass the class and packages defined by the brackets in Figure 20.4. This project will require that we define the packages and objects we will need to build the application as well as specifications for how these objects will interact with each other. The value-at-risk application will present a subset of the features of UML, but will give you an understanding of the steps necessary to create an objects and program document with UML.

VALUE AT RISK

Value at risk (VaR) is a single number that estimates the possible dollar loss on a portfolio of securities and derivatives over a specific time horizon within a given confidence level. This VaR number aggregates all the risks, including those that might offset each other, in a portfolio into a single number so as to facilitate analysis of hedging strategies and the discussions about risk with nonquant personnel. In the different markets, there have always been specific risk measurements, such as duration for bonds, delta for options, and even the much-debated beta for stocks. With VaR, however, we can estimate the aggregated risk of a portfolio containing positions in each of these instruments.

According to VaR theory, losses greater than the VaR number can be expected only with a specified probability. For example, a large trading institution with several hundred positions in dozens of markets may quantify its value at risk by saying that there is a 5 percent chance that the firm will lose more than $1.5 million over the next month given the current portfolio.

As with most theories in finance, VaR is not without its detractors. Indeed, it is important to understand the limitations of VaR analysis. VaR does not estimate event risk, nor does it take into account liquidity differences among the various constituents of a portfolio. Furthermore, just about every model for calculating VaR assumes that the portfolio under consideration will not change over the time horizon. And lastly, VaR models also generally assume either that historical price movements contain information about the future distribution of returns or that future returns will be normally distributed, neither of which may be true. To overcome the issues inherent in trying to predict the future, several methods for calculating VaR have been proposed by industry professionals and academics.

In general, the approaches to VaR calculation fall into three main categories—delta normal or parametric, historical simulation, and Monte Carlo simulation. As we will briefly explain, each of these three approaches has its strengths and weaknesses.

Delta Normal Approach

Delta normal, or parametric, approaches to VaR define risk as the standard deviation of a portfolio's log returns. We have actually examined a version of this approach in Chapter 10. Although they are fast and straightforward, the quality of estimates generated by delta normal VaR methodologies break down when instruments with nonlinear payoffs, such as options, are added to the portfolio or when nonnormal events exist in the distribution of returns.

Delta normal VaR usually assumes a normal distribution for both the changes in market prices and the changes in portfolio value, and the calculation is usually a simple transformation of the estimated covariance matrix.

Delta normal methods work well for portfolios with a very limited number of options positions. Generally these methods incorporate options by replacing them with a delta-equivalent position in the underlying stock, a process called mapping. That is, an option on a stock is thought of as a position in the stock according to the delta since for small changes in the stock price, the option acts like the stock. So once we have made this replacement, we can estimate the risk of the portfolio as a portfolio of stocks. However, this replacement method typically misstates the risk since delta itself changes with changes in the stock.

For many options positions, reliance solely on delta can be misleading. Rather, delta and gamma together must be used to predict changes in option prices given a change in the value of the underlying stock. The error will likely be small, however, for VaR computations done over short time horizons, because short horizons tend to imply small movements in the stock. The misstatement becomes significant, though, when measurements are taken for longer horizons of, for example, 2 weeks or a month. Larger changes in time result in larger changes in the price of the underlying, and VaR estimates generated using a covariance matrix should not be relied upon for portfolios with significant numbers of positions in options.

Another issue related to delta normal methods and the presence of options is the difficulty in incorporating random changes in volatilities, which, of course, greatly affect the valuation of options. In the end, historical and Monte Carlo simulation methods are better for portfolios with complex or nonlinear instruments.

Historical Simulation

Historical simulation expresses a hypothetical distribution of portfolio returns. Each return is calculated as though today's portfolio were held on a day's past market movements.

Given a portfolio, we can obtain the historical values of the factors affecting that portfolio for the past, say, 5 years. Then we can subject the current portfolio to the factor changes experienced over, say, 1000 different rolling 22-day time periods within those 5 years to arrive at a discrete distribution of hypothetical monthly returns. Ranking these returns will allow us to find, for example, the 50th worst loss, which is then the 1-month VaR at the 5 percent level.

Historical simulation methods work well on portfolios with options because they recompute the entire portfolio value for each outcome of the underlying factors. Furthermore, historical simulations can easily be extended to include a distribution of volatilities.

By recomputing based upon the existence of several factors, historical simulation methods better estimate a distribution of returns on portfolios with options. Moreover, the historical simulation method is easy to implement as long as reliable historical data is available. If time-series data for the relevant factors is not available, implementation will be very difficult.

While an improvement over parametric methods, historical simulations are not a panacea. Although it is free from the assumptions of the normal distribution, the historical time period chosen limits the range of potential outcomes. The distribution of portfolio values generated can be misleading if the historical sample is not indicative of future values.

Monte Carlo Simulation

Monte Carlo simulation also calculates risk by building a histogram of hypothetical returns. As opposed to historical simulation, Monte Carlo simulation finds hypothetical returns by choosing returns at random from a given distribution, the parameters of which may be estimated by historical data. So Monte Carlo VaR methods are not limited by actual historical returns. Furthermore, Monte Carlo simulation can easily incorporate stochastic volatilities.

Given a portfolio, we can make assumptions about the distributions of the underlying factors affecting that portfolio. Then we can estimate the parameters of those distributions and run thousands of scenarios to build a histogram of possible future returns. For each scenario, we revalue the portfolio. As with historical simulation then, the distribution of hypothetical returns will allow us to rank the outcomes and find, for example, the 1-month VaR at a specific probability.

As with the previous methods, Monte Carlo simulation is not perfect. For one, Monte Carlo methods often require long computation times, especially as the number of random variables and the number of iterations increase. For two, financial engineers must estimate the parameters of the distributions from which the random values are being drawn, and these estimates may not be indicative of the future distributions of factor movements. The distribution of portfolio values generated by Monte Carlo simulation depends upon these assumptions. Despite the caveats, however, Monte Carlo is widely used in the industry for large portfolios of positions containing complex, nonlinear derivative instruments.

STRESS TESTING

Stress testing measures the impact of an abnormal market move on a portfolio. Running abnormal scenarios allows us to quantify the move's effects on a portfolio, and if these effects are unacceptable, the portfolio composition may need to be revised. Scenarios are often historical in nature. For example, what would have happened had this portfolio gone through the crash of 1987, or September 11? What would happen if all our correlations go to 1? If our firm is engaged in dynamic hedging or constant rebalancing of portfolios, what would happen if a major shock occurred overnight and market liquidity dries up? None of these scenarios is statistical in nature, but clearly there are nonzero probabilities associated with them that must be addressed.

Now let's incorporate UML design techniques and Monte Carlo simulation into a simple VaR calculator.

STRUCTURAL DIAGRAMS

Structural diagrams show the static architecture of a software project.

Class Diagram

A full class diagram displays an overview of an entire system including the constituent classes and the relationships between them. However, class diagrams are static and only show what relationships exist, but not when they happen.

UML notation for a class is a rectangle with three parts, one each for the class name, the attributes, and the member methods or functions. An individual class is represented in Figure 20.5. Here Monte Carlo is the name of the class, and it represents the definition of a Monte Carlo simulation object. The − and + signs define the private and public visibility of the attributes and methods. Although not shown, # would define protected visibility. MyMarket, CurrentPortfolio, dblIterations, and dblDaysAhead are all private attributes of the Monte Carlo class. The dblDaysAhead attribute, for example, will hold the time horizon of the

F I G U R E 20.5

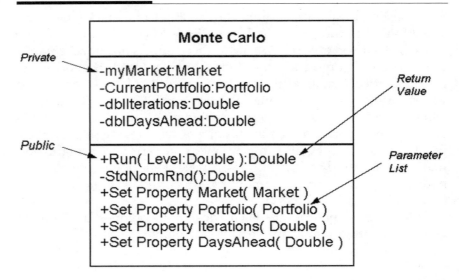

simulation in terms of the number of days. DblIterations will hold the number of times the simulation will run.

The member functions are listed in the bottom box and include the property gets and sets. The signatures of the respective methods are also shown outlining the input and output argument types. The New() method, of course, is the constructor, and StdNormRnd() is the function described in Chapter 5 that returns a standard normal deviate. In this case the properties are all WriteOnly, and so only sets are listed.

In addition to the classes themselves, we can also represent in UML the class relationships. Relationships between classes are shown as connecting links and come in five varieties—dependencies, associations, composition, generalization, and aggregation. These links should also define the relationship's multiplicity rules, which we will discuss shortly.

When a class has as a member another class, we say that it depends on that class. This is then a dependency relationship and is drawn as a dotted line with an arrow pointing to the containing class. In the example shown in Figure 20.6, the Monte Carlo class depends on the Portfolio class and has a constraint that the

F I G U R E 20.6

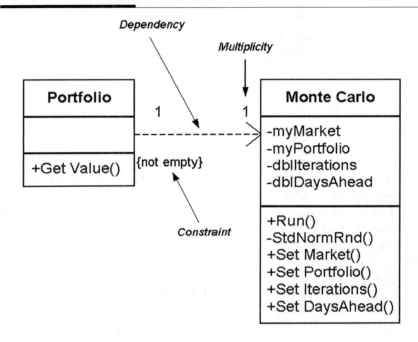

relationship not be empty. Of course, if there is no portfolio, there is no value at risk to calculate. A constraint, written in braces {}, requires that every implementation satisfy a condition. As you can see from Figure 20.6, as we begin to move outward and take a look at the bigger picture, we may start to abbreviate or even omit details at lower levels.

An association is the most basic relationship and in UML is drawn as a line connecting the two classes. As Figure 20.7 shows, an association relationship exists between the Portfolio class and the Algorithms Package.

If a class exists only as a member of another class, then the relationship is referred to as a composition within the containing class. A composition is drawn as a line with a solid diamond at the containing class end, as shown in Figure 20.8. In our trading system example, the OleDbConnection, OleDbDataAdapter, and DataSet

F I G U R E   20.7

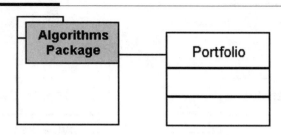

classes, collectively referred to as a Data Package, will exist only as members of the Market class.

A generalization is equivalent to an inheritance relationship and is drawn as a line with a hollow arrow pointing to the base class, as you can see in Figure 20.9. Inheritance—or in UMI-speak, generalization—shows that Portfolio is a derived class of HashTable, and of course inherits all the attributes and methods of the parent. The Value property has also been added to the class Portfolio.

An aggregation is a relationship in which several instances of a class belong to a Collection class. An aggregation is drawn as a line with a hollow diamond pointing to the collection. In Figure 20.10, an aggregation exists between Portfolio and Stock. The asterisk near the Stock class and the 1 near the Portfolio class represent the multiplicities. A single portfolio can have many stocks. Thus there is a one-to-many relationship between Portfolio

F I G U R E   20.8

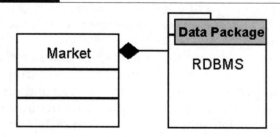

F I G U R E   20.9

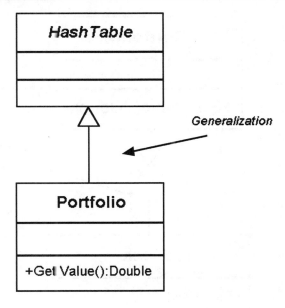

and Stock. Since a Portfolio has Stocks as elements, the diamond is positioned near the Portfolio box. We could also add a StockOption to represent another type of element in a Portfolio.

The multiplicity is the number of instances of a class that may be associated with a single instance of the class at the other end. The following table describes the most common multiplicities.

Multiplicity	Description
0..1	Zero or one instance
0..* or *	Zero or more instances
1	One instance
1..*	One or more instances

The class diagram in Figure 20.11 models the entire Monte Carlo simulation application we will create later in the chapter. As you can see, the central class is the Monte Carlo class.

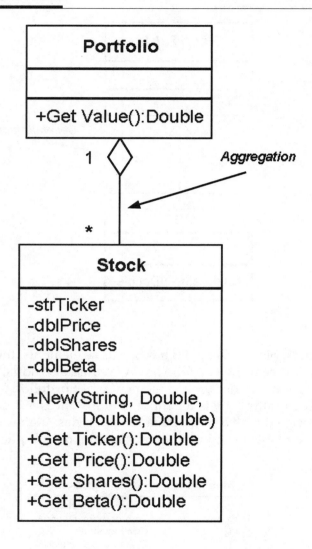

Object Diagram

An object diagram is simply a snapshot of all the objects at any given time. Object diagrams show instances of classes, and objects come and go, sometimes rapidly. So object diagrams are useful for

F I G U R E 20.11

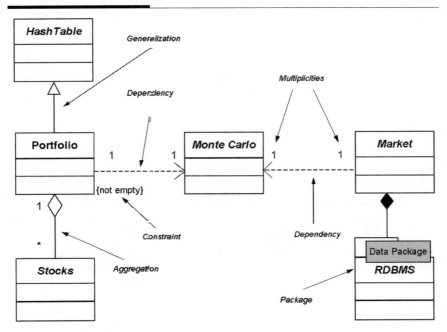

explaining very small project pieces with highly complicated relationships, especially recursive ones. The object diagram in Figure 20.12 instantiates the class diagram, replacing it with a concrete example. Each rectangle in the object diagram corresponds to a single instance of a class. Instance names are underlined in UML diagrams. Class names are often omitted from object diagrams since the meanings are usually clear.

Component Diagrams

A component diagram describes the physical units of a software system and the dependencies between them. Software components, such as the executable files and library files, are often combined into a single system and as a result have relationships and dependencies between them.

In UML, components are drawn as rectangular boxes, with two smaller rectangles sticking out the left side. Dependencies are

F I G U R E   20.12

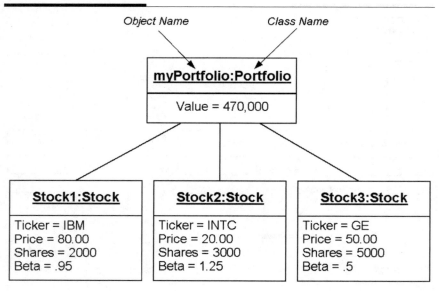

dashed lines with arrows pointing from the client component to the supplier component upon which it depends. The TraderAPI component contains an interface, shown in Figure 20.13 as a "lollipop." The dependency relationship within this diagram indicates that the .exe file component refers to services offered by the TraderAPI component via its public interface.

Deployment Diagram

A deployment diagram illustrates the physical organization of hardware in a system. Each node on a deployment diagram represents a hardware unit, and communication relationships exist between nodes. Nodes are drawn as three-dimensional boxes and contain software components.

Since the VaR model we have been following does not require any Internet or even LAN communication, we will show the hardware structure of an automated order routing system. The

F I G U R E 20.13

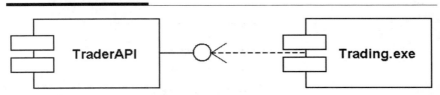

deployment diagram shown in Figure 20.14 lays out the communication relationships between the hardware components involved in automated trade entry.

BEHAVIOR DIAGRAMS

A behavior diagram represents the different aspects of a system's behavior.

Use Case Diagram

A use case diagram describes from an outside observer's point of view what a system does, but not how it does it. A use case explains what happens when a hypothetical user or actor interacts with the system. An actor is someone or something that initiates an interaction with the system. Actually a use case is very much like a scenario or a simple case study where an actor interacts with a system and is provided services by it.

The picture shown in Figure 20.15 is a simplified run VaR simulation use case. The actor is a financial engineer. The connection between actor and use case is a communication.

Use case diagrams are helpful in determining system requirements. In fact, new use cases often bring to light new requirements as the system undergoes an evolutionary design cycle and changes are made. Further, their simple, graphical notation facilitates communication.

A simple use case diagram can be expanded with additional features to display more information. The use case diagram in Figure 20.16 expands the original VaR simulation diagram with additional features for a simplified trading system. In this

F I G U R E   20-14

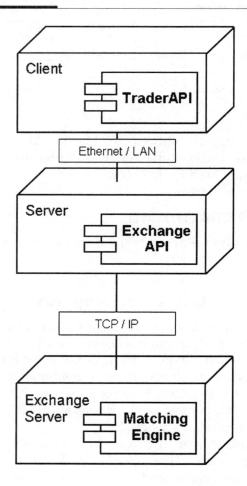

expanded design, we could include the ability to place trades and populate a portfolio.

Note again that the use case diagram does not represent any sequence; it simply shows the list of scenarios. A system boundary rectangle separates the system from the external actors—the financial engineer and the exchange. The ≪uses≫ relationship links use cases to additional ones, such as in the case Calculate Portfolio Value in Figure 20.16. Uses relationships like the one

F I G U R E   20.15

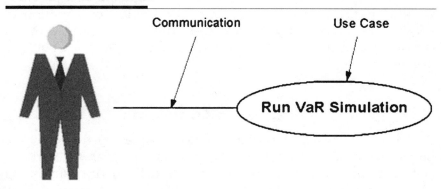

Communication   Use Case

Run VaR Simulation

Financial Engineer

shown are especially helpful when the same subtask can be factored out of other use cases. In Figure 20.16, both Select Trades and Run VaR Simulation use Calculate Portfolio Value as a subtask. In the diagram, the uses relationship is drawn as a line from the base use case to the used use case. Calculating the portfolio value is not of the type Run VaR Simulation, but is a task that constitutes a piece of the overall run simulation use case.

F I G U R E   20.16

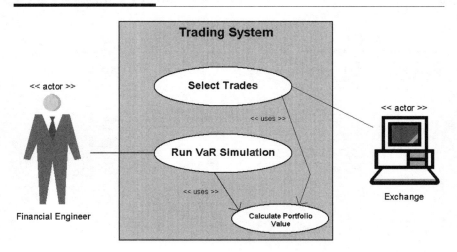

Although not shown, extend relationships are also possible. Extends indicate that one use case is a version or variation of another use case. Extends are also drawn as lines with an <<extend>> label. An extended case can be thought of as a subtype of a use case.

Sequence Diagram

A sequence diagram describes the flow of messages as they are passed from object to object. Whereas class diagrams describe a static structure, sequence diagrams illustrate the nature and timing of the interaction between classes.

Figure 20.17 is a sequence diagram for running a Monte Carlo simulation. The object initiating the sequence of messages is a Form1 GUI window. The sequence of events proceeds as we move down the diagram, and the objects are displayed from left to right according to when they become part of the sequence. The dotted lines, called lifelines, show that the portfolio exists before the Monte Carlo is run and continues to exist afterward. On the other hand, the Monte Carlo object itself and the Market object cease to exist after the simulation is completed, as denoted by the large Xs.

Message calls are represented by arrows from the sender to the receiver's lifeline. The activation bars, the hollow rectangles, represent the length of time of the execution of the message. These

F I G U R E   20.17

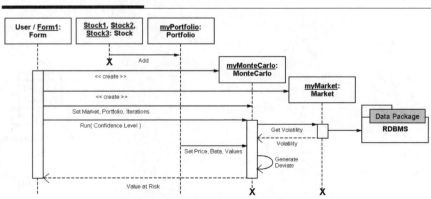

bars indicate the scope of a method occurring in a particular object. The dotted lines show return values coming back to the calling object. Notice that myMonteCarlo issues a self-call to generate a new random number.

So to populate the portfolio, Form1 creates stocks and adds them to myPortfolio. A user, presumably a financial engineer, inputs data into the GUI. Form1 creates myMonteCarlo and myMarket. The GUI sends messages to myMonteCarlo pertaining to the parameters of the simulation. Then myMonteCarlo gets the volatility from the market, and finally the simulation runs and the value-at-risk number is returned to the GUI.

Collaboration Diagram

In a large software system, objects have to collaborate, and so we have collaboration diagrams. A collaboration in UML-speak is an interaction between two classes. Collaboration diagrams, while conveying the same information as the previous sequence diagrams do, focus on the roles that objects play in the overall scheme, as opposed to the sequence of messages being sent.

Each message in a collaboration diagram has a sequence number. The top-level message is numbered 1. Messages at the same level have the same decimal prefix but have suffixes of 1, 2, etc., according to when they occur.

In Figure 20.13 the financial engineer, through the GUI, collaborates with myMonteCarlo by means of a button click and some property sets and the run method. Then myMonteCarlo collaborates with myPortfolio via three property gets and the value method. And myMonteCarlo collaborates with myMarket by means of the volatility get method.

State Chart Diagram

State chart diagrams allow us to picture the life cycle of an instance of a class and the timing of external events affecting it. State diagrams consist mainly of two elements—states and transitions. An object has states, which depend upon its current activity or

F I G U R E 20.18

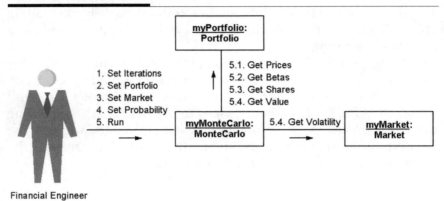

Financial Engineer

condition, and transitions, which describe how the object responds to outside influences.

An object performs an activity while in a particular state. Whereas actions are usually thought of as processes that are performed quickly, activities take much longer to process and may be interrupted by external events. An event, which could be a button click, or could be a system-generated event, or even could be internally generated, causes a transition or change in the state of an object.

As you can see in Figure 20.19, an object's initial state is shown as a black circle. Intermediate states are rounded rectangles, and the end state is shown as a black circle with another hollow circle around it. Transitions are arrows from one state to the next. A description of the event that triggers a transition is usually written beside the transition arrow.

Our example state chart diagram—Figure 20.19—illustrates the states and transitions of the Monte Carlo object. After creation, the object waits while the user enters a valid portfolio and market, a number of iterations, and a confidence level. Then the simulation executes. The setup and execution can be factored into four nonoverlapping states: getting simulation data, getting market volatility data, running the simulation, and calculating value at risk.

F I G U R E 20.19

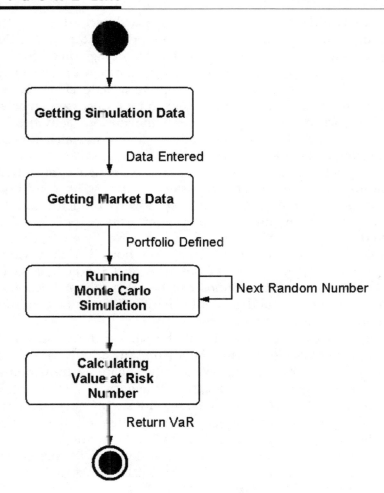

While in its running-the-simulation state, the Monte Carlo object does not wait for outside events to trigger a transition to the next state. The completion of the running simulation activity causes its transition to the subsequent state.

ACTIVITY DIAGRAM

An activity diagram is very much like a flowchart. An activity diagram follows the flow of activities in the order they occur. Being in an activity state means that an object is doing something. That something could be an event, such as a button click or form load, or the execution of a class method. Unlike a state chart diagram, which concentrates on a single object and its processes, an activity diagram focuses on the process and the flow of activities from object to object. In brief, an activity diagram states the basic sequencing convention the system should follow.

The activity diagram describes the sequence of activities including any conditional or parallel behavior. A condition is shown as a branching in the activity flow. A branch separates a single transition into multiple outgoing transitions. So if bad data is entered, the program flow will proceed down one branch. If the data is good, the other branch will be followed. Either way, the program activity flow merges again later on. Obviously, since only one of the outgoing transitions can be taken, the conditions are mutually exclusive, and a merge marks the end of conditional behavior. See Figure 20.20.

Some activities can occur at the same time or in parallel. Although not shown, parallel behaviors are drawn as forks and joins. As with a branch, a fork has one incoming transition and several outgoing transitions. In a fork, however, when the incoming transition is encountered, all the outgoing streams are taken at the same time. In the end a join occurs when all the incoming transitions have completed their individual activities.

Activity diagrams are sometimes shown with object lanes, often called swim lanes (see Figure 20.21). Lanes define which object is responsible for which activity.

Now that we have completed all the diagrams for our value-at-risk program, we are ready to code.

> **Step 1**   Create a new VB.NET Windows application named MonteCarlo.
>
> **Step 2**   Create the GUI shown in Figure 20.22. Name the text boxes txtIterations, txtLevel, txtDays, txtValue, and txtVaR.

F I G U R E 20.20

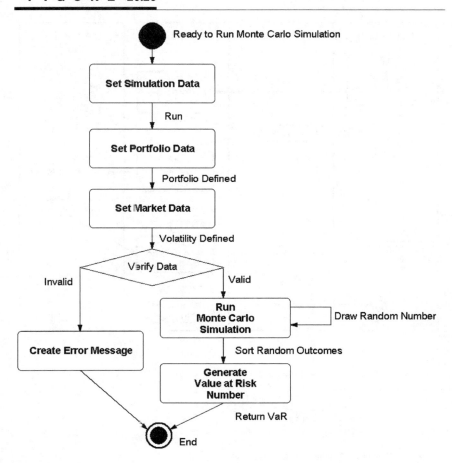

Before we can run a Monte Carlo simulation, we will need some stocks and a portfolio.

Step 3 Add a class named Stock. We will try to keep the classes simple to illustrate the overall design, so add the following definition:

```
Public Class Stock
    Private strTicker As String
    Private dblBeta As Double
    Private dblPrice As Double
    Private dblShares As Double
```

F I G U R E 20.21

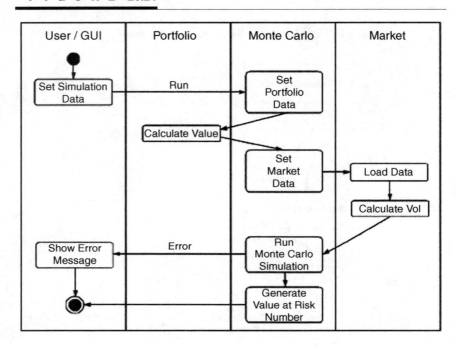

```
Public Sub New(ByVal strTick As String, ByVal dblP As Double, _
               ByVal dblB As Double, ByVal dblS As Double)
    strTicker = strTick
    dblPrice = dblP
    dblBeta = dblB
    dblShares = dblS
End Sub
Public ReadOnly Property Ticker()
    Get
        Return strTicker
    End Get
End Property
Public ReadOnly Property Beta()
    Get
        Return dblBeta
    End Get
End Property
Public ReadOnly Property Price()
    Get
        Return dblPrice
    End Get
End Property
Public ReadOnly Property Shares()
```

F I G U R E 20.22

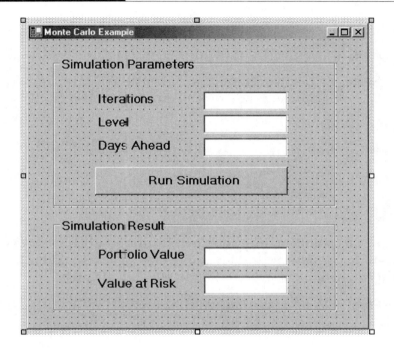

```
        Get
              Return dblShares
        End Get
    End Property
End Class
```

We could calculate a stock's beta using the historical price database, Finance.mdb, but for the sake of simplicity, we will leave this step out.

Step 4 Add a Portfolio class. This class will inherit from the Hashtable class and add a single Value property as shown.

```
Public Class Portfolio
        Inherits Hashtable
    Public ReadOnly Property Value()
        Get
            Dim dblPortfolioValue As Double
            Dim enumerator As IDictionaryEnumerator = GetEnumerator()
            While enumerator.MoveNext()
```

```
                    dblPortfolioValue += enumerator.Value.Price * _
                                         enumerator.Value.Shares
            End While
            Return dblPortfolioValue
        End Get
    End Property
End Class
```

Step 5 Now that we are ready to set up the portfolio, add the following code to the Form1_Load event:

```
Dim myPortfolio As New Portfolio()
Private Sub Form1_Load(ByVal sender As ...) Handles MyBase.Load
        Dim stock1 As New Stock("IBM", 80, 0.95, 2000)
        Dim stock2 As New Stock("INTC", 20, 1.25, 3000)
        Dim stock3 As New Stock("GE", 50, 0.5, 5000)
        myPortfolio.Add(stock1.Ticker, stock1)
        myPortfolio.Add(stock2.Ticker, stock2)
        myPortfolio.Add(stock3.Ticker, stock3)
End Sub
```

At this point you may want to run your program to make sure everything is in order so far. Now we are ready to add a Monte Carlo simulation object according to our class diagram.

Step 6 Add a class called MonteCarlo.

```
Public Class MonteCarlo

    Private myMarket As Market
    Private CurrentPortfolio As Portfolio
    Private dblIterations As Double
    Private dblDaysAhead As Double
    Public WriteOnly Property Market()
        Set(ByVal Value)
            myMarket = Value
        End Set
    End Property
    Public WriteOnly Property Portfolio()
        Set(ByVal Value)
            CurrentPortfolio = Value
        End Set
    End Property
    Public WriteOnly Property Iterations()
        Set(ByVal Value)
            dblIterations = Value
        End Set
    End Property
    Public WriteOnly Property DaysAhead()
        Set(ByVal Value)
            dblDaysAhead = Value
        End Set
    End Property
    Public Function Run(ByVal Level As Double) As Double
      Randomize()
```

```
    Dim x, y, z As Integer
    Dim dblPortValue As Double = CurrentPortfolio.Value

    Dim enumerator As IDictionaryEnumerator = CurrentPortfolio _
                                                .GetEnumerator()
    Dim randomprices As Double() = New Double(CurrentPortfolio.Count - 1) {}
    Dim PortfolioValues As Double() = New Double(dblIterations - 1) {}
    Dim PortfolioMoves As Double() = New Double(dblIterations - 1) {}
    Dim dblNextMarketReturn As Double
    Dim dblVol As Double = myMarket.GetVolatility()
    For x = 0 To dblIterations - 1
      dblNextMarketReturn = StdNormRnd() + dblVol * Math.Sqrt(dblDaysAhead _
                                                                / 256)

      z = 0
      While enumerator.MoveNext()
              randomprices(z) = enumerator.Value.Price * _
                      Math.Exp(dblNextMarketReturn * enumerator.Value.Beta)
              PortfolioValues(x) += randomprices(z) * enumerator.Value.Shares
              z += 1
      End While
      enumerator.Reset()
    Next x
    For x = 0 To dblIterations - 1
          PortfolioMoves(x) = PortfolioValues(x) - dblPortValue
    Next x
    System.Array.Sort(portfoliomoves)
    Return portfoliomoves(Level / 100 * dblIterations)
    End Function
    Private Function StdNormRnd() As Double
        Return Rnd() + Rnd() + Rnd() + Rnd() + Rnd() + Rnd() + Rnd() + Rnd() + _
            Rnd() + Rnd() + Rnd() + Rnd() - 6
    End Function
  End Class
End Class
```

Step 7 The market volatility is set by accessing the Finance.mdb database and calculating the standard deviation of log returns on the SPX over the entire data set. Add a class for the market with the following definition:

```
Public Class Market
  Private myConnection As OleDb.OleDbConnection
  Private myDataAdapter As OleDb.OleDbDataAdapter
  Private myDataSet As DataSet
  Public Function GetVolatility()
    Dim dblVolatility, x As Double
    myConnection = New OleDb.OleDbConnection("Provider=Microsoft.Jet. _
                        OLEDB.4.0;Data Source=C:\ModelingFM\Finance.mdb")
    myDataAdapter = New OleDb.OleDbDataAdapter("Select ClosePrice _
                                        from SPX", myConnection)
    myDataSet = New DataSet()
    myConnection.Open()
    myDataAdapter.Fill(myDataSet, "SPXdata")
    myConnection.Close()
    Dim intLength As Integer = myDataSet.Tables("SPXdata").Rows.Count
```

```
    Dim dblSPYreturns As Double() = New Double(intLength - 2) {}
    For x = 1 To intLength - 1
      dblSPYreturns(x - 1) = Math.Log(myDataSet.Tables("SPXdata").Rows(x). _
                 Item(0) / myDataSet.Tables("SPXdata").Rows(x - 1).Item(0))
    Next x
    dblVolatility = StDevP(dblSPYreturns)
    Return dblVolatility * Math.Sqrt(256)
  End Function
End Class
```

As you can see, the class definition also requires that we include the definition of the StDevP() function as a private method. The StDevP() method necessitates also the VarP() and Average() functions.

Step 8   To the class definition of Market, add as private methods the functions StDevP(), VarP(), and Average() from the CD.

F I G U R E   20.23

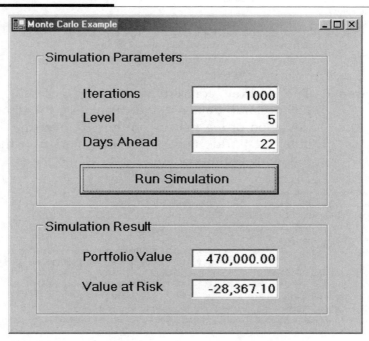

Step 9 To the Button1_Click event, add the following code to set the simulation data and run the simulation:

```
Private Sub Button1_Click(ByVal sender As ...) Handles Button1.Click
        Dim dblIters# = txtIterations.Text
        Dim dblLevel# = txtLevel.Text
        Dim dblDays# = txtDays.Text
        Dim myMarket As New Market()
        Dim myReturns As Double
        Dim mySimulation As New MonteCarlo()
        mySimulation.Market = myMarket
        mySimulation.Iterations = dblIters
        mySimulation.Portfolio = myPortfolio
        mySimulation.DaysAhead = dblDays
        myReturns = mySimulation.Run(dblLevel)
        txtValue.Text = Format(myPortfolio.Value, "###,###,###.00")
        txtVaR.Text = Format(myReturns, "###,###,###.00")
End Sub
```

Step 10 Run the program (see Figure 20.23).

SUMMARY

In this chapter we covered each of the 12 diagrams in UML, the Unified Modeling Language, and applied them to a Monte Carlo simulation for a portfolio of stocks. The chapter example program was built from these diagrams. According to the Kumiega–Van Vliet Trading System Development Methodology, we should build an objects and program document before programming. This document should lay out in UML all the classes, with their attributes and functionalities as well as system design and behavior.

PROBLEMS

1. Describe each of the 12 UML diagrams in your own words.
2. Explain the three methods described for calculating value at risk.
3. How would you create an objects and program document using UML?
4. Describe each of the three categories of diagrams.
5. What is a package?

PROJECT 20.1

The beta of stock is the covariance of the stock with the market divided by the standard deviation of the market according to the following formula:

$$\beta = \frac{\sigma_{s,m}}{\sigma_m}$$

Create a historical simulation program that uses data in the Finance.mdb database to calculate the betas. The program should select market returns at random from its distribution of historical ones.

PROJECT 20.2

Add a connection to TraderAPI.dll and/or OptionsAPI.dll so that the user can buy and sell assets and build a portfolio of stocks and options and calculate value at risk using a Monte Carlo simulation.

References

CHAPTER 1

Bernstein, Peter. 1992. *Capital Ideas*. The Free Press.

Norman, David. 2002. *Professional Electronic Trading*. John Wiley & Sons (Asia) Pte Ltd.

Van Vliet, Benjamin, and Andrew Kumiega. 2000, Winter. "Obsolescence of the Naked Trader." *Journal of Global Financial Markets*, pp. 21–23.

CHAPTER 2

Boehm, Barry W. 1998, May. "A Spiral Model of Software Development and Enhancement." *Computer*, vol. 21, no. 5, pp. 61–72.

Kumiega, Andrew, and Benjamin Van Vliet. 2001, October 23. "A Software Development Methodology for Financial Markets." Paper presented at the 11th International Conference on Software Quality, Pittsburgh, PA.

Kumiega, Andrew, and Benjamin Van Vliet. 2003. "An Automated Trading System Development Methodology." A working paper.

Rawlings, Bruce. 2003. "In Sample versus Out of Sample Testing for Financial Markets." A working paper.

Royce, Winston W. 1970, August. "Managing the Development of Large Software Systems."

CHAPTER 4

Kolb, Robert W. 1997. *Understanding Futures Markets*, 5th ed. Blackwell Publishers.

CHAPTER 5

Alexander, Carol. 2001. *Market Models*. John Wiley & Sons Ltd.

Bollerslev, T. 1986. "Generalized Autoregressive Conditional Heteroscedasticity." *Journal of Econometrics*, vol. 31, pp. 307–327.

Engle, Robert F. 1982. "Autoregressive Conditional Heteroscedasticity with Estimates of the Variance of UK Inflation." *Econometrica*, vol. 50, pp. 987–1007.

Garman, M. B., and M. J. Klass. 1980. "On the Estimation of Security Price Volatilities from Historical Data." *Journal of Business*, vol. 53, pp. 67–78.

Nelken, Israel. 1997. *Volatility in the Capital Markets*. Glenlake Publishing Company.

Parkinson, M. 1980. "The Extreme Value Method for Estimating the Variance of the Rate of Return." *Journal of Business*, vol. 53, pp. 61–65.

CHAPTER 6

Black, F., and M. Scholes. 1973. "The Pricing of Options and Corporate Liabilities." *Journal of Political Economy*, vol. 81, pp. 637–654.

CHAPTER 7

Whaley, Robert E. 2000, Spring. "The Investor Fear Gauge." *The Journal of Portfolio Management*, pp. 12–17.

CHAPTER 8

Hull, John C. 2000. *Options, Futures and Other Derivatives*, 4th ed. Prentice-Hall.

CHAPTER 9

Engle, Robert F., and Joseph Mezrich. 1996, August. "GARCH for Groups." *Risk*, vol. 9, no. 8, pp. 36–40.

CHAPTER 10

Nelson, Charles R., and Andrew F. Siegel. 1987. "Parsimonious Modelling of Yield Curves." *Journal of Business*, vol. 60, no. 4, p. 89.

Wilmer, Ram. 1996, June. "A New Tool for Portfolio Managers: Level, Slop and Curvature Durations." *Journal of Fixed Income*.

CHAPTER 11

Hernandez, Michael J. 1997. *Database Design for Mere Mortals*. Addison-Wesley.

CHAPTER 13

Bowman, J. S., S. L. Emerson, and M. Darnovsky. 2001. *The Practical SQL Handbook*. Addison-Wesley.

CHAPTER 15

Deitel, H. M., P. J. Deitel, and T. R. Nieto. 2002. *Visual Basic.NET: How to Program*, 2d ed. Prentice-Hall.

CHAPTER 16

Melamed, Leo. 2002. "Derivatives Exchanges in a Changed World Order." *Handbook of World Stock, Derivative and Commodity Exchanges*. Mondo Visione Ltd.

CHAPTER 17

Black, Keith. 2003. "Applications of Optimization in Financial Markets." A working paper.
Cernauskas, Debra. 2003. "Maximum Likelihood Parameter Estimation for Financial Model Building in Excel." A working paper.

CHAPTERS 18 AND 19

Bradley, Ronan. 2002, October 21. "XML and the Financial Services Industry." expoQ Daily, *www.ebizq.net*.
FIX Protocol, Ltd. 2003. *www.fixprotocol.org*.
International Swaps and Derivatives Association. 2003. *www.FpML.org*.
Pierce, Ryan. 2001, February 26. Townsend Analytics, Ltd. "Transitioning to Advanced Versions of Messaging Standards." Presented at FIXML Professional Training Course, New York.

CHAPTER 20

Alhir, Sinan Si. 1998. *UML in a Nutshell*. O'Reilly.
Jorion, Philippe. 2001. *Value at Risk*, 2d ed. McGraw-Hill.
Roff, Jason T. 2003. *UML: A Beginner's Guide*. McGraw-Hill/Osborne.

Acronyms

ADO	ActiveX Data Objects
API	Application programming interface
ATM	At the money
BOX	Boston Options Exchange
CBOE	Chicago Board Options Exchange
CLR	Common language run time
CME	Chicago Mercantile Exchange
COM	Component object model
COTS	Commercial off the shelf (software)
DOM	Document object model
DTD	Document type definition
DTMS	Data transformation management system
ECN	Electronic communications network
FCM	Futures commission merchant
FIX	Financial Information Exchange (protocol)
GARCH	Generalized Autoregressive Conditional Heteroscedasticity
GUI	Graphical user interface
HTML	Hypertext Markup Language
IDE	Integrated Development Environment
ISE	International Securities Exchange
ISO	International Organization for Standardization

MSIL	Microsoft Intermediate Language
NQLX	Nasdaq Liffe Markets
NYSE	New York Stock Exchange
OOP	Object-Oriented Programming
RCW	Run-time callable wrapper
RDBMS	Relational database management system
RDM	Relational database model
SQL	Structured Query Language
STP	Straight-through processing
TT	Trading Technologies, Inc.
UML	Unified Modeling Language
VBA	Visual Basic for Applications
VIX	S&P 100 volatility index
XML	Extensible Markup Language

INDEX

About the Authors

Benjamin Van Vliet is the associate director of the M.S. in Financial Markets program at the Stuart Graduate School of Business, Illinois Institute of Technology in Chicago, where he teaches courses in · quantitative finance and modeling. He is also a principal at the Office for Market Technology, Inc., a consulting company that provides its clients with trading automation solutions, corporate training, and research in the financial markets.

Robert Hendry is an independent software development consultant specializing in client/server and Internet projects for Fortune 500 companies. An instructor at the Illinois Institute of Technology, Hendry is editor-in-chief of the *PowerBuilder Developers' Journal*, product reviewer for *Wireless Business & Technology* magazine, and a member of the *USA Today* Technology Panel.

CD-ROM WARRANTY

This software is protected by both United States copyright law and international copyright treaty provision. You must treat this software just like a book. By saying "just like a book," McGraw-Hill means, for example, that this software may be used by any number of people and may be freely moved from one computer location to another, so long as there is no possibility of its being used at one location or on one computer while it also is being used at another. Just as a book cannot be read by two different people in two different places at the same time, neither can the software be used by two different people in two different places at the same time (unless, of course, McGraw-Hill's copyright is being violated).

LIMITED WARRANTY

Customers who have problems installing or running a McGraw-Hill CD should consult our online technical support site at http://books.mcgraw-hill.com/techsupport. McGraw-Hill takes great care to provide you with top-quality software, thoroughly checked to prevent virus infections. McGraw-Hill warrants the physical CD-ROM contained herein to be free of defects in materials and workmanship for a period of sixty days from the purchase date. If McGraw-Hill receives written notification within the warranty period of defects in materials or workmanship, and such notification is determined by McGraw-Hill to be correct, McGraw-Hill will replace the defective CD-ROM. Send requests to:

McGraw-Hill
Customer Services
P.O. Box 545
Blacklick, OH 43004-0545

The entire and exclusive liability and remedy for breach of this Limited Warranty shall be limited to replacement of a defective CD-ROM and shall not include or extend to any claim for or right to cover any other damages, including, but not limited to, loss of profit, data, or use of the software, or special, incidental, or consequential damages or other similar claims, even if McGraw-Hill has been specifically advised of the possibility of such damages. In no event will McGraw-Hill's liability for any damages to you or any other person ever exceed the lower of suggested list price or actual price paid for the license to use the software, regardless of any form of the claim.

MCGRAW-HILL SPECIFICALLY DISCLAIMS ALL OTHER WARRANTIES, EXPRESS OR IMPLIED, INCLUDING, BUT NOT LIMITED TO, ANY IMPLIED WARRANTY OF MERCHANTABILITY OR FITNESS FOR A PARTICULAR PURPOSE.

Specifically, McGraw-Hill makes no representation or warranty that the software is fit for any particular purpose and any implied warranty of merchantability is limited to the sixty-day duration of the Limited Warranty covering the physical CD-ROM only (and not the software) and is otherwise expressly and specifically disclaimed.

This limited warranty gives you specific legal rights; you may have others which may vary from state to state. Some states do not allow the exclusion of incidental or consequential damages, or the limitation on how long an implied warranty lasts, so some of the above may not apply to you.